MW01537125

# Filming the Line of Control

# Filming the Line of Control

*The Indo-Pak Relationship through the Cinematic Lens*

*Edited by*
**Meenakshi Bharat**
**Nirmal Kumar**

**Routledge**
Taylor & Francis Group

LONDON AND NEW YORK

First published 2008 by Routledge

2 Park Square, Milton Park, Abingdon, Oxfordshire OX14 4RN
52 Vanderbilt Avenue, New York, NY 10017

*Routledge is an imprint of the Taylor & Francis Group, an informa business*

First issued in paperback 2019

Copyright © 2008  Meenakshi Bharat and Nirmal Kumar

Typeset by
Star Compugraphics Private Limited
5-CSC, First Floor, Near City Apartments
Vasundhara Enclave
Delhi 110 096

All rights reserved. No part of this book may be reprinted or
reproduced or utilised in any form or by any electronic,
mechanical, or other means, now known or hereafter invented,
including photocopying and recording, or in any information
storage or retrieval system, without permission in writing from the
publishers.

Notice:
Product or corporate names may be trademarks or registered
trademarks, and are used only for identification and explanation
without intent to infringe.

British Library Cataloguing-in-Publication Data
A catalogue record of this book is available from the British Library

ISBN 978-0-415-46094-1 (hbk)
ISBN 978-0-367-27314-9 (pbk)

*To the ties that still bind us*

# Contents

## RAPPROCHEMENT

## INTERVIEWS

# Introduction

When, in 1947, India threw off the shackles of British colonial rule and the Muslim state of Pakistan was born, there was no way of knowing how this one historical act would reverberate down the years, in sphere after sphere.

Patently, the immediate historical spin-off was the unleashing of a five-decade period of a protracted and ongoing troublesome relationship of war and hostility between the two new nations. India and Pakistan have been involved in three major cross-border confrontations in 1948, 1965 and 1971. The Kargil face-off of the 1990s may not have been a major skirmish but it served as an ugly reminder of the unsettling relationship between the two countries. The crippling and atavistic travel restrictions between the two countries, the recurrent use of political strong-arm tactics, and the rhetoric of hate and intrigue have taken up much of the energies of the two nations.

Possibly, the bitter experience of the partition-related carnage could excite no other response. The violence that hacked complete families off the face of the subcontinent, the horrendous assault and rape of thousands of women, and the staggering loss of property had the nations reeling. One looked to intellectuals and artists for meaningful comment on this historical act. Writers like Manto, Intezar Hussain, and Chaman Nahal may have recorded their responses almost immediately, but from the comparative fledgling arena of cinema, there was little or nothing forthcoming. It was as if a pall had descended on both sides. With people either too ashamed or too traumatised to speak of their experiences, this silence was understandable. Giving cinematic voice to this hurtful subject at this early juncture was quite unthinkable. The immediate national imperative was the painstaking erection of the edifice of new nations; cinema inevitably came to be commandeered for the purpose. Indian cinema, in its earliest stages, mouthed the lofty ideals of nation-building in patriotic and venerating references to political makers of modern India like Gandhi, Nehru and

Lal Bahadur Shastri. It is to be noted that, though these references were abundant, references to Pakistan were conspicuous by their absence. All allusions to the 'other' nation were assiduously avoided. It is in this nebulous beginning, that is yet extremely vocal and evocative in its silence, that the wellsprings of the interest of this volume lie. The trajectory of this relationship through celluloid representation affords an insight valuable and crucial to the understanding of the evolving identities of the two nations.

This initial silence was followed by a discourse of animosity and cultural antagonism which found its way into the cinematic text, manifesting itself in various ways, from cultural shadowboxing to open Pakistan-bashing. One of the earliest films in Hindi, which make direct references to Pakistan, was *Upkar* (The Favour, 1965). Though the theme of Pakistan and India's relationship with it was merely an adjunct to the larger concern of tracing the changing façade of independent India and extolling the potential of agriculture, stressing the importance of the 'Jai jawan jai kisan' (Hail the soldier, hail the farmer) slogan of Shastri, it is significant that Pakistan figured at all in conjunction with larger concerns of patriotism and nationalism in an emergent nation.

With *Hindustan Ki Kasam* (Swear by India, 1973) the India-Pakistan theme moved up several notches to become a major concern. Set against the backdrop of the India-Pakistan war of 1971, this film clearly identified Pakistan as the enemy, and set the trend of the deployment of a strong anti-Pak sentiment in the ongoing exercise of forging and discovering an Indian national identity. Following this, many films, both good and bad, both hits and flops, were made with Pakistan as the central theme or, at least, as a central reference point. But recently, there has been an opening up and responses other than deep hatred towards the enemy nation have wended their way in. Though the release of a rabidly anti-Pakistan film *Gadar* (Tumult, 2001) continues to be met with box-office success, films like *Main Hoon Na* (Don't Worry, I'm Here, 2004) essay portrayals of Pakistan that are rather more neutral if not more positive.

The reason for this is, of course, the ostensible easing of the political tension between the two countries. The thaw in relations has resulted in the opening up of the padlocks on the iron gates separating them, for both cultural and academic exchange. The coast is now clear for Pakistan-friendly films. Already, the Yash Chopra hit, *Veer-Zaara*, has romantically verbalised the need for both countries to foster a positive relationship. The change of heart is seen in the new state policy of Pakistan that has allowed the screening of Hindi films in Pakistani cinema houses. Cultural exchange at the level of acting has also picked up, with Pakistani and Indian actors picking up projects with makers from across the line.

Obviously, this is the time to take stock. This volume is a first effort in this direction. Academics and filmmakers from all over the world have come together in this commitment to a fresh, cultural assessment and integration of the subcontinent, all recognising the fact that the time has come for cinema and cinematic colloquy across the border to be taken seriously. Even otherwise, cinema has been recognised as one of the most powerful of the visual media, needing to be studied for its representations, for the creation and perpetuation of stereotypes, and for the construction and deconstruction of tradition. But in the context of the dynamics of subcontinental relations, the need for this attention becomes more piquant. As has already been pointed out, the theme of patriotism in our films has been a veritable barometer of the political climate of the two countries. The essays included in this collection help trace the historical trajectory of these relations: how films are reflective of the tensions that simmer along the line of control, and how cinema ultimately becomes a means to understand the complex agenda of forging a sense of 'nationality' and the concept of nationhood in films and how it sometimes moves away from political rhetoric to iterate the need to maintain links of love and common heritage.

A need to fully comprehend the dynamics of this popular showing of culture, in the light of the improved, ever-changing political atmosphere between India and Pakistan, led to the idea of putting together a book documenting the history of the relationship between the two countries as represented in films. The need was also felt to study films made in the two countries, to construct the history of Indo-Pakistan relations, locating and discussing the aspects that link the two sensibilities either in divergence or in a coming together from a unique perspective. Hence, the response to films with this thematic brunt, and to Indian films in general, both within the two countries and amongst the Pakistani and Indian diaspora, has become an important part of this study. The involvement of contributors from across the globe, of different nationalities and ethnicities, goes a long way in proving the basic premise of this exciting study: that the interest of arriving at a better awareness of one of the most crucial political and historical relationships in the continent does not merely have a limited, 'localised' value pertinent only to the subcontinental scholar. The recognition of the key role of this relationship in world politics and in the shaping of world history is critical for the world scholar. This is a first holistic effort at enhancing cultural and sociological understanding through the focus on the unique confluence between history and film studies. Through this, readers through the world—not only those who claim some relationship with the Indian subcontinent, however tenuous it may be, by virtue of ethnicity or nationality—but all alert world citizens who have their eye on the burgeoning importance of the subcontinental players in the global arena. It is hoped that this first, committed multi-pronged approach would spur more such works, to bolster Indo-Pak studies, indeed Indo-Pak relations.

## II

With the motivating principle being the 'honest' impulse to arrive at a fresh understanding of the India-Pakistan association through its treatment in cinema, this volume wilfully embarked on a journey and methodology that would allow space for more than one genre of cinema, more than one linguistic foray and more than one kind of approach. The first essay, by Kishore Budha, attempts an assessment of the overall situation by subjecting it to a deep and incisive look. He traces 'genre development' in the context of the current market conditions, with special emphasis on the rise of the war film. He links the rise of this genre to the growth of nationalistic fervour and the formation of a national identity in the Indian subcontinent.

With the scene thus set, Adrian Athique goes on to examine the visualisation and narrative construction of the India-Pakistan border. He focuses on the southern portion of this border that runs from the southern bank of the Sutlej river across the Thar desert to the Arabian sea, and on the human interactions across that liminal space, as depicted in two films directed by J. P. Dutta, *Refugee* (2000) and *Border* (1997). Athique foregrounds the necessary problematics of articulation that constitute these films and their attempts to reconcile the obvious accidents of twentieth-century nation-building in the subcontinent and the physical implausibility of the border itself, within a redemptive nationalist rhetoric.

This analysis clears the ground for Rajinder Dudrah to zoom in on key scenes from select films since post-2000 that have explicitly dealt with the border in contemporary Bollywood cinema. He offers a close textual reading of the framing and representation of the border as actual physical and symbolic space in two films, in terms of aesthetic intent and possible audience effects. Introducing his thematic with preliminary remarks on *Lakshya* (The Objective, 2004), he analyses in detail two mainstream cinematic texts, *Main Hoon Na* and *Veer-Zaara*.

The presence of the border automatically recalls the act of border making. In the case of the subcontinent this holocaustic event has been the one most definitive and identifying event in its history, coming back to prey on the minds of subcontinental denizens over and over again. Little wonder that it has repeatedly spurred filmmakers to take it up for cinematic representation. Taking cognizance of this important historical truth, Meenakshi Bharat looks at the dynamics and politics of the adaptation of literary originals to the cinematic medium, focusing on *Pinjar* (The Skeleton, 2003) and *Earth 1947* (1988). The essay seeks to engage with the changes in the perceptions of this single cataclysmic historic event that cleft the Indian subcontinent into two, India and Pakistan, as these novels get transformed into visual montages. Bharat lays bare the dynamics of the politics of adaptation that underlies the making of the two films, making for two totally different perceptions and positions on the event. Claudia Preckel zeroes in on the treatment of women in films dealing with the Partition, while highlighting the complicating and defining factors of community, religion and nationality in *Gadar*, *Pinjar* and *Earth*. Savi Munjal's ' "Broken Memories, Incomplete Dreams": Notes towards an "Authentic" Partition Cinema', vindicates realism in contemporary cinema by examining the ways in which the choice of genre colours the ideological leanings of Partition cinema. It adopts a relativist approach towards history and argues for a plurality of equally credible histories. The article examines Sabiha Sumar's *Khamosh Pani* (Silent Waters, 2003) as an example of feminist historiography and compares it to mainstream Bollywood melodrama. The central premise is the treatment of the *auteur* as a historian who uses the visual-auditory discourse to transpose history onto screen. Kamayani Kaushiva treats of the other front of the Partition, the part of the 'Indo-Pak' border that is normally sidelined and never gets cinematic coverage—the eastern front. She takes up the central and continuous concern of Partition and its impact in Ghatak's evocative Bangla trilogy, *Meghe Dhaka Tara* (The Cloud-capped Star, 1960), *Komal Gandhar* (E-flat, 1961) and *Subarnarekha* (The Golden Line, 1962).

But sixty years down the historical line, a generation removed from the experience of Partition, possibly born of parents who are themselves post-Partition children, has come to occupy centre stage. Sunny Singh points out that, distanced from the Partition of 1947, the generation that is now increasingly coming to the fore as filmmakers and viewers of Hindi commercial cinema are thus marked by changed historical perceptions, which impact on national self-image and identity formation. In the past ten years, commercial Hindi cinema has begun addressing these changes in a variety of ways. Drawing on films as different as *Maachis* (Matchstick, 1996), *Border, Gadar, Phir Bhi Dil Hai Hindustani* (Yet the Heart is Indian, 2000), *Sarfarosh* (The Martyr, 1999), *Lakshya, Main Hoon Na, Veer-Zaara*, and *Khakee* (Uniform, 2004), among others, the essay considers how these films mediate, legitimise or, indeed, subvert entrenched Pakistan-centric political discourse through the use of content, theme, star-power or, indeed, *auteur*-intent. It attempts to demonstrate the gradual but distinct move by Hindi cinema from a Pakistan-centric and Partition-related construct of the national self-image to an increasingly self-reflexive and self-reflective one.

Carrying this reflective strain forward is Nirmal Kumar's essay in which he examines the irony of two cinematic cross-border love stories being filmed by directors who originally hail from Punjab, the state most devastated by the Partition of the Indian subcontinent. *Veer-Zaara* and *Henna* (1991), made in different times and by two widely different kinds of directors, represent a combination of astute market savviness and popular filmmaking. He analyses the thematic concerns of these films both at the wider political level and at the level of gender, taking into account the complications that arise at the knitting junctions of these two threads.

Aparna Sharma takes up the genre that is often forgotten when the 'biggies' come up for consideration. She closely examines the ethnographic documentary, *My Brother, My Enemy* (2005), set against the backdrop of the Samsung India Pakistan Cricket series, made by two young filmmakers from India and Pakistan, positing it as a presentation of a complex view involving personal histories where politics, propaganda and history intermingle. She specifically studies the film's camera choreography, in particular its use of the telephoto lens, which she argues parallels the filmmakers' ideological stance in the film that is clearly critical of the mindless jingoism both nations display in relation to one another, embedding the discussion in the cinematic philosophy of French philosopher Giles Deleuze, and the constructivist discourse within the ambit of film theory and social anthropology.

From behind the camera, Shakuntala Banaji moves beyond it to the reception of the finished product. Intrigued by the partisan nationalist sentiments, the xenophobia and anti-Pakistan rhetoric in India and amongst sections of the diaspora in everyday contexts, that have frequently been called upon and utilised by governments and/or fascist organisations, with divisive and traumatic consequences, she chooses to conduct an extended, in-depth qualitative study into texts and contexts, personal and group identities. In an effort to analyse the unremitting concern expressed about the effects of Hindi films, especially ones that choose to represent Pakistan and Pakistanis, she carried out interviews over a two and a half year period outside and inside Hindi film showings at cinema halls in Bombay and London, two cities with large Hindi-film viewing populations. This article is a distillation of around eighty brief public interviews conducted with young Indian and South Asian viewers, both individually and in groups, and thirty-six in-depth interviews lasting between one and four hours, engaging issues of religion, nation, romance, violence, ethnicity, family, gender, and sexuality in life and films. Whilst at the same time considering the *ways* in which these young viewers from different classes and locations experience films about the nationalist conflict between India and Pakistan and religious violence in the present historical arena, this article specifically addresses questions about the *political significance* of the meanings attributed to film representations of romance and national identify as well as religious and xenophobic violence between Indians and Pakistanis and, in India, within communities with different histories and experiences. Banaji argues that the ways and contexts in which commercial Hindi films choose to depict issues of India-Pakistan tension and violence, although often accurately labelled by critics as dangerously conservative and ideologically suspect, can have unanticipated implications for—and be interpreted in surprising, critical and liberatory ways by—some young viewers.

Having thus given honest space to both the film theorist and the practitioner of the craft, to the sophisticated, 'literate' viewer and the 'ordinary' spectator, finally come the voices of the people who are making cinematic history, filmmakers, directors, and commentators. First, from across the border, is the voice of Aijaz Gul, leading film critic, himself desirous of subjecting Pakistani films to the kind of scrutiny that we have endeavoured to give to films in this volume. His observations about the Pakistani film industry and the link between the two nations as seen in films give the reader the much needed 'other' perspective. To complete the picture, Tavishi Alagh, herself an independent filmmaker, draws out the responses of three stalwarts from the Hindi film industry who have, at some point or the other in their work and in their lives, given thought to the erection and demolition of The Fence: M.S. Sathyu, maker of *Garam Hawa*, the quintessential film that critiques the drawing of the border, the first real Partition film; and Javed Akhtar, with his sensitive yet sharp comments on the 'ghost' of the dividing line, both in films and in reality and how the two ultimately converge. Mahesh Bhatt comments on the connection between the two countries in his blood and in his work.

## III

Keeping in mind the wide embrace of the approaches thus essayed in the volume, and acknowledging the burgeoning importance of the vibrant field of film studies, this text attempts to locate a fresh dynamic entry point into this area of enquiry, examining a sphere not hitherto touched. The effort has been to steer clear of adding to what Ashis Nandy calls 'the proliferation of insipid, mechanical works on cinema' (Nandy 2003). The intention has been to enable fresh scholars at the local level to see the possibilities in the field and to facilitate an analysis of the intersections of the various aspects of such a study. At the broader level, those who have never been exposed to such views will be brought face to face with 'insiders' perspectives'. Further, the volume recognises the importance of maintaining an inter-disciplinary alertness to historical, sociological and even economic reverberations. It is this in-depth multi-pronged approach that marks the commitment of the researchers and editors of this volume. We are invigorated by the newness of the foray and hope that this will spur more such works, to bolster Indo-Pak studies in general, and thus to create the space for a healthy intellectual and genuine dialogue.

# Negotiating the Border

# Genre Development in the Age of Markets and Nationalism: The War Film

## Kishore Budha

*Not only do industrial and journalistic labels and terms constitute crucial evidence for an understanding of both the industry's and the audience's generic perceptions in the present; they also offer virtually the only available evidence for a historical study of the array of genres in circulation, or of the ways in which individual films have been generically perceived at any point in time.*
—Stephen Neale, Genre and Hollywood, *1999*

*'We have never had a war film ... all we have had are love stories told against a backdrop of a war.'*
—Aamir Hussain, quoted in Pearson, 'War pix storm theatres', *2003*

Film criticism in the media has played a key role in sustaining Indian cinema. Indeed, in the absence of journals such as *Cahiers du Cinema* or sustained academic study, journalistic criticism and reporting has helped shape the industry. Higson places film criticism as one of the ways to explore national cinemas.[1] Furthering this approach, Darrell William Davis has proposed three 'models of reflections'—or criticism—about a national film industry. These are: the reflectionist model, which evaluates a national film industry in relation to national politics; the dialogic model, which examines the similarities and differences between a national cinema and other national cinemas; and the contaminated model, which considers national cinema to be a compartment of a larger international institution (see Davis 1996: 17–25). The study of national cinemas in an age of globalisation is considered essential to examine perceived threats of assimilation within larger transnational systems of entertainment, culture, and economics.[2] It has been argued that economic deregulation, ushered in the early nineties, has impacted the media industries to cause historical disjunctures.[3] It is in the above-mentioned contexts that this paper examines discussions of the war film in English-language newspapers between 1997 and 2006. The public space is a rich site to understand the collective of interest groups. These discussions reveal in various nuances the concepts, concerns, and themes about the war film in industrial, aesthetic, ideological, cultural, and political terms. Thus, through a discursive analysis of statements and journalistic criticism published in newspapers, this article reveals three major themes—nationalism; the state, economics and cinema; and aesthetic criticism of form and style. The discourse substantiates historical continuities in cinema's relationship with dominant socio-cultural formations, late capital's inability to formally subsume cinema, and journalistic criticism obsessed with (western) cinematic realism. Here, the conclusions point to a validation of Higson's argument that an analysis of national cinema:

> ... would need to take into account the range of and relation between discourses about films circulating within that cultural and social formation and their relative accessibility to different audiences. (Higson 1995: 279)

It is argued that the tension between intellectual discourse and political discourse about patriotism needs to be negotiated by the industry. Thus, the industry needs to put forward an institutionalised class of texts by setting rules and expectations about the concerns of the genre, instead of letting the vagaries of India's relationship with Pakistan prevail on film production and aesthetics. This would require working closely with journalist-critics, who are well placed to counter dominant political discourse.

In their seminal study of 'classical' Hollywood, Bordwell et al (1988) demonstrated how, besides modes of production and norms of narratives, discourse played a crucial role in setting the rules and expectations about the concerns of a cinema—such as film form, genre and modes—in the form of statements and assumptions found in trade journals, technical manuals, memoirs, and publicity handouts. The repeated articulation of these notions helped the industry to cement a distinct approach to film form or style. Examining the case of the Hindi film industry, Prasad (1998) and Pendakur (2003) have argued that the Hindi film's disaggregated nature is the cause of the fragmented ideological nature of the Indian state; the mercantile nature of capital in the film industry; the role of the state in regulating cinema, especially through the instrument of censorship; and the elite nature of film criticism biased towards verisimilitude. They have argued that late capital would formally subsume the production process, thereby rationalising film form. Here it is important to look at the relationship between industry and genre development. Altman (1984) Neale (1999) and Schatz (1981) have argued that genres are defined by the industry and accepted by the audience, and the genre reaffirms what the audience believes at both individual and communal levels. Altman (1984) states that genres negotiate the relationship between a specific production system and a given audience. This implies that greater managerial and professional control over the way film texts are conceived, produced, discussed, and sold would lead to stable genres and new aesthetic possibilities.[4] Indeed, cinema is seen as part of a larger scheme of 'deregulation' and Indian industry's inevitable assimilation into global consumption. For example, Sudip Talukdar (2004), writing in *The Times of India*, argued that the film industry was a mismatch with other industries, which had been globally competitive. This belies the deterministic view of critics who see cinema eventually realising a global aesthetic of realism. The phenomenon this paper seeks to highlight is the dichotomy of this position with the reality of the way the industry sees itself—firmly embedded in the ideology of the nation-state. A close examination of journalistic discourse, industry statements, and right-wing politics reveals positions that are continuous with the period preceding deregulation. Late capital has been unable to certify the genre and this makes the war film open to interpretations and cooptation by right-wing politics. Different interest groups push competing agendas, and fears of political-commercial propagandist takeover are exaggerated, though, going by the fears expressed by filmmakers such as Mahesh Bhatt, the threat has not gone away. This can be attributed to the fact that, despite active journalistic support for change, the industry has been unable to advance a stable genre structure. Instead, the sporadic success of jingoistic films made by independent filmmakers gives them a larger space in the media, though the war film in its current form has been proven to be unreliable at the box office. This has significant implications for industry practices, as negotiating the genre with the audience directly would help reduce the linkages between production and right-wing politics. Some answers lie in the success of films made by newcomer directors aimed at urban audiences that challenge the dominant war-film form. The article is divided into three sections—right-wing politics and cinema; economics and the war film; and journalistic criticism.

# Nationalism, Patriotism

## The Context: *Border* and Right-wing Politics

Discussions of the war film have to be placed in the context of the rise of right-wing politics during the 1980s, the eventual electoral victory of the BJP in 1998 and the box-office success of *Border* (J. P. Dutta 1997). After *Haqeeqat* (Reality, Chetan Anand 1964), Dutta's *Border* (1997) is considered a landmark film. On release, it played to packed houses while generating protests amongst Muslims as far as Bradford in the UK. While denouncing the film for its 'concomitant rancour against the more brutal, less intelligent and unduly aggressive opponent' (Nikhat Kazmi cited in Varma 1997), critical reaction to the film was mixed. Mitu Varma argued that the film was after all a 'Bollywood film' with its formulaic fare of romance and songs. On a more critical note, Firoze Rangoonwalla and Nikhat Kazmi played down the film's media effects (cited in Varma 1997). Despite the critics' dismissal of the film's significance, Mitu Varma reported that the film had generated concerns in certain quarters about the timing of the film, given the ongoing diplomatic engagement. There is clearly anxiety and excitement over the perceived power of mass media—on the one hand it warrants anxiety and fears, while belief in media-effects makes it a target to be coopted for the purposes of propaganda. This creates the conditions for filmmakers to take sides with those in power and undermine the industrial development of genre.

## War Films, Right Wing Politics, Patriotism

Right wing politics has always seen mass media as propagating conservative ideas of nationalism and patriotism. Their arguments stem from the belief in media effects as well as the soft power of Hindi cinema in creating and sustaining imagery, myths and legends about the nation. Pratibha Advani, daughter of BJP leader Lal Krishna Advani, produced a documentary on the 'essence of patriotism in Hindi films'. The documentary, *Ananya Bharati*, stressed the role of Hindi films in promoting patriotism (see Pisharoty 2005). Writing in the journal of the BJP's ideological mentor, the RSS, she explained:

> As an art form that strikes the chords of both emotion and intellect, the power of cinema is unmatched. Naturally, Indian cinema has contributed immensely to the cultivation of this uniting and uplifting feeling of

nationalism. Patriotic films, as a special and much-admired genre of Indian cinema, have had a tremendous impact on our people, cutting across religious, regional, linguistic and economic identities. Moreover, they have also proved their unsurpassed power of communicating both to educated and illiterate masses.

For most Indians, cinema is the enduring source of the image of their nation as a vast and diverse land bound by the Himalayas in the north, surrounded by oceans on three sides, girdled by sacred rivers like the Ganga, Yamuna, and Godavari, and blessed with captivating natural beauty and rich resources. For them it is also the primary source of knowledge about our national heroes, martyrs, the struggles and sacrifices of our forefathers, the work of our social reformers, the wars of the pre-and-post-Independence era, including the recent and ongoing war against cross-border terrorism, and our achievements as a free and democratic nation.

Thus, few can contest Indian cinema's, particularly Hindi cinema's, unmatched contribution to strengthening the bonds of national integration, countering divisive feelings, educating the people about our shared national history and, through all this, re-enforcing in them pride and love for the Motherland. (Advani 2005: 22)

The BJP's media policy, outlined in 1998, clearly articulates a normative function position:

The BJP believes that, a healthy polity and democracy cannot survive without the support of an extra-political moral order which the democratic political order cannot itself impose on its citizens. This belief is also the emerging belief of more advanced democracies that are experiencing a steep slide in morality which is endangering the very idea of orderly society. (BJP 1998)

Filmmakers such as J.P. Dutta echo piety to this argument and remind the industry of its patriotic duties and obligation towards the martyr:

I don't care about the industry.... They would rather have me shoot inane films in Switzerland. I only care for the mother of a dead war hero who rings me up and blesses me. (J.P. Dutta cited in Unnithan 2003)

Dutta's enthusiasm and willingness to be appropriated by the BJP discourse was fed to a large extent by the production assistance he received from the Indian Army and by his proximity to politicians who found his sympathies useful to further their own goals. In return for his patriotic championing he received production support from the

Indian Army[5] while hobnobbing with right-wing politicians helped him gain publicity for his film. Key ministers from the BJP government cabinet, including Prime Minister A. B. Vajpayee and Deputy Prime Minister L. K. Advani, turned up for the premiere of *LOC—Kargil* (2003; see Gelder 2004). News reports observed that the promotional events preceding the release of *LOC—Kargil* played up the militaristic posturing. The release of the film music was marked by the presence of officers who took part in the Kargil war, fiery speeches, and a degree of nationalism not 'normally seen in the otherwise bubblegum world of Bollywood' (see Mirani 2003). In the political arena, Pakistan and India were used in gendered metaphors, i.e., to create imageries of the vulnerability of the Indian nation, necessitating extreme caution, military empowerment, and the normalisation of violence against a Muslim Pakistan by avenging the wrongs of the past atrocities against a Hindu India.[6] At the height of the BJP's rise, the spectre of atrocities against Indian women was invoked to justify the nuclear bomb. The naming of the external Muslim enemy also functions to indirectly remind India of the internal manifestation of that enemy, the Muslim citizen. Emboldened by the US declaration of the 'war on terror', the BJP raised the stakes of the game by talking of a swift victory against Pakistan to teach it a lesson. At the same time, the party was busy 'fanning the nationalist sentiment created by the crisis with Pakistan', in the hope that it would benefit the party in crucial state elections later in 2002.[7] Shiv Sena, an important right-wing ally of the BJP, engaged in lumpen activities such as digging up cricket pitches before India-Pakistan matches or issuing threats to film actors who engaged in any activity with Pakistan.

Such political developments created the environment for the film and television industries to believe that there was a market for content centred on jingoistic patriotism. During the rule of the BJP from 1994 to 2004, many films were made with storylines and attitudes reflecting the party's conservative stance, emphasising family values and religious patriotism. A survey of the news media shows that the television and film industries had appropriated the Kargil conflict by announcing a slate of films, producing chat shows, inserting war into existing soap plots, and releasing patriotic music compilations. The retail industry too organised special sales towards the war veterans fund, while painters and fashion designers organised fund-raising events. 'Kargil is a cake and everybody wants a slice' (Jain et al. 1999). Some editorials sarcastically commented that the film industry's fixation with the war was so as to cash in on the situation rather than to develop a war-film aesthetic. This view was based on a comparison with Hollywood films such as *Saving Private Ryan*, which, such editorials argued, were 'masterpieces'. The Hindi war film was criticised for its 'absurdity, clumsiness, bizarre plot twists, and canned nationalism as a prop for the standard mundane love story'. This judgement rested on comparisons with what was considered true representations of the Vietnam war with fears that comparative representations in Hindi films led to 'the trivialisation of the issue by well-meaning but entirely misguided individuals' (Anon 1999). It was a different matter that the industry was unable to sustain commodified nationalism, as a majority of the 'patriotic' films failed at the box office during 2002.[8]

## Economics, the State, and the Film Industry

### Pakistan as Market—Threats versus Opportunities

In comparison to the enthusiasm shown by the media industries to capitalise on the anti-Pakistani rhetoric unleashed by the extensive media coverage of the Kargil war, the lowering of Indo-Pak tensions by 2004 led to a dramatic turnaround. The Indian film industry today is no longer considered an unorganised sector that is funded, managed and organised by mercantile capitalists. Well integrated into the economy and recognised by government and industry bodies,[9] the new capital seeks to maximise itself rather than occupy itself with concerns of genre development. In the lowering of the rhetoric against Pakistan, producers see economic opportunities in a large Pakistani market. However, it is only a shift in discourse that permits voicing such opportunities. The Film Producers Guild of India, a significant industry body, has been emboldened by developments to openly acknowledge the opportunities offered by the Pakistani exhibition market. Komal Nahta, a trade analyst, claimed that the Pakistan exhibition could provide the leading producers excess revenues of 50 million rupees (see Ansari 2004).

Not only does this reflect the new liberal economics of the country, but also masks the hegemonic ambitions of the Hindi film in the region. Pakistani producers are acutely aware of this threat but, unable to acknowledge their own vulnerability to the soft power of Hindi films, they raise alarms of damage to the moral fabric of Pakistani society. The problem has been exacerbated by satellite television and home video, both of which have undermined the local exhibition sector. Though exhibitors stand to gain from the screening of Hindi films, analysis of policy statements of the Pakistan Culture Ministry reveals that Hindi cinema is viewed with hostility, requiring intervention by the state by encouraging tie-ups with other film industries—even when the proposed tie-ups are with film industries that have little or no aesthetic similarities. In a recent national conclave on the future of the film industry, the Federal Culture Ministry invited producers and filmmakers to find ways to arrest the decline of the exhibition sector. Given that the woes of the distribution and exhibition sectors could be alleviated by allowing access to Hindi films, it appeared odd that their representatives were kept out of the conference. Said minister G. G. Jamal: '...the government would encourage Pakistani filmmakers to co-produce films with those from other countries such as Iran and China, and the culture ministries of Iran, China and Pakistan would hold talks in this regard soon' (Ahmed 2006). The official support for production partnerships with countries other than India, within a week of declaring that no more Indian films would be screened in Pakistan, betrays the fears of a cinema that is perceived as hegemonic (see Anon 2005; Anon 2006a; Anon 2006b; Kamal 2004).

## The Film Industry and War Films

Despite the opportunities offered by the Pakistani market, the Indian film industry is unable to leverage a position of strength. This is partly due to governmental control via the instrument of censorship, which has created a culture of self-restraint, and the proximity of influential independent filmmakers who are reported to be close to the political elites. Evidence demonstrates that filmmakers have historically reconciled to governmental control over what can and cannot be shown on film screens. Thus, cinema functions as a reflector of the political establishment instead of acting as an independent intellectual force. Given the powers of the Central Board of Film Certification, which, by its own admission, argues that censorship is 'not only desirable, but also necessary',[10] the film industry finds it necessary to acquiesce to the dominant political ideology. Pendakur and Prasad have adequately highlighted the role of censorship in regulating cinema. This leads to constant shifts about what constitutes a successful film, largely dependant on political dispensation. The interdependence between reception and production, which Neale (1999) and Schatz (1981) argue is driven by mutual negotiation leading to genre development, is instead manipulated by political discourse. Thus, genre development is based on the sporadic success of films that are linked to political events. Trade analysts attributed the rash of war films in 2001 to the success of anti-Pakistani rhetoric in *Gadar* (Tumult, 2001) and the colonial-era nationalist film, *Lagaan* (The Tax, 2001; see Bamzai 2001). In contrast, by 2004, while the political discourse became amiable to relations between India and Pakistan, producers were 'busy working cross-border camaraderie into their scripts' (Ansari 2004). That year, *Times of India* reported that Nitin Manmohan's *Vande Mataram* (Salute to the Motherland, 2004) on the 1971 war had been shelved and *Sarhad Paar* (Across the Border, 2006), a war film starring Sanjay Dutt, was

> being adapted to the peace mood, even though the film was largely in the can.... More significantly, director Anil Sharma, whose last two films: *Gadar—Ek Prem Katha* and *The Hero*—unabashedly rode the jingoistic wave, seems to have amended the tone of his latest film, *Ab Tumhare Hawale Watan Saathiyon*. (Ansari 2004)

Filmmakers such as Mahesh Bhatt, considered uncompromising in their stand against right-wing politics, see the mellowing as hibernating patriotism. 'If right-wing Hindus come to power on anti-Pakistan rhetoric, then this wave will fade away. I would say that we're on the edge. Hatred is a very difficult emotion to neutralize.' (Bhatt cited in Browne 2004). Given the change in relations between the governments of India and Pakistan, filmmakers were quick to distance themselves from positions that were cheered earlier. Director Farhan Akhtar took pains to clarify that *Lakshya* (The Objective, 2004) merely used the war as a backdrop to explore struggles of individuality (see Ansari 2004; Kumar Singh 2004; Singh 2004). The failure of *Maa Tujhe Salaam* (Salute to my Motherland, 2006) led Sunny Deol to distance himself from patriotism and stick to 'straightforward dramas' (cited in Deshmukh 2002). This change in tactics can be attributed to change in political climate, coupled with extensive media coverage of the Indian cricket tour of Pakistan, which portrayed lay Pakistanis positively. Some filmmakers completely reshot parts of their films, toning down the anti-Pakistan rhetoric. Notwithstanding the differences of opinion surrounding genre theory, filmmakers' constantly shifting arguments about the structure of the war film indicates a general inability to put forth 'an institutionalised class of texts'—films that are systematically negotiated with the audience through conceptualisation, production, marketing, and modification based on extent of success. Stephen Neale (2003) stresses the financial advantages to any film industry from an aesthetic regime based on regulated difference, contained variety, pre-sold expectations, and the re-use of labour and materials. He refers to the commodification of mass-art, a necessary requirement for economic exploitation. Thus, the film industry's inability to develop a stable structure for the war film not only highlights managerial shortcomings but also the overall nature of capital within the film industry.[11] The discourse of war films shows that genre in Indian cinema is not subject to advanced capitalist conditions of production, distribution and exchange. Instead of producers and managers, the agenda of its production is defined by influential independent filmmakers, trade spokespersons and politicised members of the industry. The chair of the Central Board of Film Certification has been particularly prone to partisanship; it is a political appointment, characterised by eminent publications such as *The Hindu* and *Frontline* as a seat reserved for 'friends or sycophants'.[12] Nothing reflected this more than the arguments of Anupam Kher, its chair between 2003 and 2004. He argued that filmmakers ought to make films that benefited political realities. Dev Anand, brother of the late Vijay Anand, who vigorously campaigned for reformation of India's cinema laws, was the only voice that argued that the reality of history required wars to be examined from different sides as long as it was not propaganda (see Anon 2004b).

## Journalistic Criticism

Film critics with major publications such as *The Indian Express, India Today, Hindustan Times,* and non-Indian ones such as *Observer* and *Variety* can be considered critical and insightful in writing about Hindi films. This criticism is informative and often refers to a wide body of films within and outside India, widening the scope of the discourse. For example, Kermode (2004) finds that in the representation of Pakistanis as wicked adversaries in *Deewaar* (Luthria 2004), *Maa Tujhe Salaam, Mission Kashmir* (Chopra 2000), *Lakshya* are similar to the 'Boche of British war films or the 'gooks' of American Vietnam films'. While being critical, they also instruct readers to look beyond the 'typical Bollywood film'. It should be cautioned here that this is not reflective of all reviews and features about films and should not be considered a generalisation of the entire English-language press, though reviewers with smaller newspapers are considered pliant in their writing.[13]

## Critics and the Rhetoric of Modernisation

Film critics in media categorise the film industry as unresponsive and rigid; they characterise the industry as being obsessed with formulaic themes that are no longer relevant to contemporary audiences, who, they claim, are part of 'a new unfolding reality' and among whom, they argue, a quite revolution is taking place. Popular cultural production is argued to be out of touch with changes taking place in Indian society. While periodically admonishing the big three production houses—Yashraj Films, Mukta Arts and Dharma Productions—they cite low-budget filmmakers such as Mani Shankar, Mohit Suri and Onir, advising the big three to not 'cling to old habits' Saibal Chatterjee (2005), in particular, has consistently railed at what he sees as the film establishment, calling it an 'iron grid' of ideology that refuses to confront reality. In a particularly scathing instance, he accused it of choosing to remain in the safety of palliating productions of 'action, romance, emotions and comedy'. With particular reference to war films, filmmakers are charged with overuse of the jingoistic formula and not attending to the changing expectations of young spectators. Such critics, responding to what they perceive as the interests of their readers, actively promote an alternative aesthetic. This is illustrated in the discussions surrounding the success of *Rang De Basanti* (Colour Me Saffron, 2006) in 2006, which recommend narratives of reflexivity instead of taking spectators for granted.[14] The continuing disapproval of Hindi films by newspaper critics has shepherded filmmakers into a guarded relationship with them. While courting mass media for publicity, during pre-release they are careful to stress that their particular film is not a reissue of the war film formula. In Farhan Akhtar's interviews to the press, he was keen to distance his film *Lakshya* from earlier war films and stress that the Kargil war was merely a plot device to narrate a coming-of-age story (for example, Ansari 2004; Rao 2004; Singh 2004). Despite his box-office success with *Dil Chahta Hai* (Do Your Thing, 2001) and the film's critical acclaim, *Lakshya* met with limited box-office success, though it earned the critics' praise for its style and production values (Anupama Chopra 2005).

A key factor behind the emerging cracks in the Hindi film form is the entry of multiplex operators in the exhibition sector, which allows producers to also make urban-specific films. The emergence of multiplex exhibition provided exhibitors and distributors opportunities to juggle capacities, tap into segmented urban audiences and therefore explore newer aesthetic possibilities.[15] This audience is seen as enmeshed in the culture industry, driving the film industry to court 'elite' critics. The producers of *Tango Charlie* (2005) chartered a twenty-seater plane to ferry television and print journalists to the Indo-Pakistan border. This worked to mutual benefit, generating publicity for the film's producers while providing 'news' for the media.[16]

## Form and Style

Sustained informed critique of the war film genre, or, for that matter, other film genres is seen to be absent. Whatever critique remains, relegates cinematic discussion to the polemics of style. Sudip Talukdar wonders how, in the age of television and DVD when audiences encounter the realism and verisimilitude of Hollywood war films, the disaggregated form of the Hindi film[17] can fit with a genre such as war. He argues:

> A potential cinematic milestone has been sunk by the deadweight of songs, flashbacks and expletives, out of sync with a battle zone, where survival alone dictates every other consideration.... In other words, Bollywood, by its very being and circumstance, is rather mismatched with a genre configured on a different set of skills, attitudes, aptitudes and expertise. (Talukdar 2004)

For Talukdar, the central organising feature of war films is realism; he is representative of the English language critics' yearning for 'cinematic realism'. For such critics Indian cinema is destined to ultimately unshackle itself from the dominant—and by implication—backward film form and join the inevitable global aesthetic of realism, the same way as other industries have been unshackled from economic controls. Such critics draw parallels between film producers and other Indian industries that service global customers and exhort the former to set 'higher goals for themselves'. The assumption here is that only in the realist aesthetic can Hindi film depict true and meaningful representation. This polemic is part of a historical continuity of media discourse that is divided between a preference for continuity editing versus star publicity and gossip. Though it is Pendakur (2003) who informs us of this distinction, this research shows a new trend intensified by a rapidly expanding mass media and the influence of capitalist concerns. Previously an elite concern, contemporary mass media discourse is inclusive of producers, distributors and exhibitors shunned earlier. The entry of capitalists into what was the preserve of left-leaning intellectuals has led to the legitimisation of 'mass appeal' and the logic of the free market. It is pertinent to note that beyond arguing for mass appeal there is little analysis of aesthetics in a free market. Nevertheless, the insights of industry spokespersons appear to validate the case for active spectators. They are significant players in the shaping of the film aesthetic and underscore the gap between what the industry considers economic reality and the elite view of cinema and society. Commenting on the box office performance of *LOC—Kargil*, exhibitor Yogesh Oza said: 'The film has a lot of ingredients to make it look very real and impressive. But it is not like *Border* which had mass appeal.' Clearly, spectators do not share the critics' aesthetic opinion and seem unimpressed by realism. Some trade critics even suggest sticking to the Hindi film form and style. Komal Nahta argued that there was 'so much realism in the movie because of which it seems like a documentary on war. It is too repetitive, too realistic and too lengthy.' What follows is the prescription to stick to the 'escapist form of entertainment rather than something so real'.[18]

## The War Film Canon

There is little contention that *Haqeeqat* is canonical for war films. Eminent film journalist Bhawana Somayya signals it as 'pathbreaking' and the 'first widely-acclaimed war-film (Somayya 1997)'. However, this criticism is more an exercise in *auteur*ism than a desire to group, classify and find typicality—time honoured traditions in the acquisition of knowledge—to evaluate subsequent films. Thus *Haqeeqat* and *Border* are praised for their directorial vision and faithfulness to the motif of the heroism of the Indian solider. Talukdar (2004) emphasises that *Haqeeqat* should be recognised because its

> portrayal of the soldier's psyche, both in war and in peacetime, is unmatched for realism. Stark shots of jawans in *Haqeeqat*, bereft of equipment, numbers, supplies, artillery or air support, who die defending their posts in sub-zero temperatures against an external enemy....

Unnithan (2003) credits *Border* with validating the war-epic as a genre in the industry. Similarities are drawn with *Haqeeqat* for its motif of valour. However, unlike *Haqeeqat's* motif of unflinching gallantry in the face of defeat, heroism in *Border* culminates in victory over the adversary. The film's box office success is attributed to the novelty of this closure and the fact that a war film had been made after a long hiatus. *Border* is reported to have grossed Rs 400 million. Dutta's auteurism in straddling 'the two worlds of art and commercial cinema' was emphasised (Varma 1997), while Unnithan located Dutta's individual style in lavish budgets, harsh terrains, and casting excesses. Readings of film criticism in the mass media since 1997 demonstrate a tendency to append facts and legends about auteurs and their films rather than to build an informed discussion. There was no discussion about the vast array of subjects—war, history, nationalism, masculinity—that could have been debated. Though critics were generally unanimous in critiquing the Hindi film form, the success of films such as *Border* was met with unenthusiastic acknowledgement and the customary veering off into film form.[19] When subsequent war films failed at the box office, critics were quick to point to the rhetorical excessiveness. Remi Fournier Lanzoni argues that auteur-narrated films have a greater sensitivity towards contemporary situations and that they force audiences to be an active force (2002). The fixation with verisimilitude appears to turn the focus of mass media to criticism of form and style, rather than question the ideological fantasies of such films. What follows is a blind spot of film criticism. The constant clamour for visual realism whittles away Alexandre Astruc's argument of the tyranny of what is visual—image for the sake of it, serving the demand of the narrative, achieving the goals of realism and social fantasy (1968).

## A New Reflexive Cinema?

While it would be tempting to raise the spectre of right-wing communitarian politics, productions such as *Swades* (Homeland, 2004) and *Rang De Basanti* (2006) have not only bucked the trend, but avoided jingoism and anti-Pakistani rhetoric. *Swades* adapts Nehruvian ideology in the globalised age. Its plot has the protagonist Mohan Bhargav stumble into India's forgotten hinterland in search of his childhood nanny. This starts off a process of self-identification with rural India, which forces him to confront the bleakness of life there. Having led an economically and intellectually rewarding life in the West, he decides to stay on and help 'his people'. In his interactions with the village residents Mohan concludes that the solution to their problems lie in empowerment through self-sufficiency. Mohan demonstrates that prosperity can be attained by scientific and engineering interventions, which provides the village water and electricity. This hyphenated identification with both the individualistic wages of economic migration and the need to contribute with actions to alleviate rural poverty are attempts to recontextualise Nehruvian ideology in an era of globalisation. Gowariker's interviews to the media confirm this hypothesis: 'If you have the opportunity, you must go abroad, study, work and make your money. But after a substantial amount of time, look back at what you've left behind and see if you can contribute in any way' (Gowarikar cited in Anon 2004a) argues for the *Swades* benefits of the Nehruvian ideological state apparatus, suggesting a clearly defined programme of rural development through motifs of modernity, application of science and technology, and self-sufficiency. In such relations, rural Indians are the bearers of the incomplete nationalist project. Such portrayals ignore the reality of radical rural movements such as Naxalism and Maoist insurgencies. Instead, their politics is defined and acted out by the returning, scientifically-educated, nostalgic, and 'activist' Indian. Critics such as Saibal Chatterjee argue that a market for self-reflexive Indian cinema is slowly unfolding and filmmakers can profit from this demand by keeping the budgets low and exploiting niche exhibition. This middle-class market is the space where small-scale experiments in cinema are taking place. As argued by filmmaker Sudhir Mishra:

> The audience that goes to see *Jhankaar Beats* [Musical Beats, 2003] or *Chameli* [2004] is in the mood for something different. Besides, this is a love story. In the '90s, it was fashionable to be apolitical. But when you hear that someone like Bhupen Hazarika has joined the BJP, the younger generation is bound to react to the fall from grace of such people. The youngsters' cynicism is certainly being provoked into political consciousness. (Cited in Shedde 2004)

## Conclusion

This article has studied the lack of unity in the discourse of various interest groups, demonstrating the inability of organised capital to set the agenda and institutionalise the war film. As a result, the war film is dependent on the repetition of a formula that is inextricably bound to the politics of the nation-state. This is not only an industrial weakness but also bodes ill for the politics of the country, which is vulnerable to right-wing ideologies. It is argued here that film criticism's inability to play a constructive role in the development of the war film is symptomatic of trends rooted in history. Pendakur and Prasad have argued that journalistic film criticism has been unable to play a significant role in shaping the film industry and its practices, and this has been demonstrated in the media discourse on the war film. Media criticism is limited to debates about the form and styles such films should take, reflecting an elite and urban conception of what cinema ought to be, though there is some evidence of critical discussion and suggestions. The film industry does not appear to be able to utilise the media as a space to advance the war film as a stable genre. Instead, all critical discussion of the war film leads to the oft-repeated focus on of *Haqeeqat* and *Border*. This eventually closes all opportunities for further examination of genre. This demonstrates that far from modernising, the Hindi film continues to be influenced by socio-political formations. However, the success of some war films that have avoided Pakistan as the basis of their plot shows that spectators are open to newer forms of narrative. Sudhir Mishra has argued that there is room to engage with an audience that is unhappy with the nation they have inherited from their parents. However, to capitalise on this opportunity will require sustained discourse to develop audience and negotiate the cinematic possibilities.

## Notes

1.  Higson (1989) argues that national cinema can be explored in the following ways: a) as a production-centred industry, via 'an exhibition-led' or 'consumption-based approach'; b) with 'a text-based approach'; or c) by way of 'a criticism-led approach'.
2.  Globalisation here is understood as an age of accelerated flows of people, capital, technologies, images, and ideas. Malcolm Waters (2001) provides a good overview of the various discussions surrounding globalisation. For discussions about globalisation and national cinema see, for example, Kinder (1993); Semati et al. (1999).
3.  Madhava Prasad's work (2005) is one of the most significant arguments for a relationship between capital, ideology and aesthetics. For specific inquiries into other media in the post-nineties era see Dhareshwar and Niranjana (2000); Kumar and Curtin (2002); Scrase (2002).

4. In this context it is important to highlight the efforts by RGV and Yash Raj Films to institutionalise the genres through control over production and a consistent set of statements to the media.

5. Dutta is reported to have stated that the Indian Army, impressed by the success of *Border*, encouraged him to produce *LOC—Kargil*: 'I didn't want to go-back and shoot another war film. But the Army asked me to come over and placed the facts before me. After that, I couldn't say no'. See Nair (2002).

6. For an account of the gendered discourse of India, Pakistan and the subject, see Das (2006).

7. For more about the politics of the BJP during 2002, read Seabrook (2002) and Deshmukh (2002).

8. Deshmukh (2002) reported that, despite thousands of troops amassed at the borders with Pakistan, 'pop patriotism' was sinking at the box office.

9. For example, since 2001, the Federation of Indian Chambers of Commerce and Industry has been hosting an annual event for the film industry called 'FICCI-Frames' (http://www.ficci-frames.com), which provides an interface between the film industry, government, capital, and other industries.

10. See http://www.cbfcindia.tn.nic.in/

11. Pendakur (2003) offers an excellent overview of the Indian film industry—unorganised financed by the underworld, full of star-heavy productions and infrastructural shortcomings—and its role in shaping discourse and politics.

12. See Gangadhar (2004) and Narrain (2004) for detailed coverage of Anupam Kher's removal from chairmanship of the Censor Board, particularly the controversy surrounding the extraordinary delay in the release of Anand Sharma's anti-right wing documentary 'Final Solution'.

13. Pendakur (2003) has argued that this kind of journalism 'serves the function of creating demand for the films rather than providing any sustained critique of film and culture'. Criticism of *Lakshya* in the media tended to focus on the hype surrounding the director and the production quality of the film. For illustration see Anon 2004c.

14. In post-film release analysis, critics have argued that the time-tested formula of patriotism and bellicismo should be eschewed in favour of cinematic realism. See, for example, Doval (2006); Tyagi (2004).

15. With the earlier system of single-screen large-seating theatres, films would be made for audiences spanning large populations. Since regional distributors subsidised production costs, they would have considerable say in film narratives, given their perceptions of their audiences.

16. See Kazmi's (2005) report on the event, organised by the film's producers and covered by all leading news publications.

17. Here I refer to the term forwarded by Madhava Prasad to describe the Hindi film form. Prasad argues that the Hindi film form is a direct result of the economic nature of production. After the collapse of the studio system, the new capitalists in the industry were mercantile in nature, unable to aggregate production, distribution and exhibition, as in Hollywood. The producer, financier, distributor, and exhibitor were often separate entities. Producers, on one hand, did not own the production process and relied on various independent professionals who were hired to put the film together. This resulted in a film form that was not conceived by, strictly produced, and directed at specific audiences. On the other hand were the regional

distributors and exhibitors, who bore upon the producer plot, character, narrative, and style imperatives that they perceived as satisfying the tastes and preferences of their regional audiences. For more, see Prasad (1998).

18. Yogesh Oza and Komal Nahta's comments are in response to the failure of *LOC—Kargil* at the box office. See Tyagi (2004); Kumar Singh (2004).

19. For readings on criticism of the war film, see Talukdar (2004); Tyagi (2004); Pearson (2003); Somayya (1997); Singh (2004b); Mirani (2003).

# 2

# Aggression and Transgression on the India-Pakistan Border

## Adrian Athique

### The Performative Border

This article examines the visualisation and narrative construction of the India-Pakistan border, and human interactions across that liminal space, as depicted in two films directed by J. P. Dutta. The first of these films is the high-profile, multiple award-winning war film *Border* (1997) and the second his subsequent feature *Refugee* (2000), which was loosely described in its publicity literature as 'a human story'. Through these films, Dutta established his reputation as the leading Indian director of the 'war film', a genre marked by its relative absence in the Indian cinema prior to the 1990s. Both *Border* and *Refugee* thus constitute part of what has retrospectively been described as Dutta's 'war trilogy', along with the more recent *LOC—Kargil* (2003) which focuses on the 1999 Himalayan conflict. In the first two films of the set, which I will consider here, the border in question is not the line-of-control (LOC) that divides Kashmir, but rather the southern portion of the long border with Pakistan that runs from the southern bank of the Sutlej river across the Thar desert to the Arabian Sea. *Refugee*, moreover, is not a war film in the accepted sense, and I will make the argument that it is not so much the martial posturing which constructs the thematic inter-relation of the two films considered here but rather their attempts to naturalise the abstract barrier created by the Radcliffe line in the West.

Although the location of the India-Pakistan border itself may have been determined, and periodically re-determined, by the arbitrary separation of jurisdictions and the deliberations of technocrats, the function of the border represents a much more fundamental schism in the narrative production of South Asia. As Navtej Purewal observes: 'The border not only signifies where the nation-states of India and

Pakistan begin and end, but it also territorializes and nationalizes local populations and identities' and is employed as 'a site for the construction of a dominant national consciousness (Purewal 2003: 547).' Sanjay Chaturvedi makes the argument that one of the key defining elements of nation-building has been the reflexive production of Otherness between the two nations, where geopolitical visions are constructed through 'imaginative geographies' in which 'inclusions and exclusions, as mutually reinforcing forms of place-making, have become central—rather, indispensable—to the "nation-building" enterprise of the post-colonial, post-partition states of India and Pakistan' (Chaturvedi 2001: 149). As such, the political existence of the border is not sufficient in itself, since the *performance* of this border is an even more essential component of the processes of Othering at work in the subcontinent. Perhaps the most obvious example of this performativity is the flag-lowering ceremony conducted at the Wagah border post in Punjab, a spectacle of mutual aggression favoured by tourists that, as Chaturvedi observes, displays the common heritage of both nations precisely in the manner in which it seeks to proclaim their difference (ibid.: 156–57). Here, the locale of the India-Pakistan border itself is of far lesser significance than the complex impossibility of both difference and sameness that it is enacted, literally, to represent. However, despite the apparent enthusiasm of such performances, there appears to be some evidence that, in both its physical and symbolic manifestations, the border is not yet satisfactorily located in the realm of the 'real', and as such it

> continues to evoke action and response from both hegemonic and marginal perspectives, with fundamental questions around the border's meaning and legitimacy still being posed. The symbolic and practical implications of the border thus exhibit both border aggressions (acts ensuring its sovereign status is maintained) and border transgressions (acts which defy or challenge the processes it symbolises). (Purewal 2003: 547)

The two films that I will go on to consider here provide a useful illustration of how these aggressive/transgressive currents and actions contribute to a contradictory, and yet clearly symbiotic, affirmation and denial of the India-Pakistan border in popular discourse. Both *Border* and *Refugee* clearly demonstrate the self-reflexive instability of South Asian nationalist texts as they seek to accommodate the complex, harrowing and comparatively recent historical events that have shaped the region. In this sense, the two films elucidate some of the challenges faced by Indian filmmakers in narrating fraternity and difference in the subcontinent.

## Maintaining Boundaries

*Border* stages a dramatic account of a battle in western Rajasthan during the 1971 war. A large Pakistani force attacks during the night and a small Indian Army garrison of 120 men at Longewala puts up stubborn resistance, refusing to concede their positions until the Indian Air Force is able to come to their aid the following day. The film begins with the prelude to these events as India deploys its forces along the border. In the opening scenes, air force Captain Suraj (Jackie Shroff) is sent to establish a forward air base in Rajasthan. In transit, he meets Major Kuldeep Singh (Sunny Deol), the Sikh army officer who will command the army post at Longewala. Singh commands a detachment from a Punjabi regiment, which includes the reluctant young Lieutenant Dharam Vir (Akshaye Khanna), the bullish Sgt-Major Ratan Singh (Puneet Issar) and jocular army cook, Bhagiram (Kulbhushan Kharbanda). Bhairav Singh (Sunil Shetty), a local Rajasthani officer of the Indian Border Security force (BSF), is also assigned to the unit. The film employs the classic features of the war genre: we are gradually introduced to a small group of soldiers through half a dozen key characters who reveal their backgrounds, hopes and fears to the audience in the mounting tension preceding a victorious climactic battle against a faceless and numerically superior enemy. However, unlike the majority of western war films since the decline of the Hollywood musical during the 1950s, *Border* incorporates four musical sequences into its narrative, composed by Javed Akhtar and Anu Malik. The visual sequences for the songs are employed in two modalities: in the first part of the film, the musical interludes take place in romantic settings away from the scene of the conflict and in the second part they are 'picturised' on the battlefield itself.

The proclamation of the film, during the opening credits, as a narrative re-enactment of a real event makes a claim for situating *Border* within the web of South Asian history. However, the primary motives for India's involvement in the 1971 conflict, and its long-term political significance, both of which lie in the eastern portion of the subcontinent are consciously occluded from the account provided in *Border*. Only a brief comment by Captain Suraj to Major Kuldeep Singh, as they share a transport plane at the beginning of the film, relates the forthcoming action at Longewala to the wider context of the war.

Major Kuldeep Singh [*in English*]: Do you think we'll see action, Sir?
Captain Suraj: Going by the situation in East Pakistan it's pretty certain that they will start trouble on the western front.
Major Kuldeep Singh: As you said, Pakistan will start trouble on the western front but we will be the ones to finish it. They will fire the first bullet. We will finish off with the last.

Aside from this briefest of exchanges, the confrontation in *Border* is presented simplistically as an unprovoked Pakistani invasion of Indian Rajasthan. The audience is not invited to consider the real imperatives for the unsuccessful attempt by Pakistan to open a second front in the West in 1971. Instead, the conflict is explained as misplaced avarice for India's territory on the part of Pakistan. Indeed, given the central importance to the film of the narrative affirmation of the border as a line of defence, this is prefigured as the *only* permissible explanation for the events taking place.

However, despite the centrality of this premise to the narrative, it is thirty minutes into the film before we actually get our first glimpse of the border itself. Kuldeep Singh, accompanied by Bhairav Singh, Dharam Vir and Ratan Singh, travels the Sixteen Kilometres from the border post to visit the Radcliffe Line itself at border pillar 635. The pillar stands in the centre of a small flat between two banks of sand dunes. From a defensive position set amongst the sand dunes on the Indian side, the soldiers of the Punjab regiment watch their Pakistani counterparts stationed in the dunes opposite them. The Pakistanis, in a mirror-image montage, also watch them. One of the rank-and-file soldiers at the Indian post cautions Kuldeep Singh against standing in the open, arguing that Pakistani snipers are trigger-happy and liable to shoot him. On hearing this, Kuldeep Singh immediately leaves the cover of the post and strides out purposefully across the sand towards the border pillar. Completely in the open, he covers the short distance and stands next to the pillar itself, facing the Pakistani positions. In the next shot, we see the Pakistani soldiers in their dugout, asking their officer if they should shoot the 'mad' Indian officer. The officer indicates that they should not. Kuldeep Singh then returns to the Indian dugout and, once inside, he laughs heartily, prompting Dharam Vir to ask him to clarify the difference between bravery and madness. Kuldeep Singh explains that madness is subjective according to faith and asserts that his faith in God is sufficient to protect him, given that God is with him rather than with his enemy.

This sequence is a useful example of the border aggressions defined by Purewal, that is, performative acts seeking to affirm the sanctity of the dividing line. The posturing of Kuldeep Singh has the obvious purpose of taunting the enemy, prefiguring the inevitable conflict through an unspoken territorial challenge. The audience, of course, knows that the Pakistani Army will take Kuldeep Singh's challenge to cross the line and that they will pay dearly for doing so. So, as an act of bravado, Singh's action invites identification. There is more at work here, however, than simple playground dramatics. The fact is that this sequence is absolutely necessary for the demarcation of the space that will stand in for the wider realpolitik of the war, especially since the border itself is simply a small concrete obelisk set in a featureless sand flat in the middle of a desert. Put very simply, without the dramatised posturing of Kuldeep Singh the border is a visual non-event and cannot of itself provide a sufficient rationale for the events that follow. Rather, the border has to be made to mean something, and this difference must be marked out rhetorically. At the same time, the scene juxtaposes two sets of soldiers whose similarity is more apparent than their difference. The mirror image of the Pakistani border post, set amongst matching sand dunes, with a matching dugout and flag post serves to indicate the somewhat artificial and contingent nature of Pakistan's otherness. However, it can also be argued that this does not ultimately destabilise the production of a national other. Instead, it merely highlights the well-worn cliché of martial narratives: that the soldiers of the enemy are not much different from us (as soldiers), but soon it will be our patriotic duty to kill them nonetheless.

Taken together, the physical abstraction of the border itself, its bellicose performance (by Kuldeep Singh) and the mirror imaging of the Indian and Pakistani positions are all evocative of the Wagah flag ceremonies. The purpose, then, of this sequence is precisely the same: to provide a performative account of difference which facilitates the narration of the border as something both tangible and sacred. It is also the case that this rhetorical sacralisation of the India-Pakistan border in the early parts of Dutta's film is also intended to emphasise that this border, like other borders, is constantly under threat from acts of transgression. The transgression of the border that will take place at the climax of the film—an armoured invasion—is perhaps the most literal example, the ultimate violation of the national space. In this scene from the first half of the film, however, there is an exposition of another form of transgression, enacted through a sinister juxtaposition between Kuldeep Singh's valiant gesture at border pillar 635 and questions posed by infiltration, kinship, treachery, and retribution. The evening before they visit the border pillar, and immediately preceding that sequence in the film, the following exchange between Kuldeep Singh, Bhairav Singh and Dharam Vir takes place:

> Major Kuldeep Singh: Are the villages around the border friendly to us?
>
> Captain Bhairav Singh: They used to be, sir. Many moved across the border during the war of 1965. They're all related, and some of them are informers too, sir.
>
> Major Kuldeep Singh: Dharam Vir!
>
> Lieutenant Dharam Vir: Sir!
>
> Major Kuldeep Singh: Start a full-scale checking of the villages from tomorrow.
>
> Lieutenant Dharam Vir [*in English*]: Shall we use force, sir?
> Major Kuldeep Singh: Only if necessary.

After Kuldeep Singh's posturing at border pillar 635 the following day, the film cuts to a meeting after dark where the defence of the area is being discussed. Bhairav Singh points to the map: 'These are the villages that are most endangered, sir, because they use these very paths for movement.' At this point an enlisted man interrupts them, with the news that their Pakistani counterparts are requesting to speak to Kuldeep Singh on the radio. In the exchange that follows, the voice from Pakistan indicates that the Pakistani military is aware of the deployment of the Punjabi unit at Longewala and of the identity of its officers, and proceeds to taunt and threaten Kuldeep Singh, who responds furiously. At the conclusion of the call he turns to his junior officers and says in English: 'Gentleman, they have got the full information, that the 23rd Punjab is at the Longewala post and the commanding officer is Kuldeep Singh Chandpuri. They have got informers.' Dharam Vir cannot restrain himself and cries out: 'Bastards!'

At this point, the film cuts to a shot of the officers travelling in a jeep past a set of ruined buildings where a fire is being kept. We hear Bhairav Singh's voice: 'It's the villagers who must have passed the information to them. They keep going across the border very often.' The camera remains static on the buildings as the jeep reverses back into the shot. Looking at the light coming from the buildings, Bhairav Singh says: 'I wonder who they are and what they are doing here?'

The officers enter the camp and challenge the men they find there, who claim, in Rajasthani, that they come from the village of Dongra and are 'travelling to Tanuad for a visit to the goddesses temple. Singh translated this from Rajasthani for the benefit of the Punjabis. Searching the men, they find nothing, but as they leave the camp, Bhairav Singh notices that the men's camels are being fed on freshly cut green grass. He draws Kuldeep Singh's attention to this: 'Out here in the deserts we don't have green grass for miles' and, after a pause, 'Across the border in Pakistan, however, they do have such grass.' This is enough to confirm their suspicions, and they return to conduct an extra-judicial execution of these men, whose camel's culinary habits have exposed them as 'infiltrators' from across the border. The men have remained confined in the small enclosure of their camp and are shot down without warning by the Indian officers using their handguns. The execution is graphic and begins in slow motion that allows the fetishised hyperrealism of the close range headshots to have full effect. Once the killing is underway, one of the men recovers hidden automatic weapons—thus confirming the status of the men as agents of Pakistan. Nonetheless, Dharam Vir, for all his earlier anger, finds himself unable to 'finish off' a wounded man, despite a direct order to do so. This provokes Kuldeep Singh's wrath: 'Wars are won by slaying the enemy! You have to kill them!'

The interpolation of the sequence at border pillar 635 within this narrative of informers and infiltrators creates a powerful juxtaposition between an ideal situation, the affirmation of the border marker by daylight, and a murkier reality after nightfall, where the border is frequently being transgressed. There is also the implication of a transgression that is still worse: the identification of an enemy within. The account of the villagers who inhabit the border regions is quickly transformed by the events shown in this scene. At one moment of articulation, the Indian soldiers must protect the villages located near the border that are endangered by attack, but in the next, they must also remember that the villagers themselves cannot be trusted. The villagers are accused by Bhairav Singh of harbouring informants and making frequent transgressive crossings. It becomes clear, therefore, that the villagers may be an even more disturbing threat than the Pakistani army since they *do not respect the border or its rules*. An explanation for their strange behaviour has, of course, already been provided: 'they're all related' to the people on the other side. In the context of India-Pakistan relations, and their history, the invocation (and conflation) here of discourses of 'infiltration' and 'relational' loyalties is very clearly marked. After all, it is India's Muslims who have relatives over the border in Pakistan, and whose loyalty has been most often the object of scrutiny by the military apparatus of the state. The people who inhabit the borderlands are shown to be reluctant members of the Indian nation who, if not adequately policed, would prefer to maintain their communal affiliations with villagers on the Pakistan side, rather than demonstrate the patriotism for India that the heroes of the film so vocally espouse. The possibilities for those wishing to read metaphorical parallels between the unreliable Rajasthani villagers and India's most significant minority cannot be easily overlooked. Here then, the nationalist discourse being constructed around the border is full of ambivalences marked by a paranoid suspicion and hostility towards a significantly marked segment of India's own citizens. The lack of the 'good Muslim' character, so often used as a redemptive device in Indian cinema, amongst the main heroes in *Border*, perhaps for reasons of historical accuracy, taken along with the periodic affirmations of patriotic religiosity made by the Sikh and Hindu protagonists, can be seen as a very powerful moment of absence throughout the film. This can only be highly significant when set against the doctrinal precepts of the Hindutva politics that flourished in India during the 1990s.

There is a very obvious discontinuity arising from the shooting down of the infiltrators and the relish with which it is presented, when this event is set against the 'peace message' that serves as the denouement of the film. At the film's ending, following the major sequence that relates the failed attack on Longewala by the Pakistani 22nd Armoured Regiment, we return to the border itself. After a night of desperate fighting on the ground, followed by Captain Suraj's decisive strike from the air after dawn, Major Kuldeep Singh takes in the aftermath of the battle. As the omnipotent camera tracks across the battlefield, we see border pillar 635 again, this time surrounded by the bodies of fallen Pakistani soldiers. The hand of one corpse clasps a photo of a young woman; we see a ring of Muslim women lamenting. Now that victory over the enemy has been achieved it becomes possible for Kuldeep Singh, hitherto the very caricature of the belligerent Sikh, to display feelings of compassion towards his defeated foes. This message is powerfully scored by the Anu Malik—Javed Akhtar song *Mere dushman, mere bhai–* (My enemy, my brother). The film ends with a shot of the two national flags, the superimposition of flying doves, the sun setting in the West, and the phrase 'begining of a lasting peace' [*sic*] that appears across the screen in the stencil typeface that has become requisite for the war-film genre worldwide.

This final montage provides formal notice that equilibrium has been re-established, that the border has been maintained and can, if it is respected, offer the hope of peace. Of course this is a victor's peace, and the fraternity that is offered in this brief sequence sits uncomfortably with earlier suggestions made in the film that those who have relations in/with Pakistan help to foster infiltration and invasion, and that retribution for such treachery should be swift and subjudice. It would be unrealistic, however, to expect a nuanced presentation of the difficulties of inhabiting border-zones or the traumas of familial separation that are caused by the imposition of borders in this particular film. It would also be self-deceiving to expect a sustained pacifist message from *Border* which, after all, is so consciously a war film. With such an agenda it is not surprising that *Border* received generous co-operation from the Indian military, as the (stencilled) credits of the film make explicit: 'Without these forces behind J. P. Films, "Border" would not have been possible.' Nonetheless, Dutta has responded to criticism of the film as 'jingoistic' by seeking to make a distinction between being pro-army and anti-Pakistan: '*Border* wasn't meant to open wounds. It tried to instil a sense of pride within all Indians regarding the Indian Army which has upheld some values even when there has been a discernible drop in moral standards in all walks of life. *Border* wasn't meant to indulge in Pakistan bashing' (Jha 2000a).

## Crossing Borders

*Refugee*, J. P. Dutta's 'sequel' to *Border*, was released in 2000. This film focuses again on the India-Pakistan border, this time as it stretches across the Great Rann of Kutch further to the south, demarcating Indian Gujarat and Pakistani Sind. While, in the first film, the narrative progression begins with the national border being affirmed and then defended against transgression, *Refugee* inverts this structure. Here, the border is transgressed in the first part of the film and then affirmed in the second. The narrative of *Refugee* focuses on the cross-border transgressions of a young man: Refugee (Abhishek Bachchan), conveniently unmarked by family, community or nationality, who works as a smuggler of both goods and people across the India-Pakistan border in both directions across the Rann of Kutch. The first part of the film narrates the efforts of a family of 'Bihari Muslims' who have fled Bangladesh by 'infiltrating', and then crossing India in order to reach the border with Pakistan. They hope to cross illegally in order to re-settle in the homeland that abandoned them after Bangladesh seceded from Pakistan in 1971. Refugee assists them in reaching their goal, and then becomes romantically involved with the daughter of the family, Naazneen (Kareena Kapoor). However, in the latter part of the film, Refugee, who claims to have no allegiances to either country, is ultimately forced to take sides as his people-smuggling unwittingly facilitates an infiltration of terrorists from Pakistan, who conduct a bombing in Delhi with the aid of his 'bad' brother Shadab (Shadaab Khan).

The plight of the Bihari Muslims, with which the film begins, presents an entirely different set of problematics around the border, not least because the primary aim of the protagonists is to breach the border in order to *leave* India. The Bihari Muslims of *Refugee* are the 'stranded Pakistanis' of Bangladesh, Urdu-speaking Muslims who originally migrated from the eastern parts of India to the eastern wing of the newly-created Pakistan in 1947, as well as their descendants. It is estimated that some 700,000 Muslims from West Bengal, Orissa, Assam and, in the majority, Bihar, migrated to East Pakistan. Initially well-received in East Bengal as Muslim migrants during the creation of Pakistan in 1947, relations between Bihari immigrants and the Bengali majority in East Pakistan became increasingly strained as relations between the western and eastern portions of Pakistan turned sour. After India's intervention in the civil war and the declaration of Bangladesh as an independent nation, some 160,000 West Pakistanis were repatriated from Bangladesh. However, Pakistan was only willing to take those non-Bengalis from the former East Pakistan who had been in government service or formerly domiciled in its western provinces. Thus, most of the non-Bengali minorities in the former eastern wing who had migrated there in 1947 were left behind after 1971 in a Bangladesh that refused to accept them as citizens. As such, the 'Bihari Muslims' lack the citizenship of either Bangladesh or Pakistan, with as many as 300,000 of them living out their lives in refugee camps in Bangladesh (Ahmad 2003:173). This complex tale of multiple displacements and disavowals, shifting borders and nation-splitting is recounted in the opening voice-over of *Refugee*:

> In 1947 when our country was partitioned, people from Bihar left their
> homes and set out for East Bengal, which had become part of Pakistan,

with dreams of a better life. But those dream were fragile. Then came 1971 and the dreams were completely shattered. East Pakistan became Bangladesh and these Muslims from Bihar became refugees once again. Once again, stateless. Bihar they could never return to, like the tree that can never throw roots into the very soil from which it has been uprooted. Now they embarked upon a very long journey from Bangladesh to Guwahati, from Guwahati to Delhi, from Delhi to Ajmer and then onwards to Ahmedabad. From there to Bhuj and finally to Haji Pir. The journey to Pakistan would take them through the Rann of Kutch, illegally. For miles stretch the salt-infested wastelands and marshes. No man, no animal, not even a blade of grass in sight for miles. There are these men, professionals, who specialise in evading the border guards and smuggling them out. One of them is the young 'Refugee', who has no home, no family, no parents to name, maybe that's why they call him Refugee. For Manzoor Ahmed and his fellow travellers from Bangladesh, perhaps he is the kind of man they have been looking for.

Abandoned by their contacts, Manzoor Ahmed (Kulbhushan Kharbanda) and his family languish on the Indian side of the border. Manzoor assesses their plight with a statement of contrition: 'Out first mistake was in 1947 when we left Bihar and went to Bengal.' His aged mother supports him with her own assertion that the family have been cursed for forsaking the graves of their ancestors in Bihar. At this moment, they are approached by a local villain who offers to help them cross over into Pakistan. Taking their savings as payment, he takes the family to meet Jaan Mohammed (Anupam Kher), the Muslim headman of a village near the border. Before they arrive, we see Jaan Mohammed addressing a group of villagers as he articulates the impositions that the border villages have suffered since being divided from their kin across the border:

> All I'm saying is that Pakistanis eat the same food as we eat, right? And they dress the same as us and think the same as us. We've friends, brothers and relatives on that side, and on this side too. We want to wed our daughters to their sons. And we want our sons to wed their daughters. It used to happen this way before Partition didn't it? What seals the relationship is a bond of sweet love. But these leaders and those men in uniform. They won't let us live in peace [*gestures into the distance*] nor them. And when things go out of control they go counting heads. All because we live near the border.

With this speech, Jaan Mohammed provides a rationale for the border transgressions that are to follow. The motivation being articulated here is similar to that given in *Border*, that the villagers who inhabit the borderlands do not respect the border, and prefer to maintain the ties of kinship that it has sundered. The treatment of this position is much more sympathetic here, as it is throughout *Refugee*, but the coding of the explanation is remarkably similar. The compulsions for fraternity with Pakistan are much greater for those Indians who 'eat the same food', 'dress the same' and 'think the same', that is for Muslims. If Indian Muslims are represented only by a powerful absence in *Border*, then in *Refugee* they become central to the narrative, and thus central to the didactic message of the film, which addresses them directly on the inherently dangerous nature of fraternisation and transgression. The non-Muslim audience is positioned implicitly as sharing this instructional address to their compatriots on the crucial matter of unambiguous loyalty, an imperative that speaks back to Jaan Mohammed as the events that transpire in the film unfold. For now, Jaan Mohammed greets Manzoor Ahmed and his family and, having taken their money from the middleman, introduces them to his 'adopted son', Refugee, who will take them across the border to Pakistan, where they will be assisted by Jaan Mohammed's brother whose village lies on the Pakistan side.

Under the cover of darkness, Refugee leads the Biharis out towards the border. The party includes Manzoor, his elderly mother and his wife, their daughter Naazneen, as well as Asghar Ali, his wife and their daughter, Selma. Evading the searchlights of the Indian watchtowers and the patrols of the BSF, they move out towards the Rann. As they move through the night, a series of coy exchanges foreshadows the romance between Refugee and Naazneen. They eventually reach border pillar 423, set in the midst of the great salt flats, and Refugee informs them that they are now in Pakistani territory. Manzoor's mother, however, collapses in fatigue against the border pillar, asking them fatalistically: 'How long will you carry this corpse'? Refugee tells them that it is too dangerous to remain by the pillar and, taking Manzoor's mother upon his back, leads them on onwards into Pakistan. Her plight has slowed them down, however, and they cannot pass the Pakistan border posts before sunrise. They are forced hide in the scrub, to avoid detection by the Pakistan Rangers in the watchtowers and to wait out the daylight before moving on. This is too much for Asghar Ali, who, believing that he has reached his promised land, refuses to wait: 'Are they going to stop me? Are they going to kill me? One of their brothers? They are my people. This is the land of my dreams.' Closely followed by his wife, Asghar Ali runs towards the Pakistani watchtowers shouting: 'I am home, it's me, Asghar Ali!' The border guards, predictably, shoot them both down, and Refugee and his charges are forced to slip away hurriedly as Pakistani troops search the area.

As the bodies of the Alis are brought back from no man's land by the Rangers, a local guide tells their commander, Mohammed Ashraf (Sunil Shetty): 'They look like refugees attempting to infiltrate' and reveals that there had been others there who had slipped away. Ashraf declares that a sweep of the border villages must be conducted. Once night has fallen again, Refugee, still carrying Manzoor's mother, guides the reminder of the party (Manzoor and his wife, Asghar Ali's distraught daughter Selma and Naazneen) across the border to the safety of Jaan Mohammed's brother's home. As they are resting, Mohammed Ashraf and the Pakistan Rangers sweep through the village, and the Biharis are saved from exposure by Jaan Mohammed's brother, Altaf Mohammed, who claims that Manzoor Ahmed is an old friend who is visiting the area to find a match for his daughter. After Ashraf departs, Refugee reveals to Manzoor that his mother has been dead ever since the shooting of the Alis, and that now she must be buried. Having carried her corpse through the night, Refugee has demonstrated his noble nature and, in this way, he relieves Manzoor of the family curse: he will now be able to bury his mother in the Pakistan that she has reached finally, only in death.

In the sequences that follow, Manzoor and his family, along with Selma, continue to live in the village of Jaan Mohammed's brother. Here, we see a world much like that on the other side. The villagers make money from the activities of smugglers like Refugee with a stream of people and goods, from narcotics and guns to Lata Mangeshkar cassettes being moved across the border. The transgressive space of the border is politically marked here in partisan terms by the dangerous nature of all the Pakistani exports (drugs, guns and eventually terrorists) as opposed to the benign Indian exports (Lata Mangeshkar and stranded Bihari refugees). Stripping the politics of this aside, however, the role played by cross-border smuggling in the border regions is a crucial component for the creation of transgressive spaces. This is the socio-economic nexus of the borderlands where, as Purewal observes: 'The market and trade run by smugglers on both sides for such goods as alcohol, dry fruits, electronics, videos, and cigarettes has been influential in mapping out the routes across the border' (Purewal 2003: 549).

Given the importance of the cross-border economy, the people of the villages on the Pakistani side are as cautious and evasive of the Pakistan Rangers as their counterparts in India are of the Border Security Force. The morality of the borderlands and its inhabitants shown in the film is a rich mix of greys where there are army informants in the villages on both sides, just as there are army personnel (again on both sides) who pass information to the smugglers. It is within this dangerous, yet also close-knit and familial, world that the romance between Naazneen and Refugee develops as Refugee moves backwards and forwards across the Rann between India and Pakistan.

The stability of this transgressive cross-border society is soon threatened, however. Refugee unwittingly assists a group of terrorists to cross over, who enlist his wayward younger brother's aid in carrying out a bomb attack in Delhi. Horrified, Jaan Mohammed disowns his younger, legitimate son, but the damage now has already been done. The profitable life led by Jaan Mohammed and Refugee, undisturbed by any particular national loyalties, is about to come apart. Following the Delhi bombing, the commanders of the two opposing border forces meet at a tent on the border for their quarterly 'border flag meeting'. Their meeting begins with an exchange of sweets, *balushahi* from India and *sewaiya* from Pakistan. As they eat, Raghuvir Singh provokes an exchange with Mohammed Ashraf by telling him that he hopes that he is enjoying his Indian sweet, because it is 'soaked in the blood of Indians'.

Mohammed Ashraf: What was that you said?

Raghuvir Singh: From Delhi to Coimbatore, when the bombs explode, India bleeds. Pointing to the sweet. Surely a drop or two will splash over here.

Mohammed Ashraf: Raghuvir sahib, before levelling that allegation, you should have considered that from Peshawar to Karachi, subversives are having an orgy of blood. This sewaiyan you eat is soaked in Pakistani blood.

Raghuvir Singh: So now the thief accuses? Are you alleging...?

Mohammed Ashraf: No. Not at all, sahib. I am just asking you to eat a sweet.

Raghuvir Singh: Ashraf, enmity, like friendship, can never be one-sided. It's both-sided.

Mohammed Ashraf: From day one it is an enmity that you have scored.

Raghuvir Singh: Mr Ashraf, this is your misconception. For centuries it has been the tradition for sons to move out of their homes once they are grown up. So we give them a separate house to live in. But even after you have been given [a separate house], you are still unhappy?

Mohammed Ashraf: That's provided you leave us in peace. And what is this everyday heckling. You have cut off one of our arms. That which you call Bangladesh today.

Raghuvir Singh: Revenge? We haven't cut off anyone's arms. But with this feeling of vengeance, blood will flow. The blood of innocents. On our side, on your side too.

Mohammed Ashraf: Both sides must think. We must stop the enemies of humanity.

Raghuvir Singh: Not the handful of terrorists who are pawns for hire. The real enemies are the ones who employ them, who do not want us to live in peace with our neighbours. They want us to keep on fighting, so that attention is diverted from the real enemy.

Mohammed Ashraf: The problem is no one knows who the real enemy is. The real enemy is hunger, poverty, helplessness.

Raghuvir Singh: For which we are the ones responsible. The ones who trade in the merchandise of war. We buy planes, ships worth millions to bomb each other. Without a thought to how many schools we could build with that money, how many hospitals.

Mohammed Ashraf [*in English*]: Right. [*Nodding*]. Anyway, our countries are large and our borders vast, but in the areas under our command we can stop the enemies of humanity.

Raghuvir Singh: That's what I'm here to tell you. Far better would be to start searching the villages near the border.

Refugee, meanwhile, is caught trying to re-cross the border to India. He is beaten unconscious by Pakistan Rangers and packed off across the Rann on a camel laden with explosives by Mohammed Ashraf's sadistic and lecherous second-in-command Tausif Ahmed, who turns out to be in league with the terrorists. As Refugee recovers in hospital on the Indian side, Raghuvir Singh confronts him over his smuggling activities. Contrite, Refugee elects to finally become an 'Indian', volunteering his services to the BSF to atone for his past activities. He is quickly made an officer in the BSF and informs on, and then helps arrest, his former colleagues. The one drawback to this new life is that he is unable to cross the border to see Naazneen, now pregnant with his child, on the Pakistan side. At this point, the terrorist group decides to invade India and annex Jaan Mohammed's village, counting on the Muslim population's support. Manzoor's hitherto meek host in Pakistan, Altaf Mohammed, is suddenly transformed by religious zeal and joins with the terrorists. Mounted on their camels, the terrorists and the Pakistani villagers cross the border and seize Jaan Mohammed's village of Astalkot. Jaan Mohammed refuses to join in their insurrection and is shot dead by his brother, thus finally discovering that he does not 'think the same' as those over the border, and that he really is an Indian after all. Refugee and Raghuvir then lead the BSF forces in a counter-attack which liberates the village.

This somewhat unlikely turn of events in the second part of the film works to re-establish the authority of the border that is undermined in the first half of the film. From the entry of the terrorists that confirms the sinister side of the smuggling network, *Refugee* begins its switch away from arguments for transgression towards supporting the same discourses on infiltration as *Border*. At the flag meeting, Mohammed Ashraf and Raghuvir Singh make a formal assertion of this position as they conclude that peace is only achievable if they work together to defend the integrity of the border. This agenda is played out in the events surrounding the sudden 'invasion' of Astalkot by the terrorists and the Pakistani villagers. Here, the film works to separate and delineate the competing loyalties of the people of the border villages. This provides a parallel to the discourses on Indian Muslim identity structuring John Mathew Mattan's contemporaneous *Sarfarosh* (The Martyr, 1999), as identified by Vazira Fazila-Yacoobali (2002: 183–198). Here, the permissible attachments for Indian Muslims are spelt out through the concepts of *ghar* (home/family), *qaum* (community/faith) and *mulk* (homeland/nation). In *Refugee*, Altaf Mohammed shows that he is ready to kill his brother for qaum and mulk whereas Jaan Mohammed defies the terrorists on the basis of ghar and mulk. Here qaum and ghar are formally separated and each becomes joined to mulk in a mutually exclusive arrangement. This opens up the possibility/requirement for Indian Muslims to become fully Indian by privileging mulk over qaum, homeland over faith. There is also another layer to this message in *Refugee* that functions as a restoration of the equilibrium of difference that marks the border itself, as those who have privileged not only qaum, but also ghar, over mulk in the first part of the film ultimately see their family split along national lines and destroyed. Refugee alone is redeemed by his earlier decision to put his nationality first and to respect the authority of the border, thus adopting the standard cinematic role of the 'good Muslim'. During this transition, his first adopted father, Jaan Mohammed, and the community of villagers and smugglers is replaced by the patriarchal Raghuvir Singh, and the community of the Indian military and its service to the state.

In the final scene of the film, Mohammed Ashraf organises for Naazneen to attend festivities taking place at a shrine located in the border area. Raghuvir Singh and Refugee, as officers in the BSF, are also present. In a gesture of magnanimity, Ashraf arranges for a priest to wed the heavily pregnant Naazneen to Refugee. As the two Indian officers are escorted back across the border, Naazneen's labour begins and she reaches out for the border pillar and hangs on to it for support. With the aid of a handful of women who are gathered at the border fence to watch the celebrations on the other side, Naazneen and Refugee's baby son is delivered on the ground next to the border pillar, just as fireworks start going off in the sky above them, because the moment of this birth is also the midnight between the 14th and 15th of August, India and Pakistan's two independence days. As the film ends, Raghuvir and Ashraf haggle amicably over the nationality of the baby. Raghuvir notes that, since this is an international border area, the child belongs to neither country. This makes the child, as Ashraf puts it 'neither, both, a citizen of the world'. In reply, Raghuvir says: 'He will make a place for himself. A land with no boundaries. A land where comings and goings are not restricted. His country will be called the kingdom of mankind.' Together they conclude: 'No passport. No visa.'

## Equilibrium

J. P. Dutta has been insistent that *Border* and *Refugee* were both films that promoted a message of peace between India and Pakistan (quoted in Jha 2003). Nonetheless, it remains the case that *Border* was accused of being an anti-Pakistan film and was therefore banned in the Middle East markets where Hindi films are commonly exported. *Border* provoked violent agitations against video stores by Muslim South Asians overseas (Varma 1997). *Refugee* was somewhat better received offshore but did less business in India than its predecessor. Despite the self-conscious peace messages with which both films end, Dutta has been much criticised for his supposedly one-sided portrayal of the issues dividing India and Pakistan. Anish Khanna, reviewing the less provocative *Refugee*, still declared it to be 'less than subtly biased' (Khanna 2000). So, even though both films end with the invocation of a post-confrontation subcontinent, as one amateur reviewer comments: 'One can't help suspect that J. P. Dutta imagines such a world would be established on India's terms rather than Pakistan's (IMD 2001). Dutta, however, is unrepentant: 'I'm trying to tackle a serious bilateral issue here. At least I have the guts to bring such a sensitive subject in a mainstream Hindi film' (quoted in Jha 2000b).

In commenting on the two films Dutta has said: '*Border* was a war film. But I don't think *Refugee* was a war film' (quoted in Jha 2003). In other respects, however, particularly in their primary focus on the border itself, the two films are discursively inter-referential. Indeed, in many ways, *Refugee* can be seen as a rejoinder to the many criticisms of *Border*: the complexities of Indo-Pak relations receive more recognition, the questions surrounding nationalism and Muslim identity are considered, and the people of the border regions are given more sympathetic and substantial treatment. It is, of course, far from insignificant here that Hindi (or perhaps more accurately Hindustani) cinema has a large following in Pakistan. For filmmakers, the importance of audiences on both sides of the border has to be balanced by what constitutes a permissible articulation of India-Pakistan relations within India's political-economy. Needless to say, the political implications of any cinematic account of inter-state relations in India are subject to an explicitly national(ist) censorship regime. Nonetheless, for their part, Pakistani audiences for Hindi films seem prepared to take the occasional jingoistic outburst with a pinch of salt. Whereas *Border* presents a narrative in which hostilities between the two countries are relatively black-and-white, *Refugee* goes some way towards nuancing the many grey areas that provoke the nationalist anxieties that feed conflict in the region. Nonetheless, despite the contrasting affirmative/transgressive positions towards the India-Pakistan boundary with which the two films begin, their concluding positions are remarkably similar to official Indian doxa: conflict will continue as long as enemies outside the nation are trying to enter, the loyalties of border communities are suspect and must be policed, a secure border and the establishment of a clear demarcation between the two states and the adoption of unequivocal national loyalties are the only means of achieving peace.

Whether they are engaged in military confrontation over the border, or collaborate in its operation, both states have a fundamental stake in the existence of the border. As such, the films of J. P. Dutta work consistently towards reconciling the constant problem of the border, making it the central problem of nationalist confrontation in South Asia. The considerable challenge of its visual incongruity, arising from its literal existence as an artificial cartographic intervention in real space, is met with considerable creativity through a whole series of dramatic metaphors staged around the border pillars. Unable to discount the accidents of history entirely, however, or to negate the lingering bitterness caused by Partition, the meanings that seek to establish themselves in these border narratives direct themselves towards a mythic future where the border is no longer transgressed. They seek to suggest that once the border is finally naturalised, and everyone has positioned themselves unambiguously within two nation states that have each ceased to make claims upon the territory of the other, then peace can be achieved. The unfinished business of partition *in a strictly territorial sense* thus becomes both cause and solution to the nationalist problem, with the border serving as the fulcrum between secure and contented national spaces.

However, this message, while seemingly clearcut, is undermined by a number of subtexts that construct another implicit, and contradictory, agenda. Here, the narrative treatments given to the people of the border regions and to their relationship to the state, and the focus on the ambiguities of belonging which are assumed to concern Muslims in particular, suggest with equal force that the true meaning of the border arises from human, rather than spatial, geography. The need, five decades after Independence, to continue striving for a clear boundary in terms of political and cultural identity is a visible reminder (for audiences on both sides of the border) of the impossibility of a purely cartographic expression of cultural differences. Paradoxically, the India-Pakistan border in the films of J. P. Dutta emerges not as a physical location, but as a psychological condition underpinned by a regime of violence.

# 3

# Borders and Border Crossings in *Main Hoon Na* and *Veer-Zaara*

## Rajinder Dudrah

Lieutenant Karan Shergill (Hrithik Roshan) stands at the edge of the border landscape between India and Pakistan in the Kargil-region mountains in the film *Lakshya* (The Objective, 2004). Accompanied by his Indian-Muslim army Captain, Jalal Akbar (Sushant Singh), Karan is driven to the LOC (Line of Control) to be shown what he is to defend as part of his duties as an officer of the Indian armed forces. Karan and Capt. Akbar stand in the same frame looking onwards over the Indian border and into Pakistani territory. The camera films a long shot over the top right angle of the Indian *chowki* (army bunker) and looks across into the distance at the Pakistani chowki. Capt. Akbar interrupts the diegetic sound of the mountain terrain:

> Capt. Akbar: Karan, do you see the Pakistani bunker over there?
>
> Karan: Wow! It's unbelievable.
>
> Capt. Akbar *(Pointing to the pillar in between the distance of the two bunkers)*: That pillar marks the LOC and from here to there is no man's land. Not ours not theirs. Even so, we exchange fire almost everyday. If there's firing we also retaliate.
>
> Karan: That's amazing. It's like I've always known, but somehow...I've never felt this Indian before. *(Pauses as he looks on, over the border)* I'm an Indian.
>
> Capt. Akbar: I still remember seeing these borders for the first time. I understand how you must feel. Come, let's go.

A mid-shot remains on Karan as Capt. Akbar moves out of the frame. Karan stands still. He is momentarily captivated by the sight of the physical geography in front of him, demarcated as Pakistani by the Pakistani bunker. The final closing shot of this scene is a long shot, from Karan's point of view, of the Pakistani chowki from across the Indian border.

The sequence of this scene is composed of silent and natural diegetic physical sounds (like that of the wind whistling through the mountains), the insertion of non-diegetic music (when Capt. Akbar points out the pillar marking no man's land, a slow and gradual orchestral score begins signalling a military motif that remains implicit in the background), and long- and mid-shots that are edited to suture the characters, landscape and, by implication, the predominantly Indian viewers of the film into a symbiotic relationship where the nation is invoked and shown to be in need of border controls and *raksha* (protection).

This scene is telling of the moments in recent popular Hindi cinema, through which the border is conveyed on-screen through audio and visual gestures, and how it comes to signify certain kinds of under-standings that are created by filmmakers for possible kinds of inter-pretation by Bollywood film audiences. In this instance from *Lakshya*, narratives, symbols and metaphors of Indian self versus Pakistani other, as versus them sameness versus difference, and defence versus attack are articulated together and can be deciphered by paying attention to the audio and visual style of the film.[1] Audio and visual style, is a useful indicator of the motifs and politics that operate throughout a large part of the film *Lakshya*. The film has been crafted in the predominant mode of a war drama set during the Kargil conflict between India and Pakistan in 1999 and, as such, its polarities of the Indian 'self' and the Pakistani 'other' are marked in clear ideologically and culturally hegemonic ways that are used to demonstrate India's legitimacy to defend itself against an invading Pakistan. But what of the moments also in contemporary Bollywood cinema where the use of the border and, by implication, the Indo-Pak self/other dichotomy is not as easily coded and perhaps allows for more fluid representational possibilities at and across the Indo-Pak border?

This essay will provide a close reading of some key scenes from two select films of the post-2000s that have engaged with the border in contemporary Bollywood cinema. It offers a close textual reading of the use of the border as actual physicality and symbolic space in two different and select films in terms of aesthetic intent (how the border appears, is framed and represented) and in terms of possible audience effects (what kinds of pleasures and meanings the use of the border generates).

The films that are focussed on in terms of their audio and visual style around the border are *Main Hoon Na* (Don't worry, I'm here, 2004) and *Veer-Zaara* (2004). The reason for the choice of these films is twofold: First, they appear in the context of flashpoints of both aggression and opportunities for peace across the Indo-Pak border: post-millennium South Asian themes that the two films engage with.[2] Second, the two films interpret and create meanings about the border (i. e., they speculate on the consequences of borders) and, especially in *Veer-Zaara,* they also invoke border crossing as a possibility and aesthetic pleasure that transcends easy and conservative constructions of Indians and Pakistanis in problematic binary terms.

The methodological imperative, in this essay, of articulating together screen textual analysis and socio-cultural commentary draws inspiration from scholarship in border studies, particularly relating to the Indo-Pak region. Recent work on the history of the simultaneous independence and violent partition of India that resulted in the 3000 km-long Indo-Pak border has argued for the need not only to intervene in the political formation of borders, but also the terminology that defines borders to carefully consider (Kalra and Purewal 1999; Purewal 2003).[3] A border can be considered an actual and physical place—literally, a line of control and division. Arising from an intervention into the plight of the people who live near or are connected (even through diasporic or transnational routes) to borders, the term 'borderland' is an apt way of addressing the socio-cultural space that is created and exists as a possibility that can encapsulate the pleasures, pains and politics of residing near and sometimes crossing, and at other times wanting to cross, actual borders. As Gloria Anzaldua puts it, 'A borderland is a vague and undetermined place created by the emotional residue of an unnatural boundary. It is in a state of constant transition' (Anzaldua 1987: 3). Navtej Purewal, elaborating on borderlands, argues for the importance of analysing the formations of culture in these spaces: 'The significance of culture in those places and spaces around borders presents a challenge to the political science of international borders in which it is not merely formal arrangements between nation-states that are of importance' (Purewal 2003: 541). Borderlands, then, can become sites of creative cultural production that require investigation. For the purposes of the present chapter, it is argued that *Main Hoon Na* and *Veer-Zaara* both attempt representing and engaging with the Indo-Pak border as actual physical place but more so as symbolic borderland space. What kinds of cinematic borderland spaces are constructed in these two case study films will be evaluated in the conclusion.

## Main Hoon Na

*Main Hoon Na* was the hit film of the summer of 2004, both in the domestic Indian and overseas Bollywood markets. *Main Hoon Na* is the story of Indian Army Major Ram Prasad Sharma (Shahrukh Khan) who is involved in events to ensure that 'Project *Milaap* (Unity)'—the releasing of innocent captives on either side of the borders of India and Pakistan—can take place as a sign of trust and movement towards peace between the two nations. Opposed to this project is an ex-Indian Army officer, who parades under the pseudonym of Raghavan (Suniel Shetty) and, together with his group of ex-army militants, terrorises those involved in Project Milaap in an attempt to prevent its occurrence.

   *Main Hoon Na* has been made in the mould of a classic *masala* film—having ample ingredients of action, romance, melodrama, and elaborate song and dance spectacles. Like almost any other Bollywood masala film, it too draws on one of the predominant mythic and religious texts of India, the Ramayana. Evidently, Shahrukh is cast as Ram, his younger brother (played by Zayed Khan) literally as Lakshman, the villain is a reworking of the name of the demon king Ravan, and Shahrukh's role can be read as averting a threat to the nation, India. Ram also has to bring together his separated and bickering family. However, the film's creative team, headed by renowned dance choreographer Farah Khan in her directorial debut, has deliberately gone against the grain of applying this Hindu text in a right-wing nationalist vein. *Main Hoon Na* can be situated in recent popular Hindi cinema as following on from the anti-Pakistan, anti-Muslim slanted films of late such as *Gadar—Ek Prem Katha* (Revolution—A Love Story, 2001) and *The Hero* (2003), both starring Sunny Deol. *Main Hoon Na* is a conscious attempt to move away from the depiction of Pakistan as the constant wrongdoer or sole villain. Instead, it reinterprets the Ramayana predominantly as a story of reconciliation and diplomacy, in which the nation of India has to deal with its internal enemies and terrorists, as in the character of Raghavan, that pose a threat to the possible peace process between India and Pakistan. Ram's bickering family unit, a metaphor for the social condition of the nation, must also be restored through dialogue and love.[4]

The depiction of the border features throughout *Main Hoon Na*, at crucial points in the development of the main plot of Project Milaap. The opening scenes of the film take us into the world of public debate in urban India through the current affairs programme of *Jan Manch* (People's Voice). A discussion is being filmed in front of a live studio audience that stands in for sections of the Indian public. Here, the inception of Project Milaap is being discussed by the show's host and the brainchild behind the initiative, Indian Army General Amar Singh Bakshi (Kabir Bedi). The merits of small steps towards possible peace are being discussed. General Bakshi explains the reasons for wanting to release fifty Pakistani captives in Indian jails, some of whom have been in prison since 1971 and many who have accidentally crossed over the Indo-Pak border looking for water, not realising that they have done so. As Bakshi says: 'Our borders are not properly sealed.' Accompanying this exchange, images of everyday, ostensibly poor village folk are displayed on the several television screens in the studio. Stills of men, young and old, in handcuffs and chains, encapsulated by barbed wire, and in dark prison cells are shown, accompanied by an angelic, enchanting musical score. Throughout this sequence, the camera shifts between General Bakshi and images of the Pakistani captives on the screens, to a slow pan-shot across the audience members of the *Jan Manch* show—the audience are watching and thinking. Bakshi goes on to say: '…Some of them didn't even know that they have crossed the border…. We feel it's time to send them back home.' The studio audience applauds.

This opening sequence, then, is as much a signpost of the challenges, trials and hopes towards initiating a reciprocal friendship that await our hero, Ram, as it is a preferred ideological mediation of the possibility of an enhanced peace process between India and Pakistan. India is seen as starting off the steps towards diplomatic friendship, via the release of captured Pakistanis, and, later in the film, Pakistan also follows suit with the release of captive Indian villagers who crossed over its borders. What is also of significance here is the implicit ideals given to a version of Indian democracy, in which the main protagonists are hailed as urban and middle class Indians. In the studio, the audience members are all dressed in cosmopolitan urban western attire—the men wear suits, shirts and trousers, and the women wear dresses. These signifiers of a modern and urban Indian setting are juxtaposed with the images and attire of the Pakistani prisoners in Indian jails. The captives are wearing white cotton tunics and everyday basic village clothing. A polarity is set up in terms of class and access to power—the poor relatively powerless villagers on the borders of India and Pakistan, and the middle class city dwellers who have the cultural autonomy to debate, discuss and thereby partake in generating ideals of active public citizenry through the talk-show format. Interestingly, then, it appears that the urban metropolises of India are where the fate of the borders and its people are discussed and decided.

The second point in which the border features in the film is in the flashback scene as backdrop story to Raghavan's formation as the film's villain. Through Raghavan's recollection, the audience views the arrest of several Pakistani villagers across a nameless desert region of India, where Raghavan, as an Indian Army officer, is in charge of the patrol. The Pakistanis have mistakenly crossed over, looking for water, echoing and making real the earlier reference to the border from General Bakshi's dialogues in the *Jan Manch* studio sequence. Raghavan lines up the Pakistanis, telling them that they are now on Indian soil, misuses his power, and 'tries' and executes them on the spot with a pistol shot to the backs of their heads. Raghavan is subsequently court-martialled and dismissed from the army. It becomes clear that Raghavan's violent hatred for and mistrust of Pakistanis comes from the death of his young son, allegedly caused by Indo-Pak fighting across another border—in the disputed region of Kashmir. The border and the consequences of border crossing in this instance are shown as a literal place of danger, where territorial control and the possible abuses of its laws and powers lead to abhorrent executions. The border becomes an ongoing contested margin, resulting in the fuelling and escalation of Indo-Pak tension.

It is in the final segments of the film, as it moves towards its climax, that the border is actually physically shown for the first time. Of course, it is a constructed and fictitious border—one that is never explicitly named or geographically identified. The border is set amidst a desert landscape, with winds blowing and sand flying in the air for atmospheric effect. Through the use of the Indian villagers' clothing and appearance, the area might well be considered Rajasthani. Project Milaap is about to be realised as Pakistan has agreed to release fifty Indians. The frame consists of two large border fences running parallel to each other. In between is no man's land. Two gates are strategically positioned on opposite sides of the fence as the only official entry and exit points. The gates are the conduits through which the release and exchange of the Indians and Pakistanis can take place across the border.

The release and exchange sequence is set amidst another exchange—an exchange of wits, physicality, and a battle for life and death as Ram and Raghavan have their final showdown and fight each other, fist to fist, at a separate location. The highly stylised and martial arts choreographed action sequence between Ram and Raghavan takes place parallel to when Project Milaap is underway and the two sequences are sutured together through the film's editing.

As Ram and Raghavan face each other, white doves fly around them.[5] At the border, the militaries of India and Pakistan are gathered, as are the families and villagers from either side to receive their loved ones, and the media are also present to mark this historical occasion. String instruments are used to create music of anticipation as the camera cuts to images of the villagers looking on over the border fences. Cut to Ram and Raghavan exchanging blows and kicks. The music here is electronically generated—synthesised sounds and electronic drumbeats punctuate the physical offensive of the two bodies; angelic chanting is laced over the music as if this attack on each other requires divine intervention. Cut to the gates opening at the border and the two generals of India and Pakistan shake hands and congratulate each other on the success of Project Milaap. Violin, wind and piano instrumentation builds up to a triumphant orchestral score as the prisoners from either side walk across no man's land together in a line. As they pass each other they rub shoulders, becoming a single indistinguishable line of South Asian men on the screen. Their relatives and villagers clap with joy on either side of India and Pakistan. Cut to Ram and Raghavan who have now fought their way on to a rooftop that has been planted with explosives. An army helicopter arrives to rescue Ram from the roof; Ram's brother Lucky is on board. The roof begins to explode and Raghavan is killed. Ram runs off the roof, leaps across the air and catches on to the legs of the helicopter, in the mode of an action blockbuster hero. Cut to the prisoners reuniting with their families. Cut to Ram falling on top of Lucky, both embracing each other. Cut to the families on either side of the border hugging and physically reconnecting. These scenes are filmed in slow motion as if to accentuate the powerful achievement of the two events: Project Milaap and Ram's success after the battle. The families laugh and cry—universal signs of human emotions across the border. An Indian man bows down on his knees, picks up sand from the desert and rubs it across his forehead. A Pakistani in a similar pose gets down as if he is praying and touches his forehead on Pakistani soil. Violins and a *bansuri* (an Indian flute) play, evoking a reconciliatory mood: a mood that is almost otherworldly, as if the angelic, chanting sound from earlier has now turned into angels sighing with relief. Cut to the helicopter where Ram and Lucky yell out in joy. The closing shots of this sequence are of two other brothers on the Indian side of the border—they hug. One brother picks up the other in glee.

The final sequences of *Main Hoon Na*'s finale are a way of bringing together the disparate blends of the masala genre (melodrama, action, religious texts in the light of globalisation, emotive music), and the trials of the hero as a personal battle that literally becomes a battle for the sake of national honour and better prospects with neighbouring Pakistan. The reuniting of Ram and Lucky as brothers and the coming together of Indian and Pakistani families both offer an ideologically preferred solution for the bickering nations of India and Pakistan to resolve their differences through diplomacy. This possibility is a cause worth fighting for as exemplified in the personal, physical and political trials of our hero Ram. The border, then, is a physical and manmade construction that can be mediated for means other than the abuse of power and mindless violence that has been seen in the capturing of innocent Indo-Pak civilians and Raghavan's murder of Pakistani villagers.

### Veer-Zaara

If *Main Hoon Na* extols the virtues of overcoming the border through diplomacy and personal actions, then a slightly later film in 2004 (also starring our leading mediating man Shahrukh Khan) explores the pleasures and trials of border crossing. Released in the autumn months to coincide with the religious festivals of Diwali and Eid, *Veer-Zaara* was the international Bollywood hit of the closing months of that year. It is the love story of the Indian male and Pakistani female protagonists who are separated due to personal and political hurdles that come in their way. The story is told predominantly through flashbacks from the prison cell in Lahore, Pakistan, where Veer is unjustly held captive. The Human Rights Commission in Pakistan appoints Veer a lawyer, Saamiya Siddiqui (Rani Mukherjee), to argue his case and Veer gradually opens up to her. They become friends and he recalls his ordeal: Veer Pratap Singh (Shahrukh Khan) is a helicopter squadron leader in the Indian Air Force that operates on the border geographies of India and Pakistan. On one of his rescue

missions in the mountains, he saves and meets Zaara Hayaat Khan
(Preity Zinta). Zaara has left Pakistan in order to fulfil the dying
wishes of her elderly nanny, Bebe (Zohra Sehgal). Bebe is a Sikh
woman living in Pakistan since Partition and requests that her ashes
be immersed in the river at the Sikh pilgrimage site of Kiritpur in
Punjab, India. Concerned, that Zaara is a lone woman traveller,
Veer decides to accompany Zaara on her journey to Kiritpur. At Kiritpur,
he invites her to his village in the Punjab to meet his family and fellow
villagers. Veer and Zaara kindle a strong liking for each other that
slowly develops into love. Zaara returns to Pakistan to get married
but realises that she is in love with Veer. Veer travels to Pakistan as a
visitor in order to win back Zaara but obstacles are put in their way
by Zaara's fiancé, at whose behest, Veer is blackmailed and wrongly
imprisoned under espionage charges. Veer spends twenty-two years
of his life in a Pakistani prison and pledges a vow of silence in order
to protect Zaara's and his real identity, and hence their love for each
other. Simultaneously with Veer's decision to stay in the Pakistan jail,
Zaara makes a similar decision. She crosses the border to the Indian
side and spends several years (until she is reunited with Veer) with
Veer's family in their village. Saamiya takes Veer's case to court and,
despite mounting odds, she wins. Veer and Zaara are reunited and
they return to India together as an elderly couple.

The use of the border as a clearly identifiable representation and
apparatus of state control appears only twice in the film: once at the
railway station of Atari that borders on the northwest fringe of India's
geography with Pakistan, and in the final scenes of the film when Veer
and Zaara return to India by walking across the Wagah border from
Pakistan into India. These are two relatively short episodes in the
film's  length of over three hours and we shall return to their virtues
and ideologies in a short while. What allows the border to manifest
itself throughout the film as a discursive and implicit reference is the
diegetic world of the film where the possibilities and pleasures of
border crossing are more paramount than the border itself. This is
not to offer a reading of *Veer-Zaara* in terms that the Indo-Pak border
does not matter as a line of control and divisive entity (as that it clearly
does); rather, the reading put forward here proposes to account for the
pleasure the film aims to encourage around the idea of the Indo-Pak
border, at the level of plot, dialogue, and audio and visual style.

The border is implicitly crossed countless times throughout the film
through the development of its plot (e. g., in the first instance and as

the opening credits roll, Veer is dreaming a song and dance sequence of him and Zaara together, which is in an imagined geography that could be anywhere in India or Pakistan; Veer's reality wakes him and us up in a Pakistani prison in Lahore; Zaara is shown in Lahore with her family; Zaara arrives in India to take Bebe's ashes to Kiritpur, and so on). The plot is audio-visualised as narrative that is sutured through the continuity edit cuts that allow the viewers to make sense of the unfolding story. Even at the level of script, the spoken dialogue by the key characters, and in at least two songs in the film, the border is referenced as either crossed or to be negotiated in terms of a barrier to the lovers meeting (e. g., the frequent references to '*sarhad paar*'—across the border). What marks out the pleasures of Indo-Pak border-crossing, in rich and suggestive ways, are the audio and visual signatures that the film leaves as impressions with its viewers, as both invested with transcendental possibility and the emotional and political strife that accompanies a mixed-race, mixed-religious (Veer is a Sikh and Zaara a Muslim), two-nation love, across the Indo-Pak divide.

The initial reason for a young free-spirited Pakistani girl to leave her homeland and venture into India for the first time to fulfil the dying wishes of her Bebe appear to be bestowed by a certain sense of adventure and spirituality that are inspired by the character of Bebe herself. The exact reasons for Bebe to be in Pakistan are unclear. However, the brief dialogues that Zaara and Bebe share make clear that Bebe was brought over to Pakistan by Zaara's grandfather at the time of Partition and Bebe had chosen to stay with Zaara's family ever since. Whether Bebe had been abducted at the time of Partition or was in love with Zaara's grandfather and came over of her own volition is left unexplained, but Bebe remains a Sikh woman who visits Nankana Sahib, a Sikh *gurudwara* (place of worship) in Lahore, regularly. She is also considered a part of Zaara's family and is given spacious and separate living quarters in the Hayaat Khan household. Zaara is shown accompanying Bebe to the gurudwara, and bowing down and praying before the Guru Granth Sahib (the holy book of the Sikhs); afterwards they eat ice cream together and giggle like two young sisters or close friends. In this way, it is suggested that Bebe has been a personal and spiritual guide in Zaara's life as well as her nanny. The interfaith aspects of Zaara's religious openness are referenced and elaborated on throughout the film, through references to the different mystic saints in both the Sikh and Islamic traditions of faith, either pictorially through images, through song lyrics and through Sufi shrines that are flagged up at key moments in the plot development. From the outset, then, with the introduction of Zaara and Bebe's relationship and Zaara's commitment to the journey to India to deliver Bebe's ashes, an audio and visual style of openness is established that refuses to be pigeonholed as simply and exclusively as India/n and Pakistan/i; rather, it is one that reaches across both borders and creates a diegetic world of fluid exchanges through its sights and sounds. This becomes the primary pleasure of Indo-Pak border crossing in the diegetic world of *Veer Zaara*.

As Veer accompanies Zaara across the fields and countryside of the Punjab to Kiritpur, then on to Veer's village and then to the Atari train station for Zaara's return journey to Lahore, they embark on a personal adventure that slowly brings them closer to each other. The *mise en scène* is full of rich textual metaphors of lush greens, open valleys, flowing rivers, picturesque mountains, and the meeting and greeting a panoply of everyday Indian characters that give an added human dimension to Veer and Zaara's travels. They move across rivers together on an overhead pulley crossing, where Veer carries Zaara in his arms across a river bridge when she twists her ankle. The music that gives expression to these actions is composed of playful *shehnaii*s a traditional wind instrument associated with celebration, and string and percussions instruments, both eastern and western, which are used to signify an upbeat tempo. Often, when Veer and Zaara are together in the same frame, the music is signalled neither as Indian or Pakistani but a mixture, a blend of the two signifiers being evoked as one through the audio and visual registers. These registers take on a spiritual and transcendental quality that is in keeping with the tradition of the mystic saints in both Sikhism and in Sufi Islam that profess the oneness of mankind and the immeasurable sweet pain and longing for a loved one that is akin to the yearning of the soul's quest for union with its divine source.

The uplifting mood of this journey together is both elaborated further and interrupted when Veer and Zaara arrive at the Atari train station. As a border station, it is heavily policed. Tall metal grilled fencing with barbed wires is constructed between the two train lines— one set of tracks operates train traffic within India, and the other set operates trains from Pakistan into India. It is here that their friendship begins to explicitly turn into desire and love for one another. This is especially the case when faced with the prospect of separation via the entry of a human division in Zaara's fiancé, Raza Shirazi (Manoj Bajpai). The three characters meet on the platform bridge. Raza is crossing over from the side of the train's arrival from Pakistan—he is literally and symbolically signified as Pakistani and also as the film's central negative character, akin almost to that of the villain's entry in popular Hindi cinema. He is dressed in a regal black Pakistani *sherwani*-style suit and the music signals him through strings, percussions, and vocal chords that create associations with Islamic sounds and the stature of an aspiring mogul (Raza's political ambitions and his arranged marriage to Zaara as a political alliance between the two families becomes apparent upon Zaara's return to Pakistan).

Cut to a moment later: Veer and Zaara find themselves waiting on the platform together—Raza is away making arrangements for his and Zaara's return journey—and Veer confesses his strong liking for Zaara and his contemplation of a marriage proposal to her. Zaara is stunned speechless, though not altogether caught unaware; her feelings for Veer have also been kindled deeper. Raza rejoins them, and in the verbal exchange between the two men Veer almost confesses his love for Raza's fiancé. During this entire exchange Zaara remains quiet; she does not utter a word. What is further interesting is that this scene occurs at the border—a negotiation is taking place with the woman as the site of the transaction, yet she is unable to speak or chooses to remain silent. Rather than cast this encounter at the border in the film as one where the heroine is simply subjugated by the authority of the two men, we need to follow the movement of this scene as it unfolds into a complex and rich expression of the self through coded audio and visual registers.

As Veer and Zaara turn their backs to each other to go their separate ways, a song begins: '*Do pal ruka khwabon ka caravan*' ('For two moments our caravan of dreams stopped and then moved on'; playbacked by Lata Mangeshkar and Sonu Nigam'). The song is filmed as part day-dream sequence and part magical intervention, as the characters express their true feelings for each other without letting them be known in public: Veer sings to Zaara and Zaara to Veer in an antiphonal call and response style, yet they both imagine the other singing; neither sings at the same time in the same frame. They confess their love to each other through the use of their imagination. It is here that Zaara communicates openly and clearly amidst the hustle and bustle of the border train station. The song sequence is deployed, in one of the conventional formats of its usage in popular Hindi cinema, as a narrative accelerator, to enunciate the unspeakable in a conservative social setting at a border crossing.

As the song ends, the action returns to the actual social world of Veer and Zaara at the train platform. Zaara has now boarded the train. Veer turns around to look at Zaara for one final time at this juncture in their meeting, anticipating a return glance that will confirm her interest in him.[6] Zaara steps back into the frame of the train compartment's doorway. She sends a Muslim greeting of *adaab* to Veer—she gestures towards her forehead with a gently bowed head and a slightly cupped right hand with polite deference and a slightly concealed smile. As they perform this coded etiquette, the music of the song is drawing to a close and the two have secretly confirmed the sentiments of the lyrics—to each other and to the audience. The pleasures of the Atari train station scene arise from the impossibility of Veer and Zaara's situation, manifested at a border crossing: our hero and heroine are unable to fully express their true feelings for each other due to the intervention of Raza; and their perceived difference in terms of Indo-Pak social identities is the obstacle. The border crossing is given added resonance as it creates a moment of exchange, social danger (the fiancé is nearby, as is the Indian police), possibility (if only they could speak openly to each other), longing, and sadness in parting—in accumulation, the scene bears all the hallmarks of a classic Hindi film's emotional and melodramatic moment. The border and the pleasure and problem of how to overcome and cross it effectively constructs an intended relationship of affect with the viewer.

The border features again in the film's closing scenes. This time it is the Wagah border that crosses over from Pakistan into India, and vice versa, across the divided state of Punjab in both lands. Filming on this actual location is an attempt to give credibility to the issue of people and love being separated by manmade political boundaries in the film. What is worthy of comment at this border sequence is the representation of the return of Veer back to his homeland after over two decades in Pakistan, now with Zaara as his partner. Accompanying them to the Pakistani side of the border is their solicitor and new friend, Saamiya. They exchange dialogues of thank you and good wishes. Saamiya presents a small box of *sindoor* (red powder used by Hindu married women to adorn their foreheads), inviting Veer to make Zaara his forever. Veer completes this predominantly Hindu wedding ceremony by marking Zaara's forehead with the red powder.

Veer says to Zaara, 'Come, let us go home.' Veer bows down and pays respect to the land of India while the tricolour (the Indian flag) adorns a border gate behind him in the frame. Veer and Zaara walk over into India, past a line of border guardsmen. They turn and wave to Saamiya, who waves back; she turns away from them, wipes her tears, smiles and walks out of the frame back into Pakistan.

A dominant reading of this scene, and arguably its intended effect, is one of an ideological climactic resolve that goes against the grain of the fluid pleasures of border crossing and the creation of eclectic borderland spaces demonstrated elsewhere in the film, as has been discussed earlier. Zaara is Hindu-ised as Veer's elderly bride and they return to the bounded nation identity of India as their home. Yet, this dominant ideological conclusion, which lasts for around three minutes, is small compared to the three-plus hours of border crossing that the film has just explored. The intended dominant Hindu-Indian inscription imposed upon the resolution of the film is at odds with the eclectic cultural, social and aesthetic exchanges that have been presented earlier in the film. Thus, the ending is askew and perhaps not the most remembered or exemplary scene of the film, if it is one of the scenes remembered at all by the film's global audiences. This is an argument that would best be tested through a qualitative audience study of the film, which is beyond the remit of this essay. Nonetheless, what is possible is the speculative conclusion that the episodic nature of many popular Hindi films, *Veer-Zaara* as present case in point, are viewed and engaged with in sporadic ways, and whose pleasures and possibilities are not simply curtailed by endings that betray the accumulative effects and affects that have been set into motion over the duration of the filmic text.

## Conclusion

If borders are a physical construct, then borderlands are contested spaces of, around and between borders. The two films studied here present depictions of borders that the films' central protagonists need to negotiate and overcome, and thereby the filmic texts become attempts at illustrating borderland spaces through the particular lens of Bollywood cinema. The films create their own cinematic borderlands that can be made sense of by deciphering their audio and visual styles. One of the central aesthetic pleasures of the films, and especially of *Veer-Zaara*, is the emphasis placed on the potentially radical act of border crossing. As Kalra and Purewal argue, 'People who engage in this process are therefore attempting to overcome the limitations imposed by hegemonic and dominant forces that construct and maintain socially congealed difference' (1999: 55). Furthermore, crossing a border may cause shifts in its boundaries, as argued in the analysis of the two films, but this does not necessarily result in the removal of the border. In both films, the political border of Indo-Pak is crossed but the border remains intact and, particularly in the climax scene of *Veer-Zaara*, it might well be argued that a preferred ideological mediation of the nation state of India is attempted. Also, the ease with which our two protagonists in *Veer-Zaara* are also able to move across the border might be a cause for lament—we never see them having to negotiate the lengthy procedures and draconian Indo-Pak measures of having to obtain a visa and then to deal with immigration officials at the border.[7] Nonetheless, this is a minor setback in the world of Bollywood cinema, as border crossing as an imaginative and transcending act is given more credence and is what marks the aesthetic pleasures of the cinematic borderland spaces of *Veer-Zaara*. Both films also avoid replicating easy acts of border aggressions (attempts at maintaining the sovereign status quo of borders), and instead aim at being part of the complex dialogue towards border transgressions (attempts at overcoming the dominant symbolic expressions of sovereign borders; see Kalra and Purewal 1999: 56; Purewal 2003: 547).

A final point for reflection is how the two films, in terms of their distribution and reception, as part of an internationalised Bollywood cinema in the contemporary moment of globalisation, might further add to understandings of acts of border transgressions. Here, both films have been viewed and supported, at the very least, by Indians and Pakistanis and their diasporic counterparts (for example, in box office returns, and DVD and video rentals and purchases, and also in the pirated circulation of DVDs, goods that have also transgressed the Indo-Pak border). These audiences have interpreted and made their own readings of the cinematic borderlands of the two films across the local and global movements of planet Bollywood that crosses numerous nation state boundaries.

## Notes

1. Paying attention to audio and visual style in the analysis of film texts is an established critical and debated area of close textual analysis within film studies. Focusing on audio and visual style in a film allows us to decipher and make readings about the

sound and visual components of the image/s as they articulate and offer meanings of the diegetic world/s being presented. Audio and visual style refers to aspects such as the overarching musical score, background music, sound motifs, the *mise en scène* and their intended projections as semiotic signifiers of aesthetic pleasure, and particular kinds of social ideology.

2. For instance, both films were made in the context of developments after the battle of Kargil in 1999; the 13 December 2001 attack upon the Indian parliament in New Delhi by Kashmiri separatists; and the initiation of various bus services between India and Pakistan since the mid-1990s to improve diplomatic and cultural ties, which have been suspended and started again according to the political climate between the two countries.

3. This excellent work builds upon the US-based debates of border studies of the late eighties and early nineties where academic research has been largely derived from the US-Mexico border (e.g., Anzaldua 1987; Chambers 1990; Giroux 1992; Rosaldo 1989). On border theory, see also Michaelsen and Johnson (1997). According to Purewal, 'Border Studies has come to constitute a broad field that attempts to understand the various processes of power, nationalism, social relations and culture at the physical and symbolic sites of international boundaries' (2003: 540).

4. Both *Main Hoon Na* and *Veer-Zaara* use the star persona of Shahrukh Khan to good effect. Shahrukh Khan has established himself as the current international Bollywood box office superstar, through his regular roles as a character that mediates various kinds of urban and diasporic Indian trials and desires in popular Hindi cinema. Aspects of his star persona are also nuanced by instances from his everyday real life that are regularly reported in fanzines and in the film trade press. Shahrukh is seen as advocating a genuine vision for a secular India and a peaceful South Asia in terms of communalism; this is often developed through his character roles—in these two films he has to mediate a path of peace and good relationships across the Indo-Pak border. Although Shahrukh often plays the idealised Hindu Indian on-screen, in real life he is an Indian Muslim with a Hindu wife, and he is well known for celebrating and partaking in both Hindu and Muslim religious festivals as part of his family affairs. On Shahrukh Khan as an urban Indian and diasporic phenomenon see Dudrah (2006).

5. The white doves symbolise peace—the tryst of Ram and Raghavan will decide the outcome for the possibilities of peace. Furthermore, as the director Farah Khan reveals in the director's audio commentary of the DVD release of the film, she has deliberately used the doves not only to make a point about the battle for peace but also as a quote from and homage to one of her favourite directors and his films—John Woo's *Face/Off* (1997), where white flying doves are used in the final fight sequence between John Travolta and Nicholas Cage.

6. This is a stylised reference in Hindi cinema, where the hero and heroine, upon meeting and in establishing their relationship to each other, return glances to confirm their liking and, later, love for one another.

7. Obtaining a visa to cross the Indo-Pak border is time-consuming and stressful. It takes at least seven hours to cross the thirty-two-mile border between Lahore and Amritsar. See Kalra and Purewal (1999), pp. 62–63.

# Drawn Lines

# 4

# Partition Literature and Films: *Pinjar* and *Earth*

## Meenakshi Bharat

*Whenever a film is on a literary subject, it is like watching literature being murdered.*
—*Chandraprakash Dwivedi, director,* Pinjar, *2003*

Literary responses to the drawing of borders in the Indian subcontinent in 1947 have been aplenty and quite steady in their appearance, starting soon after the act was perpetrated. Some early writers were Saadat Hasan Manto, Intezar Hussain and Amrita Pritam, while more recent authors who delved into the issue were novelist Bapsi Sidhwa in *Ice-Candy-Man* (Sidhwa 1988), people's chronicler Urvashi Butalia with her collection of individual memoirs, *The Other Side of Silence* (1988), a spate of anthologies of Partition stories (Bhalla 1994; Cowasjee and Duggal 1995; Darpan 2000), and a concerted translation enterprise of Partition-related literature.[1] Literary artists from both sides of the border have constantly felt compelled to relive their hurt through a recall of their own experience of Partition. In the very personal, very unique questioning and analysis of their predicament, they attempt to take stock of themselves through their writing, in the context of the far-reaching repercussions of the division. But strangely, the visual media had long been chary of handling this sensitive topic. Despite the rare appearance of a *Garam Hawa* (Hot Winds, 1973)[2] in the seventies, presenting a sensitive handling of the nerve-wracking aftermath of Partition, and a *Tamas* (Darkness, 1987),[3] five-part television serial of the late eighties, it is only recently, in the wake of resurgent critical and political interest, that this theme has found a more continuous and assertive voice. Mainstream blockbuster successes like *Gadar* (Tumult, 2001)[4] have been backed by other turn of the millennium responses, in much-acclaimed cinematic adaptations of two exploratory literary texts: Bapsi Sidhwa's *Ice-Candy-Man*, written in English, cinematically translated by Deepa Mehta as *Earth* in 1999, and Amrita Pritam's *Pinjar* written in Punjabi in 1950 and made into a film with the same name by Dr Chandraprakash Dwivedi in 2003. In these retakes on the historical splitting up, both films attempt a serious appraisal of Partition, patently indicating that the issue is pertinent even today. But in the interstices between the two art forms, somewhere on the journey from the novel to the film, a shift in nuancing takes place. The complexities arising from this interface, and the underlying agenda of the adaptive engagement, makes for a vibrant dynamics that demands thorough analysis.

That the makers of the two cinematic texts are more than conscious of the task of adaptation at hand is abundantly clear. They wilfully, almost compulsively, draw attention to the original novel. They welcome questions about this aspect, fielding them with alacrity. In response to one such poser, Chandraprakash Dwivedi, the medico turned film director of *Pinjar* (The Skeleton, 2003), found himself pushed to a corner and forced to comment that the relationship between literature and cinema was indeed problematic. He commented: 'Filmmaking is like giving birth to a child; the memories will always be painful. *Whenever a film is on a literary subject, it is like watching literature being murdered* [emphasis mine]', implying that the spirit of the literary artefact apparently suffers at the hands of the filmmaker. Though this has been the usual major evaluative stricture passed against cinematic adaptations whenever they have come up for assessment, the superiority of the written text most often being taken for granted, for a director to make such an avowal when he is himself engaged in the act speaks of the enormity of the issue. But when the adapted literary text is located at one of the most harrowing divisive junctures of subcontinental history, when a line was unimaginatively and politically etched through the heart of a people, tearing them apart with unprecedented violence, the problem becomes even more piquant. So, apart from the regular issues that cinematic adaptation raises, a specific dynamic of complex questions is unleashed. Engagement with this dynamic moves far beyond the reductive 'better than' or 'not as good as' yardsticks, far beyond even the mere establishment of adaptation as an acceptable and respectable exercise (an exercise that has met with much resistance from purists) to a direct face-off between conflict-ridden ideologies in diverse art mediums.

Both the novels in question have been written by women who personally went through the experience of Partition. Interestingly, both were simultaneously resident in Lahore at the time when the city burnt in Partition-ignited rioting. But the one was a grown woman with an adult female apprehension of the event, and the other but a mere child: Pritam (1919–2005) was twenty-eight, married and pregnant at the time and Bapsi Sidhwa only eight. The former, a Sikh from Gujranwala, now in Pakistan, was forced into refugee status in India while the other stayed on in Lahore to grow up in the 'toddler nation (*Ice-Candy-Man*, p. 140).'5 The narrative perspectives that both use in their novels are commensurate with this fact: Pritam looks over the shoulder of Puro, a young adult woman of childbearing age, and Sidhwa through the innocent, incredulous gaze of the eight year old Lenny Sethi. In that sense, both novels have an autobiographical element, though *Ice-Candy-Man* cashes in on Sidhwa's childhood experience in a more direct, concerted manner. The film *Pinjar*, for the most part, broadly carries the narrative's mono-perspective with Puro at its centre. Yet, the film unobtrusively slips into the deployment of multiple points of view, with part narration focusing on Puro's betrothed Ramchand, part on her brother, and part on her mother. They all have independent stories to tell, enjoying a space they never had in the written text. But *Earth* carries through the narrative direction of the novel quite faithfully, hemming the relation from the lame child's point of view with a voiceover by the character of grown-up Lenny Sethna.

Written in 1988, at the peak of this latter-day Partition-related creative activity, *Ice-Candy-Man* is written by a Pakistani but not a Muslim. In a theocratic state, the author's Parsi identity has significant reverberations. She occupies, simultaneously, a neutral position and an outside one, giving her a unique critiquing vantage. Also, her experience of Partition is recalled, as was Pritam's; only, it is much more distanced in time: Pritam's book was published within three years of Partition and Sidhwa's four decades after. In addition, it is significant that Sidhwa writes in English, the language of the erstwhile colonisers. Pritam, on the other hand, wrote primarily in Punjabi, having made a brief beginning in Hindi. It is but evident that the immediate target audience for the two was diametrically different. Printed at a time when the publishing industry was neither as organised nor as professional as it is today, the original publication details and dates of *Pinjar* are difficult to come by. Moreover, Pritam only reached a wider audience after her work was translated. Besides, she has written much else that has been ranked superior to this novel. In fact, the making of the film has popularised the novel, the latest editions openly cashing in on the film by using pictures of the star, Urmila Matondkar, and the rest of the cast on the cover. The film has opened the narrative to a much larger audience simply by virtue of the fact that it is a Hindi film, by far the most potent art medium in the Indian subcontinent. What is more, cast in what has popularly come to be termed the 'Bollywood' format, with song, dance and mainstream actors, it immediately became a crowd-puller. The interesting fact is that, considering the seriousness of the subject, the choice of the Bombay film pattern of colour and song seems unusual. Translation into another medium, from the literary to the audio-visual, automatically changes background texture: the use of colour, sound, song, music, and dance imbues a larger than life element to the narrative. The upshot is that Dwivedi brings serious literature to the common man. Finally, the selection of the film for screening at international forums has brought the narrative hitherto unparalleled global visibility.

That does not mean that Dwivedi was not aware of the special problems of working on an adaptation. He learnt quickly enough that organising finance for a film based on literature was a very difficult proposition because the success rate of such films was low. His importunities were met with the response, 'Why literature?' Basically, the highbrow character of literature was not considered conducive to box office success. So, if a filmmaker wanted his film to reach the masses, many compromises were entailed. In part, Dwivedi sought to achieve such success by the very deployment of the popular, mainstream layout of Bombay films already talked about: the casing of colour, song, dance, and romance. Yet, it was essential to maintain a distance from the formula of commercial films if a significant comment had to be enunciated. Predictably then, the novel *Pinjar* incorporates the format of successful commercial Hindi films while yet not emulating them. Actually, just the choice of a literary artefact, which had the solid credentials of coming from the pen of the most respected woman writer in Punjabi, who was also the recipient of the highest literary awards of the country[6] helped establish the seriousness for the project.

A similar logic applies to the transformation of Sidhwa's novel into a film. Mehta too, like Dwivedi a few years later, adapted the novel to this popular Bombay blueprint inasmuch as the use of song and dance.

But the treatment of the narrative other than this is totally western. The fact that the film is made in both Hindi and English clearly indicates that she had a western audience in mind from the outset. Once again, this film too is a brave confluence of the serious and the commercial. Also, note the astute choice of successful Bombay actor Aamir Khan to play the ice-candy-man, the Khan known for his cerebral leanings and repeatedly iterated desire to be associated with what is termed 'meaningful cinema.'

It is evident that the personalities of the directors and the actors have a direct bearing on the finished product. Deepa Mehta's western sensibility demands underplaying, though, even here, viewers have reacted to the un-ayah qualities of Ayah, with viewers criticising her too-beautiful sarees. Even though the big draw, the thinking Khan, Aamir, is in sync with the working ideology of the director, his 'Bombay' presence can never be completely forgotten. The use of 'Bollywood' intrusions like the mandatory song and dance routine bespeaks some concessions towards popular viewership. *Pinjar*, on the other hand, has been made by an indigenous, homegrown director, brought up on a diet of Bombay films. In this case, the popular draw is its heroine, Urmila Matondkar. Song and dance are an integral part of the film. Yet, the content and its treatment break away from the formulaic mould. This dual allegiance is evident even in the performances. The expressive yet restrained performance by Manoj Bajpai plumbs depths beyond the Rashid of the book, managing to garner a National Award for Best Performance by an actor for the year. On the other hand, despite an overall commendable performance, Matondkar's 'Puro' and the director fall prey to the use of another popular 'Bollywood' technique: the use of melodrama. One viewer wishes that she indulged less in 'huffing and puffing'. Another feels that her acting is rather loud in parts, as in the scene when she disguises herself as a *khes* (cotton rug) seller as part of the plan to rescue Lajo, her brother's wife and Ramchand's sister.

It follows that the process of adaptation is bound to have an impact on the carrying over of novelistic concerns into the audio-visual medium. Since both the protagonists are females created by women novelists, the gender question, 'the woman's lot' is never far from the narrative. In *Pinjar*, issues like the marriage of girls, their submerged desires, their aspirations, and their education are all seen in the light of the gendered views of contemporary society which, in turn, has its foundation in the belief of the unequal status of men and women.

The factors that limit the realisation of Puro's identity due to her sex are clearly Pritam's focus. The underlying and overt lamentation of the text is:

> Is yug mein ladki kā janm lénā hî pāp hai.
> [It is a sin for a girl to be born in this age.] (Pritam 1950: 83)

and, in the film,

> Béchāri, mardon kî mārî.
> [Poor thing, accursed by men.] (*Pinjar*)

Similarly, in *Ice-Candy-Man*, Lenny's Parsi doctor consoles her mother when the latter voices her worries about Lenny's future prospects, saddled as she is with her polio limp. 'What about her schooling?', is the parental question. He responds in the stock patriarchal manner:

> 'She'll marry—have children—lead a carefree, happy life. No need to strain her with studies and exams.'
>
> (*ICM*: 15)

In fact, Lenny is acutely aware of her own position as a girl, and sensitive to the gendered attitude of the world:

> …drinking tea, I am told, makes one darker. I am dark enough. Everyone says, 'It's a pity Adi's fair and Lenny is dark. He's a boy: Anyone will marry him.'
>
> (*ICM*: 81)

But the critical consideration is whether the films take up this theme and, if so, to what extent. The male director of *Pinjar* does echo some of the concerns of the novelist in this quarter. He shows his allegiance by almost taking Amrita Pritam's words quoted above, verbatim, and putting them in Puro's mother's mouth in the shape of a plaintive song, 'Jag mein janam kyon leti hai beti?' (Why is a daughter born in this world?) Even so, it would seem that his main objective is to make a Partition film, and the gender question remains, at best, a secondary concern as it never was with Pritam.

Quite surprisingly, the woman director of *Earth* decides to give the woman angle shorter shrift than the author does. Lenny's gender awareness is not ever brought up as an issue. The competition between the sexes is totally done away with by the absolute deletion of the characters of Adi, her brother and of Cousin.[7] It is only Mother, taking off her husband's shoes and seeing to his immediate physical comforts, who might throw some light on the skewered gender equation which is of considerable interest to Sidhwa. It would seem that the director has decided that if she has to be faithful to her theme of Partition, and if cinematic economy and cogency has to be maintained, she should not stray too far from it.

It is clear that the desire to root the film historically is the dictating factor in the making of these two films. In the case of *Pinjar*, the telescoping of the time period covered in the novel, roughly 1935 to 1948, to the two years around the severing moment of Partition signals this impulse. The film opens with the textual indication that it is 'August 1946' and ends two years later in 1948. The opening frame of the film is of Partition-associated violence in Amritsar. A Sikh faction clashes with a Muslim one. Blood splatters on the camera when a human body is sliced with a sword. Thereafter, the camera moves to Puro's home where it dwells on the family setting, building up an offsetting picture of happy domesticity. This microcosmic cosiness is disrupted by the political division of the subcontinent. The visual narrative concentrates on juxtaposing this smaller picture with the macrocosmic upheaval overtaking the nation, constantly highlighted by numerous references to the larger political scenario where the struggle for independence is in full swing. Puro's brother's participation in the freedom struggle, his soliciting of money from his father for his political engagements, and his participation in political rallies and demonstrations occupy significant cinematic space. This development of her brother's character has the effect of amplifying the political, historical and nationalist preoccupations of the film.

Moreover, Dwivedi's slogan for his title frame is, tellingly, 'Beyond Boundaries'. It is clear that 'mulk ka batwara', the division of the nation, is the major focus of the film, punctuated as it is with patriotic iterations, political speeches and the strains of 'Vande Matram' (Salute to the Motherland), the nationalist cry of the independence movement in the Indian subcontinent. The novel, on the other hand, is never so trenchant in its pursuance of this theme. Its ultimate appeal is more as a novel that voices social and feminist concerns as they are played out during difficult times. This slight novel—with the overriding themes related to women, family, children, and social divisiveness based mainly on religious affiliations—cashes in on experiences that the author has had occasion to see at close hand. Specifically, at that point of time, Pritam's main concern was to document the plight of

women in Punjabi society, which was ridden with social schisms and
tensions. Written close on the heels of Partition, she naturally grounds
her novel in that troubled scenario; she presents the fact that there
was tension between Hindus and Muslims even prior to the Partition,
the event being a build-up of earlier social tensions. The novel spans a
period from more than a decade prior to 1947, to just after Partition.
It would seem, in a way, the novel is about Partition. Yet, it is still not
a Partition novel *per se*, in that it does not focus just on the climactic
historical moment.

Dwivedi's concerns are obviously wider and more temporally
focused. He reads beyond the written word to mount characters,
frames and stories in a way that is a departure from the book. Also, in
the interest of drama, and in keeping with the condensed two-year span
of the film, Puro loses a child in childbirth. Even the mad woman's
son that she nurtures for the first months with such tenderness and
devotion is snatched away by inimical, unfeeling and divisive social
norms. In the book, not only does she have her own son but she gets
to ultimately keep the other child once he is returned to her. The film
version functions, for one, to concentrate the action around the year
of Partition. Moreover, this works very well to get audience sympathy
for Puro's plight and also to give her final decision to stay on with
Rashid immense emotional and moral power. The fact that she has
finally managed to put her past behind her, including her dreams of
marriage to Ramchand, and is able to unconditionally embrace Rashid
for all his love, understanding and support, is a sure crowd winner.
Also, this and the last show of solidarity between Ramchand and
Rashid is completely in line with the recent friendly overtures between
the two nations. The political goodwill of the moment, 2003, a crest
in the seesaw motion of Indo-Pak relations, apparently discourages
the use of anti-Pakistani sloganeering and pro-India jingoism, which
was present in many earlier films dealing with cross-border relations.
The release of the music on the Wagah border enunciated this stand
in good measure, with both director and cast proclaiming it publicly
in interviews and in public forums. The patriotic strains of the song
'Vatnan ve o mere vatna ve, bat gaye ve ri angan' (Oh my nation,
divided are the homes), too, refers to the undivided original homeland
and not to the emergent India or Pakistan. Of course, Pritam too had
no ill word to utter vis-á-vis either nation or people. But that was
because, as has already been pointed out, she was presenting a realistic
picture of the times, her eyes riveted on social issues. She was making
no 'political' statement, only uttering a humanitarian lament for the

unfortunate turn of events. But Dwivedi, while carrying forward Pritam's objective, falls in with the contemporary political agenda in his adaptation, the iteration of the desirability of political amity between two warring nations.

This political alignment between writer and filmmaker is completely reversed in the relationship between Bapsi Sidhwa's *Ice-Candy-Man* and the film *Earth*. Sidhwa, Pakistani in her allegiance and nationality, clearly shows a nationalist tilt in her novel. Jinnah is 'our Jinnah Sahib' but India is othered by 'your precious Gandhijee' (*Ice-Candy-Man*, p. 91). Gandhi and Nehru are caricatured into sex maniacs and 'enema'-fixated individuals. The references to *swaraj*, the Quit India movement, the mountbatten plan, and the Radcliffe Commission unmistakably locate the narrative in a political and historical matrix. Even the issue of colonialism is an evident political preoccupation; there is reference to the British as 'the goddam English' who are held responsible for bringing the scourge of polio to the subcontinent: 'Blame the British.' Sidhwa clearly has an agenda and does not evade taking sides. The antagonistic cries of '*Jai Hind*' (Hail India) and '*Pakistan zindabad*' (Long live Pakistan) rend the skies, aglow with the hellish fires burning in Lahore. Of course, the novelist has concerns beyond these limitations. The misinterpretation and misuse of religion to feed the rift between different communities is highlighted in every class. There is narratorial sympathy for Ayah, metaphorically standing for undivided India, with her coterie of admirers from every religion, Muslim, Hindu, and Sikh. In this context, Ayah's rape and dislocation becomes symptomatic of the scourge of Partition. Through all this, Sidhwa's Pakistani nationality and her religious and social allegiance to Parsidom are never in question.

Unlike Dwivedi, who fixes the apolitical original in a historical-political context, Deepa Mehta waters down the political affiliations of her author. She becomes a disinterested documenter of religious and cultural difference. If she is talking about Parsi culture then it is merely to present a cultural milieu in as neutral a manner as possible. She stresses this difference as the reality of the times, a perennial, continuing, iden-tifying condition of the inhabitants of the subcontinent, of humanity, indeed, of *earth,* her chosen metaphor. In adapting a novel written by a Pakistani, she strips it of the pro-Pakistani tilt and also assiduously steers clear of veering the other way. Mehta's diasporic Indian status (she is based in Toronto, Canada) may have made this stance easier to adopt since, in a way, she is an outsider. Despite her emotional and cultural allegiance with India, she is able to transcend the specific to emphasise the general and the human.

An early indication of this impulse can be seen in the title she gives her film: *Earth*, subtitled *1947*, the particular partition coming to stand for the general innate fractiousness of man. It is worth noting that her credits acknowledge *Cracking India* as the original of this film, the title under which Sidhwa's novel was published in the Americas. The deliberate naming of the specific political division of the country, *1947*, and her focus on the common condition of humanity, *Earth*, makes her intention abundantly clear. Also, with her first film *Fire* (1996), she had already publicised her plan to make a set of films based on the elements, fire, earth and water, essential ingredients of human nature.[8] With this personal agenda, she succeeds in departicularising the theme, imbuing it with a more general colour.

The relationship between the director and the author is also informative. It is bound to have an impact on the process of adaptation. When asked about Amrita Pritam's reaction to his desire to adapt the book, Dwivedi is unstinting in his praise for her 'liberal' attitude. He says that she 'frankly told me her medium is writing novels, stories and poems while filmmaking is mine. And the two are totally different. She gave me complete freedom to do what I want (Verma 2003)'. This 'complete freedom' is what allows Dwivedi to further his agenda. For Pritam, in 1950, barely three years after Partition, it was too early to posit political amity; she could but lament the division of a people at the humanitarian level. In a way then, more than half a century later, the filmmaker could verbalise the writer's early unformulated desire, marking the trajectory of the development of Indo-Pak relations towards a hopeful coming together of the two nations.

Deepa Mehta has had an even more positive involvement with the author and the book. Whereas Pritam had left the director to do his work, this director kept Sidhwa in the loop right from the beginning, working closely in tandem with the writer who became an integral part of the film crew. The degree of participative commitment is apparent in the fact that the last frame showing the 'narrator' limping away from the camera is that of Sidhwa herself. The short hair and the polio drag in one leg is unmistakable. Sidhwa, on her part, was quite taken in with the fact that her book had been chosen by Mehta. She was quite happy with what Mehta did with her novel, acceding that an adaptation meant that a lot would be thrown out. Respecting the independence of the adapting art form, she comments:

The movie stands on its own. But it has the voice of the child and it has the spirit of the book—it has objectivity and it has the story. A movie is only a two-hour affair. A book is spread over a wider expanse of time. Deepa had to get rid of many incidents and characters. I hated the fact that every time I saw the script it was shorter. Then when the film was made, scenes were thrown out until something that seemed very bare to me was left. I realise now that the film works so excellently because of the cuts. (Rajan 2000)

Mehta loved the book enough to have a script ready even before a contract was drawn up. Sidhwa was generous in her applause for the filmmaker. She felt that Mehta 'understood every nuance of the novel. She understood what was very important—the importance of the Parsi child and her passionate perspective.' Little wonder that she immediately 'told her to go ahead and make the film'. This mutual admiration is indicative of the fact that the vision of lost amity was common to both the writer and the director. There was, therefore, little call for Sidhwa to interfere with the film. Her purpose of the 'recording of a particular history in hoping that we might learn lessons from that history' was broadly maintained by the film. Not only that, Sidhwa recognised and welcomed an opening out of her own work through it:

The movie has a totally different audience, a different way of seeing things. But, the film widens the audience for the original story. The purpose for writing the story is to reach an audience, so through the film, that goal was further achieved. This wider *Earth* audience may, in turn, learn from the historical tale told in *Cracking India*. (Rajan 2000)

Mehta also carries forward Sidhwa's widely applauded quality—that of the book being the first Partition narrative from the Parsi angle. The film takes up Sidhwa's dispassionate critique of the 'bum-licking'[9] tendencies of this minority community.

These films, then, appeal to both intellectual and mainstream audiences and, as such, facilitate significant changes in the attitudes and preferences of the Indian viewing public. People who earlier could not have responded positively to such themes are now vouching for them, evidencing the fact that, in general, audiences are becoming more discerning, more demanding. The widening appeal of such films demonstrates a newfound maturity that allows filmmakers to be more adventurous in their choice and treatment of subjects. These films also pave the way for more meaningful and enriching exchanges between the realms of literature and cinema in India. It is amply clear that there is a larger directing philosophy that goes beyond these particular texts, literary or cinematic, to enunciate a shift towards the establishment of a climate of colloquy between the two nations. These are the impulses that made Dwivedi pick up a novel written so long ago. These are the reasons for Mehta instinctively choosing to adapt Sidhwa's novel. In fact, whatever the play in time, whatever the variation arising from the fact that the writer is reliving a personal experience and that the filmmaker, at a remove, is recovering and assessing another's experience, there is this common thread of belief in human values that connects all the four artistic entities.

## Notes

*Pinjar* directed by Chandraprakash Dwivedi, 2003 with Urmila Matondkar, Manoj Bajpai, Sanjay Suri in the cast. Released as 'a human saga set during the Indo-Pak Partition.' Announced that it is based on the novel by Amrita Pritam.
*Earth* directed by Deepa Mehta, 1998 based on Bapsi Sidhwa's novel *Ice-Candy-Man*. Aamir Khan, Maia Sethna, Nandita Das, Kitu Gidwani, and Rahul Khanna were in the cast.

1. The works of Manto Hyder, Pritam, and Joginder Paul, amongst many.
2. Dir. M. S. Sathyu, with Balraj Sahni leading the cast. Though initially held up by the censors, the film went on to win the National Award for its contribution to national integration.
3. The serial aired on Doordarshan and directed by Govind Nihalani, a stalwart of the parallel film industry, adapting a Hindi novel of the same name by Bhisham Sahni (1988). See Mazumdar (2005).
4. *Gadar—Ek Prem Katha* (Tumult—A Love Story), the biggest blockbuster of 2001, with Sunny Deol and Amisha Patel in the lead romantic roles, was an out and out Bombay masala film with music, song, dance, melodrama, and histrionics. This film was clearly anti-Pakistani, with a great deal of dialogue-shouting aimed at whipping up the emotions of the patriotic Indian audience.
5. Sidhwa, a Parsi from Lahore, divides her time between Pakistan and the US and is a US citizen. She makes frequent visits to India.
6. The Sahitya Akademi and Jnanapith awards.
7. The deletion of Adi also implies that the minor theme of colour, 'whiteness', as an aspiration of the colonised, does not find place in the film.
8. The first film of the series was *Fire,* followed by *Earth*. With the storm generated by the controversial theme of lesbianism in *Fire* behind her, interest in *Earth* was certain. Shabana Azmi and Nandita Das are the protagonists of *Fire*.
9. In the film, Lenny's mother says that the Parsis are called 'bumlickers'. In the book they 'run with the hare and hunt with the hound'.

# 5

# 'Millions of Daughters of Punjab Weep Today': The Female Perspective in Partition Films

## Claudia Preckel

T he Partition of India in August 1947 marked the creation of the two independent nation states of India and Pakistan and the end of British colonial power. Looking at the mere facts of these events, especially in the Punjab, one can only obtain a tiny insight into the human tragedies and terrible experiences which occurred as a result of the violence which ensued: twelve million people were forced into migration and millions were killed. Approximately seventy-five thousand women became victims of sexual violence, rape and abduction. The wounds of these violent events have not completely healed even to the present day. Partition has, in some cases, continued to be a national trauma and a personal tragedy for some women, one that still cannot be discussed publicly or in private.

Partition became a focus of major scholarly interest in 1997, the fiftieth anniversary of India's independence. But the process of 'writing history' in India as well as in Pakistan has ended up in the creation of an 'official history' of the two nation states. As a consequence, the positions and experiences of women have often been marginalised. In 1998, Urvashi Butalia published her well-received book *The Other Side of Silence*, in which she collected memories of female victims of Partition, mainly from Sikh and Hindu backgrounds. In this work, women speak, for the first time in forty years, about the violent events of Partition. This has meant reliving trauma, pain and anger, and also the start of a necessary process of introspection, remembrance and mourning (Kabir 2005: 190).

The Partition became a subject of literature as early as the 1950s, with several female novelists and writers discussing the events of Partition quite soon after it had happened, whereas it remained a strong taboo in Bollywood cinema until recently. It was only in 1973 that Bollywood first dared to depict the violent events of 1947 in *Garam Hawa* (Hot Winds, 1973). In this essay, I take for analysis three films depicting the events of Partition. Two of these films are based on novels written by female authors. They are partly fictional, partly 'faction', meaning fiction based on historical facts. The films—all of them milestone Partition films—are *Gadar* (Tumult, 2001). *Earth* (1999) and *Pinjar* (The Skelton, 2003). These have been chosen because, on the one hand, they present the female view on Partition and, on the other, they portray the difficult relations between the dominant religions of the region—Hinduism/Sikhism on the one hand, and Islam on the other—in the colonial context.

## Female Victims? Male Perpetrators? Male Victims?

The common factor in the films mentioned is that they concentrate on the fate of the female characters—Sakina (*Gadar*), Shanta (*Earth*) and Puro (*Pinjar*). All are either in danger of being abducted and/or raped, or endure these horrific experiences. In the three films, the female protagonists—irrespective of their religion—are characterised positively, whereas the men are always involved in violence. The women in these films become victims of male violence because men think that this is the way to humiliate their enemies. It seems to be an 'easy' way to destroy the enemy's honour.

The film *Pinjar* illustrates that this method of dishonouring women is not related to the period of Partition alone. *Pinjar* is based on Amrita Pritam's (d. 2005) novel of the same name. It is the story of a Hindu girl, Puro, played by Urmila Matondkar. On the day before her marriage to the rich and sensible Ramchand (Sanjay Suri), Puro is kidnapped by the Muslim, Rasheed (Manoj Bajpai), who himself is a victim of circumstances and family loyalties. When Puro successfully escapes from her kidnapper, her own parents refuse to take her back. Puro decides to live with Rasheed, marries him and becomes a Muslim named Hameeda. Following the events of Partition, Ramchand's sister Lajo meets the same fate as Puro. Puro tries her best to get Lajo released with the help of Rasheed, who suffers from the guilt of having abducted Puro and her separating from her family and religion. The families are finally reunited in a refugee camp on the Indo-Pakistan border. Puro is asked to return with her family to India in order to marry Ramchand, but she refuses and decides to live on with Rasheed.

There is a further twist in this tale of religious divide. Puro, a former Hindu, finds an orphaned Hindu baby and wishes to bring it up as her own. Rasheed and Puro are forced into a decsion to return the child to its own community where it would be cared for according to the customs and religion of its own people. This decision can be seen as a lesson learned by Rasheed that 'might is not always right' and imposing religion or values on another person is not an enlightened path towards earning love and respect.

Rasheed eventually comes to realise that in his world, men are the decision-makers and that these decisions are taken without any reference to the women's wishes or desires. By failing to take their women into consideration, their world could be considered to be out of balance. Dwivedi strictly avoids blaming any community for the terrible events of Partition. This is illustrated by the fact that the heroine Puro is abducted by Rasheed because of a family feud, the roots of which were embedded long before Partition. This also underlines the thesis that women can be victims any time and in any place.

The Partition clearly sets new limits and boundaries for the heroines and their scope of action. This is impressively shown in the film *Earth* and the fate of the female protagonist Shanta. *Earth*, the controversial film by Indo-Canadian filmmaker Deepa Mehta also earned heavy criticism from Muslim communities both within and outside India. This movie is not a typical Bollywood product and the message is subtler. Director Deepa Mehta portrays all religious communities of the Indian subcontinent, allowing her protagonists to enumerate, through the dialogue, all the stereotypes and prejudices they have against the other communities. The story is based on Bapsi Sidhwa's (b. 1938) partly autobiographical novel *Ice-Candy-Man* (Sidhwa 1990). The main character of the film is Lenny, an eight-year-old Parsi girl from Lahore. After having suffered from a polio infection, Lenny is disabled and has to wear leg callipers. Like the majority of Parsis in India, Lenny's family maintains a neutral stance among the religions of India. Lenny lives among people who belong to the Hindu, Muslim, Sikh, and Christian communities—and these people are friends. One of the most important persons in Lenny's life is Shanta, her beautiful Hindu nanny (Nandita Das). The group around Lenny and her ayah is deeply confused by the rumours about Partition. During this situation, the Muslim ice candy man Dil Nawaaz (Aamir Khan) falls in love with Shanta, but she decides to marry Hassan, the Muslim masseur (Rahul Khanna). Dil Nawaaz feels betrayed, both by the woman he loves and by the other religious communities in India responsible for cruelties against the Muslims. The story culminates when Hassan is killed by his fellow-Muslims and Shanta is abducted and is never seen again.

Whereas Shanta was free to choose Hassan as her consort and even had a premarital sexual relationship with him before Partition, her abduction and (by implication) rape spelled the end of her control over her own body and her sexuality. Rape and sexual violence are symbols of newly created borders and boundaries on the real landscape. They are signs of forcefully set marks on the body, separating 'ours' from 'the others.' By dis-honouring females of the 'other' communities, men are setting limits to the woman's free will to choose her own religious or sexual identity. The motif of sexual violence against women does not have any religious reason, nor does it orginate in romantic desire. Rather, the origins lie in an over-emphasis of masculinity, which is rooted in the patriarchal system and deeply entrenched notions of 'manhood' and the male will to enforce power over women, who—in their eyes—are the weakest part of 'the other' community.

This message is clearly conveyed in the film *Gadar—Ek Prem Katha* (Tumult—A Love Story, 2001) which deals with the fate of the Muslim heroine Sakina (Amisha Patel) during Partition. The story also focuses on the superiority of the macho hero Tara Singh (Sunny Deol) from the Indian Sikh community. The male protagonist has to cross the borders to newly founded Pakistan to rescue his wife Sakina who is detained in Lahore by her own parents. The Muslim community in India, comprising about 120 million believers, heavily criticised *Gadar*, not only because the film deals with a Sikh-Muslim love story, but also because Islam is portrayed as a violent and cruel religion. The film *Gadar* evoked strong reactions by moviegoers, which included destroying some movie theatres. It cannot be denied that the depiction of Islam and Muslims is often very negative and stereotyped: the Muslim is often shown as a traitor to Indian interests and as a terrorist; the Muslim woman is a *purdah*-clad oppressed subject to male machismo. However, elements of the film are somewhat more complicated than this. Sakina, the Muslim protagonist, comes from an influential Muslim family of landlords. Her education, however, is not a Muslim one. Sakina has been educated in a Catholic convent, largely separated from the world outside. Before Partition, when her family was still living in India, it is shown to have adopted western values. This can clearly be seen when Sakina sings the song

*Que Sera, Sera* ('Whatever will be, will be'), sung by Doris Day in Alfred Hitchcock's Academy Award-winning film *The Man Who Knew Too Much* (1956):

> When I was just a little girl
> I asked my mother, what will I be
> Will I be pretty, will I be rich
> Here's what she said to me.
>
> Que Sera, Sera,
> Whatever will be, will be
> The future's not ours to see
> Que Sera, Sera
> What will be, will be.

It is very interesting to see this song in the context of a Muslim family, as it seems that the singer of this song is at the mercy of her own fate. The ideas inherent in this song coincide quite neatly with the popular Muslim belief in *kismat*, that is the fate of an individual written by the hand of God. The lines of the song clearly foreshadow the fate of the heroines of all the three films. Their self-determined life comes to a sudden and sometimes tragic end.

The representation of the heroine as a victim of male violence forms a second level of interpretation. The female protagonist—especially a mother—can be seen as a symbol of the nation, as 'Mother India'. In all three films, the female characters emphasise the national integrity of India and do not want the Indian subcontinent to be partitioned. Instead, the female protagonists support the view that India is *one* country where all religions can co-exist. For example, in *Earth*, Shanta, meets a group of people in a local park in Lahore. The men around her belong to the Hindu, Muslim and Sikh communities. When they start talking about the Hindu-Muslim conflicts, Shanta stands up and leaves the group, shouting: 'Unless you stop talking about Hindus and Muslims, I will not come to the park.' When the communal riots break out, Hassan and Shanta are obviously deeply shocked by Dil Nawaaz's hateful speeches against the Sikhs. Hassan stresses that the Sikhs are bringing Hindus and Muslims closer. After all, the Muslim Holy Quran is kept in the Golden Temple in Amritsar, the holy place of the Sikhs. Sikhs are described as acting as a kind of intermediary between the Hindu and Muslim communities. This is exactly what the Sikh protagonist in *Gadar* does by crossing the newly created borders between India and Pakistan. He further crosses the boundaries between the religious communities, as he falls in love with a Muslim woman. The sensitive issue of forced conversion of women will be examined later in this essay.

Even in the choice of their partners, the female protagonists stress religious harmony and unity. Although Puro is abducted by Rasheed, a Muslim, she finally falls in love with him and decides to live with him as Hameeda, his Muslim wife. In the beginning of the film, however, Muslims are characterised as a constant threat to the family ideal of Puro, Ramchand and their families. Rasheed follows Puro wherever she goes, creating a dark, threatening and even demonised atmosphere whenever 'the Muslim' appears. Later, Puro/Hameeda realises that Rasheed is as much a victim of circumstances as she is. He has been forced by his family to take revenge for something that happened two generations earlier. In this respect, Rasheed himself is a victim, because he does not have the freedom to make decisions of his own free will. He has been further forced by his family to hurt the woman with whom he is in love. When Puro/Hameeda has a miscarriage, Rasheed interprets this as a just punishment by God. He tries to obtain forgiveness at the local *sufi* shrine.

At this point, we see the face of 'good Islam', namely the local shrine of the Islamic holy man. Although it is a Muslim shrine, *Pinjar* shows that access is not restricted solely to Muslims. It is to be noted that, although the setting of the shrine is on land which later becomes Pakistan, the scene is dominated by the Indian national colours, saffron, white and green. This shows that the shrine neither belongs to India nor to Pakistan. Further, the shrine is not restricted to the presence of men alone. Until the present day, women visit it in search of divine support. The shrine is the only place for public worship and prayer, as women in South Asia usually do not pray in mosques. Often, women receive help in issues of health (e. g., in case of infertility) or in difficult social situations (e. g., after being divorced or widowed.) Thus, the shrine—in contrast to the mosque—becomes a place where female problems are cared about. It is also a place free from the orthodox (and allegedly 'fanatic') male interpretation of Islam, where music and dance are prevalent, and 'good Islam' is practised, also by women. The shrine, thus, is a place for religious as well as gender equality and a place for public awareness for female problems.

When Rasheed visits the shrine, an inner development starts. Whereas earlier, he was not open to Puro's problems, he begins to realise that he has done her wrong. His violent (male) interpretation of law, custom, tradition, and religion changes to and adopts a soft (female) attitude towards family, love and religion. Rasheed's metamorphosis from the 'bad' to the 'acceptable' Muslim begins at the shrine, thus reinforcing the positive notions of sufi Islam in South Asia.

The role of the sufis as poets and 'good Muslims' is also emphasised at the beginning of the film *Pinjar*, where the famous lines of the sufi poet Waris Shah (d. 1798) are quoted:

> I call Waris Shah today:
> 'Speak up from your grave,
> From your Book of Love unfurl
> A new and different page.
> One daughter of the Punjab did scream
> You covered our walls with your laments.'
> Millions of daughters weep today
> And call out to Waris Shah:
> 'Arise you chronicler of our inner pain
> And look now at your Punjab;
> The forests are littered with corpses
> And blood flows down the Chenab.'

The lines allude to Waris Shah's *Heer*, considered to be one of the most famous works in Punjabi poetry. A parallel is drawn between the tragic love story of Heer and Ranjha and millions of Punjabi women who lost their homes and families. The poems of Waris Shah are still read and quoted in both India and Pakistan. The sufi poet—although a man—is regarded as a 'chronicler of female pain', stressing the sufi responsiveness to female sensibilities.

The character of Dil Nawaaz in *Earth* underlines the view of men as being both perpetrators and victims. At the beginning of the film, he is seen as a very handsome, sympathetic and tolerant person. His character is reflected in his name, 'Dil Nawaaz' meaning 'cherishing heart'. He does not seem to have any prejudices against other religions, and falls in love with Shanta, a Hindu woman. He tries to win Shanta's heart by playing and joking around with Shanta's charge, Lenny. Lenny stresses that Dil Nawaaz is her personal hero. She especially likes the sweets and the ice cream that the 'ice-candy-wallah' sells. Moreover, both the word 'ice candy' and 'Dil Nawaaz' evoke positive associations in the spectator.

With the events of Partition, Dil Nawaaz undergoes a negative change, which is the complete opposite to that of Rasheed in *Pinjar*. Whereas Rasheed becomes understanding, gentle and sympathetic to the fate of abducted women, Dil Nawaaz becomes more masculine than ever (both inwardly and outwardly). In the scene when he stands with Hassan, Shanta and Lenny on the roof of his house, they watch the beginning of the religious riots in Lahore. Dil Nawaaz's character has completely changed and he watches the death of several Hindus with great *schadenfreude*[1] and hate. Shanta and Hassan are deeply shocked by the complete absence in Dil Nawaaz of humanity and sympathy. In addition to the change in his character, his masculinisation becomes obvious in his outward appearance. In the beginning of the film, he dresses in the traditional Indian Muslim way, in a *pyjama kurta* or with a 'western' shirt, mostly in bright colours. In the scene on the roof of the house, his style has completely changed. His clothes are dark, he has kohl around his eyes, and he is wearing a muscle shirt. His muscles (as a symbol of his masculinity) become visible for the first time at this point in the film. As a result, he clearly resembles Sylvester Stallone in *Rambo*. Everything soft and gentle in his character has vanished, and he looks like a hard and embittered man.

But Dil Nawaaz is not only a perpetrator, he has also become a victim of political circumstances. Two of his sisters have been cruelly killed in the rioting. Before their death, they have been tortured and their breasts cut off. Their dead bodies are found in a train arriving from Amritsar. On seeing them, Dil Nawaaz, traumatised, wants revenge and it is this feeling that brings about the negative change in his character.

Hassan, the masseur in *Earth*, is shown as a kind of good Muslim counterpart to Dil Nawaaz. He is a very sensible man who neither wants to kill or to commit violence against members of other religions, especially people who have been his friends. Although he can understand Dil Nawaaz's wish for revenge, he is not ready to blame the Hindus or Sikhs for the situation. He does not want any hate between the communities, and is even willing to marry a Hindu woman. Shanta, for her part, is willing to convert to Islam before her marriage with Hassan. All in all, Hassan is the 'good Muslim'. Here again, a gendered approach to the film might be seen: whereas the character of Dil Nawaaz undergoes a 'masculinisation,' the character of Hassan undergoes a 'feminisation': the figure denies the value of a male, muscular aggressive body, but emphasises female attributes like empathy, love, understanding, and harmony. Like several of the female characters of the film, Hassan too is victimised. Battered by his religious and sexual choices, the metaphor of newly created borders becomes applicable to his body too, when it is physically assaulted. The only difference between Hassan and the women shown in *Earth* is that he is victimised by his own community, the Muslims.

Another stereotype of the bad male Muslim is Sakina's father in *Gadar*. As a member of the Muslim aristocracy, he has access to political circles. Like the Parsis in *Earth*, the family leads a bourgeois lifestyle before Partition. Their good relationship with the British is shown by the fact that Sakina attends a Christian school in which British values and culture are taught. After Partition, the family belongs to the political elite in Pakistan. Sakina's father is not willing to accept a Sikh son-in-law and therefore declares Sakina's marriage with Tara Singh to be invalid. In his eyes, Pakistan is an exclusively Muslim country, which has nothing in common with India. The family's lifestyle, seen in the interior of the house, has now become exclusively 'Pakistani'. Whereas in pre-Partition India, Sakina's father was tolerant in various ways, he develops into a despotic patriarch in Pakistan. Earlier, he had sent his daughter to a Catholic school in India; now, he is not willing to accept a Sikh son-in-law. In India, he had encouraged his daughters' freedom and independence. After the family moved to Pakistan, Sakina's father is not open to any kind of opposition concerning the arrangement of his daughters' marriages and the choice of their grooms. He makes it clear to his family that he will not tolerate any female protest against his decision to marry his daughters to Muslim husbands.

This new Pakistani identity is challenged by the Indian-Sikh Tara Singh. Tara Singh is a man who does not force himself on women and is not personally involved in any violent activity against them. He has fallen in love with Sakina a long time before Partition, but has never dared talk about his romantic feelings towards her. He gives Sakina all the time she needs and, indeed, she does fall in love in him. When Tara Singh realises this, he defends his love against his own parents who want him to marry a Sikh woman. After his parents accept his choice, the couple live a happy life in India. Warmed by her love for her husband, Sakina easily turns into a village woman used to hard work. Here, the famous film *Mother India* (1957) is alluded to: the ideal of an Indian woman is the mother living in a village and sacrificing herself for her family and the Indian nation. Sakina comes to embody this role, leaving behind her aristocratic westernised lifestyle. Her husband Tara Singh respects his wife as a lover and as the ideal mother to his children. The film emphasises that, in the end,

Indian (Hindu-Sikh) moral values and love are superior to the Pakistani Muslims' insistence on their Islamic identity. Pakistani Muslims have to accept the multi-ethnic and multi-religious state of India in which Islam plays only a subordinate role.

*Gadar* depicts the most negative image of Pakistani Islam and counterpoints it with a positive image of the Sikh. The protagonist Tara Singh has two sides to his character. On the one hand, he is a soft and gentle, interested in art and music. When he meets Sakina for the first time in the Catholic convent, he immediately falls in love with her. He gives her a snow globe, which symbolises her homeland (*watan*). It is only when he realises that his family has been killed by Muslims that he starts killing. Only Sakina's influence—when she is almost raped and killed by the Sikh mob—can stop him. The theme of violence against other religions is continued when Tara, Sakina and their son escape from Lahore to India. Tara kills hundreds of Muslim Pakistani soldiers single-handedly and destroys Pakistani military equipment such as jeeps, helicopters and a train. The ending of *Gadar* puts the film in the category of the action movie, in which Tara Singh becomes a hero with whom the male audience can identify. For some sections of the audience, Tara Singh is the person who takes revenge for the events of Partition. He is the one to show the Pakistanis that Indians are superior to them, physically, psychologically and morally.

Besides the figure of Tara Singh, all three films enumerate some stereotypes of the Sikh community—either positive or negative. *Gadar* implies that the Sikhs will never belong to Pakistan and can also never be forced to betray their identity as Hindustanis. In a key scene of the movie, Sakina's father wants Tara Singh to convert to the Muslim faith. Before the conversion is complete, the Muslim audience of this public 'event' wants Tara to shout 'Pakistan zindabad! Hindustan murdabad!' ('Long live Pakistan! Death to India!'). Tara Singh refuses and then the fighting starts. This implies that Sikhs would not agree to recognise the state of Pakistan, and would prefer to support (an undivided?) India instead.[2]

But not a single film blames one or the other community as 'being guilty' for the violent acts committed during Partition. The victims can be seen on all sides and in all religions, and in all religions, women are victimised more often than men.

All films analysed convey the same intention: it is not religion which causes conflicts, war and violence. Rather it is the patriarchal system which causes the 'beast within' to emerge.

- In *Pinjar*, the patriarchal system 'forces' Rasheed to abduct a woman because of a family feud which started many years before.
- In *Pinjar,* the patriarchal system 'forces' Puro's father to send his daughter back after she manages to escape from Rasheed who had abducted her. This system 'forces' a father to repudiate his daughter in order to guard the 'honour' of all female members of his family.

This behaviour is clearly not based on religion, but on customs and traditions. Males of a community are under social pressure from older or more powerful members. The younger men of every community adhere to male ideals of masculinity. Whereas their intention is to protect 'their own' women, they do so by dishonouring the women of the 'other' community.

## The Great Exception? The Parsi Community

Interestingly enough, the Parsi community in India is shown to be neither victim nor perpetrator in the Partition. There are no forced conversions of Parsis to other religions, nor are there any violent Parsi men. The reason might be seen in the Parsis' neutrality in religious matters.

As already mentioned, Bapsi Sidhwa, the author of *Ice-Candy-Man*, belongs to the Parsi community of India. The Parsis, who claim Indo-Aryan origin from Persia, are Zoroastrians. In India, Parsis are members of the Zoroastrian religion whose ancestry can be directly traced from Persia. The word Parsi itself is derived from the Persian word 'Farsi' for 'Persian'. In *Earth*, a traditional story of the Parsis' arrival in India is recounted. In the eighth century, a group of Parsi refugees arrived in Gujarat, looking for refuge from Islamic expansion in Persia. The ruler of Gujarat refused to give them refuge and sent a messenger to them with a glass of milk, thus signalling that the people of India are a homogenous mixture. In response, the Parsis dropped some sugar into the glass of milk. They wanted to illustrate that they would make Indian culture sweeter, while remaining invisible just as sugar in milk.

The origin of the Parsis as Persian refugees is held responsible for their neutral stand in religious and political affairs. In *Earth*, their behaviour in India is further compared to a chameleon: it is easy for them to adjust to the situation in India and to remain invisible in order to survive.

Bapsi Sidhwa claims this neutrality in her own works. As she herself and her family were directly involved in the events of Partition, one cannot say that Sidhwa remains completely neutral. However, due to the Parsis' neutrality, some critics think that Sidhwa's works might be read as a historical source or as 'history'. It is furthermore true that her novels can serve as a personal account of a female member of a minority community during the time of Partition. Her account might be regarded as 'authenthic', as Sidhwa shares many memories with her female characters. It might also be counted as an account of a person who became marginalised in many ways: as a member of the minority Parsi community, as a child, as a disabled person, and as a woman author. Not many female authors have written on the Partition; Sidhwa's semi-autobiographical novel might be regarded as one that gives a voice to women who have, for over forty years, been silent about their personal experiences during Partition.

In *Earth*, the Parsis' exceptional role among the religious communities in India is depicted. One essential part of this role is the Parsi community's relationship with the British colonial power. *Earth* shows Lenny's parents' close social relationship to the British. They invite, and are invited, for dinner; they dress in the western way and drive British limousines. The British considered the Parsis to be a 'good' religious community, to whom they gave a special status during the colonial period (Didur 2006: 60 ff; Luhrmann 1994). The Parsis are shown to imitate the British and are said to have adopted a certain awareness of their Indo-Aryan descent. Lenny's brother is described as 'white' and as looking like the British. Parsi familiarity with western culture is evident in the scene where Lenny and her mother dance the waltz. Further, it is shown that the female members of the family are able to enjoy their upper-class lifestyle (like the British people around them), whereas outside their windows their world is falling apart and their country is 'cracking'. Whereas the female members of all other religious communities live under the permanent threat of being harassed, abducted or raped, the female members of the Parsi community in *Earth* are only indirectly confronted with this possibility.

Mehta, following Sidhwa, evokes the impression that Partition was a fight between the Hindu, Sikh and Muslim communities that did not afflict the Parsi community too much. The Parsis were not driven away from their homes, nor did they suffer from the violence. As noted above, Lenny's family is shown to continue their bourgeois lifestyle even at the time of violence and murder between 'the others', clearly underlined in the scene showing Lenny and her mother dancing the waltz while other families start to leave Lahore. The only effect of Partition on the Parsis might have been the psychological trauma of seeing other people suffering, seeing violence with their own eyes. In Lenny's special case, Partition marks the end of her innocence as a child. After she tells Dil Nawaaz and the Muslim mob where Shanta is hiding, Lenny sides with those who have suffered from violence, rape and abduction. The fate of her Hindu ayah is a belated eye-opener to the fate of hundreds of Muslim women living in a Recovered Women's Camp in the very neighbourhood of Lenny's home. Lenny had heard about the so-called 'fallen women' earlier. When a little Muslim boy tells Lenny that his mother had been terribly tortured, raped and finally murdered, Lenny, who is almost speechless and who feels entirely helpless, invites the boy to have a slice of cake. The boy replies that he does not know what cake is, almost as certainly as she does not know what rape is, and the conversation ends. This scene illustrates again that the Parsis lead a life which has almost nothing in common with the hardships and problems of the other communities in India. Lenny's mother is never in danger of being raped or of suffering from other forms of physical violence—neither is little Lenny. It also seems clear that Parsis are not involved in the 'Partition nonsense', as Lenny's mother calls it. They are sure that they can stay in Lahore and even help their neighbours when they leave. As almost invisible chameleons (so they describe themselves), they can live in India as well as in Pakistan. There is also no necessity for them to change their behaviour or their beliefs. As mentioned before, the victimisation of Parsis as shown in the films is more on the psychological than on the physical basis. Although being witnesses of hate, murder and rape, the male members of the Parsi community do not undergo any masculinisation and do not become any perpetrators. The women do not undergo 'feminisation' nor experience physical victimisation. The Partition borders do not concern the Parsis as much as the other communities in India; one might also say that the borders between men and women also do not affect the Parsis as much.

## Forced Conversions—Conversions from the Feeling of Love

As a result of the masculinisation of the male protagonists, women become victims of violence in many ways: through rape, abduction, betrayal, and forced conversions, all of which are shown in the three films. In *Pinjar*, the Hindu girl Puro becomes the Muslim woman Hameeda. This is not her own decision. Her miscarriage, resulting from having been raped by Rasheed, can be interpreted as a metaphor: the forceful conversion of women cannot secure the nation. Only the woman's acceptance of 'another' faith arising from love for her husband and as a result of free will can be the basis of a 'healthy' nation. Rasheed realises this point and abandons the path of violent masculinity.

The conversion of women by force is alluded to in the film *Gadar*. Tara Singh wants to save the Muslim girl Sakina from the Hindu-Sikh mob. Thus, he marks Sakina's face with a *bindi* (a vermillion dot on the forehead, traditionally worn by Hindu and Sikh married women) formed from his own blood, stressing that she has become a Sikh now. Marking someone with one's own blood is a powerful sign of having inducted someone to one's community. The rape of a woman, on the other hand, is a forced mark to say that she, from that time on, is dishonoured and belongs to 'another community.'Although Tara Singh's mark on Sakina's head, and thus her implied conversion to Sikhism, is not her own decision, it does not have a negative connotation in *Gadar*. This conversion is further sanctified later in the film, when Sakina falls in love with Tara Singh and becomes a Sikh during a regular wedding ceremony.

The conversion of men to another religion, however, is not possible in films. This is amply illustrated in *Gadar*. Tara Singh crosses the Indo-Pakistan border. His father-in-law does not accept his daughter's marriage with a man from 'another' community and tries to force Tara to convert to Islam. Tara accepts this condition out of love for Sakina, but strictly refuses to shout 'Hindustan murdabad!' In this scene, there is an evident connection between religion and the nation, which means 'India is Hindu and Pakistan is Muslim.' Conversion to Islam—according to the film—would have meant a conversion from 'Indian' to 'Pakistani', which cannot be countenanced in that film.

## Conclusion—Crossing Borders

Bollywood films—some of them based on literature by female authors—sometimes show female perspectives on religion, violence and Partition, perspectives that have been marginalised in previous discourse. It is especially the experience of physical and psychological violence that becomes a subject of such films. The reason for the religious fanaticism and violence is seen in notions of masculinity, which are prevailing in every community. The Partition is seen as a terrible event in which men are setting borders and boundaries for women and 'other', 'weaker' men. These borders and boundaries are either real or metaphorical: from childhood to adolescence, India-Pakistan, Hindu-Muslim, love and hate, body and mind. All three films analysed show female protagonists, who, after having painfully experienced these borders, find the strength to cross them. They are no longer solely victims of the Partition, but also active subjects in their newly defined communities. Some male characters, on the other hand, are shown as feminised victims of circumstances. The films clearly show that if men—like the protagonist Rasheed—are to cross borders to achieve mutual respect and understanding, they have to feel as women. Thus, these films might be regarded as catalysts for discussions about gendered experiences of historical events and an understanding of processes underlying terror and violence.

## Notes

1. A delight in others' misfortunes.
2. Unfortunately, the Sikhs became victims of riots in 1984 after the assassination of Indira Gandhi by her Sikh security guards. Many people were reminded of the violent events of 1947.

# 6

# 'Broken Memories, Incomplete Dreams': Notes towards an 'Authentic' Partition Cinema

Savi Munjal

'For me the idea was to give a piece of life to the audience, exactly as I see it, exactly as I live with it'. Sabiha Sumar's remark about her feature *Khamosh Pani* (Silent Waters, 2003) echoes Cezare Zavattini's vindication of the Italian neo-realist aesthetic for bringing the lives of ordinary people on screen, without embellishment or dramatisation.[1]*Khamosh Pani* chronicles the life of Ayesha, born Veero, kidnapped by Muslims during the Partition, and saved by one of her abductors who married her. Stylistic resemblances to Italian neo-realism, Soviet expressive realism and the early films of Satyajit Ray are unmistakable in Sumar's inclusion of unglamorous actors and the choice of grainy footage to convey the past. The film operates at two levels—one, as a powerful social document and two, as a poignant personal story between mother and son. The social commitment and humanistic perspective of *Khamosh Pani* underlines the fact that Indian cinema banks on realism to de-centre and displace the dominant discourse of mainstream melodrama. The contention of this article is that unlike the West, where realism is inevitably equated with bourgeois ideology and consequently dismissed for being complicitous with prevailing norms, realist cinema has immense potential in Indian cinema and is central to the process of the writing of history and of nationalist myth-making. *Khamosh Pani* serves as the ideologue of a small family in a small village, and illumines the ill-documented underside of the political events. It allows the *auteur* to grapple with complex issues revolving around the Partition(s), memory and forgetting, and arouses the cognitive abilities of the audience into recognition of the traumatic past.

The complex interweaving of narrative, war, political passions, and the multifaceted cultural realities is evident at the beginning. The establishing shot of Charkhi and the repeated pan-shots of the village connote harmony that is ruptured by constant flashbacks. The grainy black and white footage of the flashbacks conveys a sense of foreboding and mars the laughter that characterises the first scene. This sets the tone for the entire narrative—scenes depicting widowhood are followed by an enactment of elaborate wedding rituals, and the turbulent past is juxtaposed against the present as Sumar's narrative negotiates with the dialectic between memory and forgetting. This provides a contrast to the excessive *mis-en-scène* conspicuously oversaturated with glaring colours in films like *Main Hoon Na* (Don't Worry, I'm Here, 2004) and *Gadar* (Tumult, 2001).[2] *Khamosh Pani* makes a conscious attempt to steer clear of melodrama as it seeks to convey the socio-political and religious conflicts of the time. Unlike jingoist Partition cinema that constantly construes Pakistan as the spatial other, Sumar uses spaces to convey a nuanced understanding of national trauma. Spatial dynamics gain resonance as the mosque, once an apt heterotopic location for a romantic rendezvous becomes the site for the propagation of mainstream extremist sentiment (Foucault 1986: 22–27).[3]

The subversive, *Khamosh Pani* seems to insist, cannot be inscribed in common cinematic language. The static taxonomy of melodramatic Hindi films, which relies on oppositions between the good/bad, Indian/Pakistani, civilised/savage, is rejected for a subtle articulation of pertinent political and social concerns. The process of Islamisation and the subsequent breakdown of pluralism in Pakistan are articulated through multiple indexes. The incorporation of General Zia's name in popular culture can be witnessed through the barber's joke:

> 'Why does Zia sir's barber always mention elections?
> Because the General's hair stands at the name of elections, allowing the barber to cut his hair.'

Sumar negotiates, within the realm of humour, with the suspension of elections during the reign of General Zia-ul-Haq in the name of ethnic cleansing and scrutinizing the malpractices of politicians. Moreover, the insidious conflation of the axis of politics and religion is betrayed by the *maulvi*'s tirade against politicians and their insistence on faith in the Almighty: 'The one who does Jihad does not have any greed or fear.' Sumar systematically dismantles the ideological state apparatus that perpetrates the internalisation of hegemonic practices. The essential attempt is to explode what Walter Benjamin calls 'the continuum of history' (Benjamin 1969: 253–64)[4] and wring mankind away from the conformism that threatens to overwhelm entire civilisations.

Interestingly, retrogressive religious practices are constantly linked to orthodox patriarchy. *Khamosh Pani* provides an insight into Islamic cultural politics in a faction-ridden and ideologically fragmented society and raises profound questions about women's civil rights. The fundamentalists' disapproval of love marriages and dismissal of girls like Zubeida shows how the misinterpretation of Islam leads to retrogression, fundamentalism and obscurantism. Photographic realism aids the director to systematically expose and dismantle power structures that gained dominance in 1979. A particularly vocal scene, which underlines the change brought about in Salim, is when he participates in building a wall around the school. 'We will do this for our mothers and sisters, we will give them the protection of covers and four walls.' The examination of links between patriarchy and oppressive political systems, which lends to *Khamosh Pani* its complexity, shows how the sexual identity of the signatory influences the ideological leanings of the film. The *auteur* articulates the debates in favour of purdah with frightening clarity only to dismiss them within the schema of the narrative. Sumar does away with the 'orientalist' view which homogenises Islam—represents a view that it as a religion which denigrates women and limits their freedom. Instead, she constantly foregrounds alternatives for women's equality from within Islam: through Ayesha, who playfully advocates shorter sleeves for the bride, and through Zubeida, who dismisses Salim's religious extremism as ignorance: 'Salim, even I read the Quran, but that does not mean I do not think.'

Sumar's 'flesh-and-blood' depiction of women starkly contrasts with the myriad representations of women in commercial Hindi films. Women in films such as *Border* (1997), which claims to be 'adapted, dramatized and fictionalized for the screen from a true happening…the Battle of Longewala',[5] are limited to playing the roles of mothers, wives and sweethearts. In the immense box-office hit *Gadar*, Sakina passes from her father to the hero, back to her father and eventually back to her husband. A sense of helplessness characterises Sakina from the beginning of the film to the very end. The dialogues betray this: 'I will only wait for him [her husband] … he will definitely come to take me.' Be it Amisha Patel in *Gadar* or Sushmita Sen in *Main Hoon Na*, cinema represents women as fetishised objects to satiate the male gaze. As opposed to the representation of women as objects of desire, a tendency that promotes what Laura Mulvey calls erotic scopophilia, *Khamosh Pani* breaks away from the paradigm of the male-hero-agent. Ayesha builds a life for herself and fiercely clings to her independence till the very end: 'I made my own life without all of you … this is my life and my house.' *Khamosh Pani* draws attention to the doubly victimised stature of women during the Partition—victimised by the enemy as well as by their own community: 'We got our wives killed…but we did not let them get to the hands of the Muslims.' The historiological narrative draws attention to the exploitation of women in the name of honour. Driven to suicide by the members of her community or abducted by the members of other communities, the woman occupies a problematic position within the self/other binary—she is destined to be neither with the 'self' nor the 'other'. Her quest for identity is constantly marred by denial or, worse still, erasure: 'There is no woman like that.' The body of the abducted woman, Veero, provides the site for mapping these anxieties. The process of rehabilitation becomes especially important as, what Foucault calls 'the techniques of power and … discourse' (Foucault 1980: 98) collude in the attempts to use women to reaffirm the idea of a nation. Construed as a passive victim by her brother and ostracised as an outsider by the Muslim community, Ayesha occupies the proverbial no man's land. The fraught topos of Samar's feminist historiography, which vocalises the trauma of women, marks a self-conscious move away from the totalising potential of mainstream melodrama. Ayesha's stoic turning away of her brother and her angry retort: 'He [her father] wanted to kill me for his own peace … and what heaven is left for me—of the Sikhs or Muslims' goes a long way in depicting the split, indeed, the schizophrenic subjectivity of the women who survived the violence. The film serves as a unique imagistic site that allows the director to articulate, as Butalia specifies, 'their speech, their silences, the half-said things, the nuances' (Butalia 2000: 100).

Sumar's characters depict the national psyche at a moment when Pakistan was undergoing Islamisation under General Zia-ul-Haq. Stark photographic realism is deployed to foreground analogies between the traumatic events of 1947 and Bhutto's execution in 1979. The political partition of India is at once a distant reality as well as something that paradoxically feeds into communal politics as late as

1979. *Khamosh Pani* insistently asks the audience to think about the presence of antagonism and communal rivalry despite the passage of time. This analysis gains resonance within the contemporary context, for, India too witnessed communal riots against the Sikhs in Delhi in 1984, and against the Muslims in Bhagalpur in 1989. Despite its obvious political engagement, the film constantly focuses on the individual and the repercussions of political events on the filial unit. The emphasis is constantly on what Eric Auerbach calls 'daily life,'[6] the everyday business of living (Auerbach 1953).

Salim changes from being a cheerful Romeo to a heedless zealot but the change is never chronicled in shades of black and white. It is the subtle shades of grey that the narrative seeks to present. Samar's vocabulary chronicles his descent into fundamentalism in the name of vindicating his nation, his *qaum,* but there is a conscious shift away from 'authoritarian certitudes and monumentalist hierarchies' (Stam 2000: 19)[7] central to the melodramatic schema. A correct aesthetic understanding of social and historical reality becomes the precondition of Sumar's obvious cinematic sophistication. Despite his descent into fundamentalism, Salim is painfully aware of what he has lost as he locks away pictures of his childhood in a trunk with his mother's belongings. At another point, he gives his mother's locket away to Zubeida. The extreme poignancy which characterises this scene betrays an immensely nuanced understanding of character.

The avoidance of melodrama is nowhere more evident that in the screen space provided to Ayesha's suicide. Ayesha's action proves to be the point of culmination for a series of close-ups of the well, interspersed throughout the movie. With the recurring snapshots of the well, the structuring *leitmotif* of *Khamosh Pani*, time makes a prominent appearance in the cinematographic image. A variation of the Deleuzian *opsign,* (Deleuze 1986),[8] the pure optical image signified by the constant close-ups, the well seeks to chronicle layers of time—past, present and future, in order to show the analogous nature of political events spanning decades. The nature of exploitation meted out to women remains the same—repeated close-ups of the well juxtaposed against the building of the well, and retrogressive dialogues of the fundamentalists show that there has been no change, no apparent progress in the position of women. Precisely: there *is* no progress; the journey is aimless, characterised by a dearth of alternatives for women. Yet Ayesha's suicide, the action that ties all narrative strands together, is represented within a split second. Ayesha dies, but the movie does not end—*Khamosh Pani* ends with Zubeida's musings. Zubeida, like thousands of women all over Pakistan, is fleshed out as an agent, while still being a victim—she is not ignorant but *chooses* to remain silent. *Khamosh Pani* seeks to give a voice to the marginalised 'other' and provides multifarious and reflexive ways of understanding women. While this cinematic exposure of power systems successfully conveys the perils of patriarchy and religious extremism, it does not pose a solution to the problem.

The film ends ambiguously. Women like Zubeida have not triumphed; they are still on the sidelines waiting to be heard. *Gadar* and *Main Hoon Na*, on the other hand, revel in closure, which seeks to unify the narrative. Sakina's father undergoes a sudden change of heart, which leads to the metaphorical 'happy ending' in *Gadar*. Moral disarray is ameliorated through utopian clarity at the end. This unification provides a point of commensurability of radical and reactionary cinema. Despite their 'emancipatory' politics, films like *Main Hoon Na* retain the segregationist logic of jingoist cinema and rely on defamiliarised caricaturisation. *Main Hoon Na* is palimpsestic; it bears the impact of earlier films and traces of neighbouring discourses. This circulation of stereotypes as signs shows how the reactionary intent of the film is an effect of its aesthetic language and generic affiliations. This is what leads us to conclude, using Stephen Neale's words, that 'even positive images can be as pernicious as degrading ones, (Neale 1993: 41–47, 163).[9] Melodrama irrespective of its radical/reactionary bent, revels in the formulaic—a dangerous tendency Deleuze sums up as 'nothing but clichés, clichés everywhere' (Deleuze 1986: 212).[10] I call it 'dangerous' because the threat of popular cinema has become more pertinent in recent times, with globalisation allowing unprecedented opportunities for the dissemination of mass forms. Mainstream melodrama, which relies on stark binaries, propagates jingoism and incorporates non-diegetic song-and-dance sequences, has far more takers in the West's media bazaar than realistic cinema. Ironically, it is the discourse of nationalism that is central to the popular appeal of melodramatic films.

The discourse of nationalism becomes especially important as it throws light on the position of the *auteur*. Viewing nation as narration, Homi Bhabha elaborates on how 'nation' is articulated in language, signifiers and rhetoric. A reflection of Bhabha's parameters can be witnessed in archetypal melodramatic cinema, which takes recourse in rhetorical strategies that rely on inciting preconscious apprehension within the audience. *Gadar*, for instance, reiterates the ideological concept of fixity through its construction of Pakistan as the 'other'. Bollywood melodrama repeatedly glosses over difference and 'ventriloquises' for whole nations and peoples in a monolithic voice. *Khamosh Pani*, on the other hand, does away with preconceived visual cues that are used to apprehend reality within melodramatic cinema. It disrupts universalising and hegemonic narratives and relies on apertures to convey a complex sense of multiple realities. Sample the exchange between the barber and the Sikh gentleman visiting Pakistan two decades after the partition:

> Sikh gentleman: 'I was staying here till 1947.'
> Barber: 'I came here in 1947.'

The narrative constantly seeks to underline the heterogeneity of the population. The forceful statement, 'The question is whose voice is Zia-ul-Haq' interrogates the lawful hanging of an elected Prime Minister by a military dictator. The popularity of Bhutto's Pakistan People's Party (PPP) in West Pakistan, especially Punjab, is brought to the fore alongside Sumar's ideological affiliations. Clearly 'realism' is a precarious concept—all cinematic renditions of history seek to forge a narrative, which is mediated by the consciousness of the director of the film. The *auteur's* subject position gains importance as she seeks to reconstruct 'facts' about the Partition from memoirs, testimonies and stories not from lived experience. However, despite the continuous entanglement of 'event' and 'interpretation', Sumar's focus on the filial unit allows for a personal engagement with history. There is a constructive, purposive and political dimension to the plot in *Khamosh Pani*. This political and historical engagement aligns Sumar's 'fictional' reconstruction to a historians 'factual' rendition of a historical event.

As a range of contemporary philosophers have shown, 'real' history can no longer be construed as a separate epistemology based on empiricism (White 1973: 51).[11] Sumar resorts to emplotment, argument and ideological mediation in order to stress on the moments of overlap between the micro and the macro narratives of history. Her prioritisation of individual histories and private memories directs the focus on issues which purportedly 'objective' renditions of history gloss over. Sumar, akin to feminist historians like Urvashi Butalia (Butalia 2000),[12] seeks to highlight the marginalised aspects of political events—how families were divided, women raped, murdered, exploited and/or silenced, how the experience of dislocation and trauma shaped their lives, and determined that of the cities, towns and villages they settled in—issues which find little reflection in written history. *Khamosh Pani* then needs to be understood as 'historiophoty' (Rosenstone 1988; White 1988)[13]: the veracity of the representation and the accuracy of detail allow Samar to fashion a distinctly imagistic filmic discourse which questions patriarchal representations of partition by foregrounding an alternative historiography. The film succeeds in the resignification of norms outside the epistemological given, and fashions a counter-discourse that manages to convey the gendered ramifications of the apocalyptic Partition in a way far more nuanced than in melodrama.

The stress on the 'individual' as opposed to the 'general' offers an alternative historical view and echoes Gyanendra Pandey's debunking of master narratives as fraudulent. According to Pandey, a self-conscious, 'fragmentary' approach to writing historical narratives is an attempt to address these contradictions, gaps, and silences. The merit of the 'fragmentary' point of view 'lies in this, that it resists the drive for a shallow homogenization and struggles for other, potentially richer definitions of the 'nation' (Pandey 1991: 559). It then becomes important to examine which version of history is visualised on screen by a particular genre.

The choice of the genre inevitably colours the politics of films on the Partition. Melodramatic films rely on a 'characteristic ensemble of manicheaism, bi-polarity, the privileging of the moral over the psychological and the deployment of coincidence in plot structures' (Vasudevan 2000: 131),[14] which generates vicarious pleasure in the symbolic triumph. *Gadar* homogenises whole peoples and relies on stark juxtaposition between the 'good' Sikh (Sunny Deol) and the tyrannical, venomous Muslim (Amrish Puri). *Khamosh Pani*, like Pandey's 'fragmentary' historical narrative, displaces this margin/centre paradigm in favour of a nuanced polyvocality. The film steers clear of comforting truisms and deconstructs polarisations to reveal the fractured fabric of post-Partition society. In contrast to the totalising methodology of mainstream melodrama, Sumar's fragmentary perspective stresses the multi-dimensional nature of political events.

Filmmakers such as Sumar, then, assume the function of intellectuals as they confront not only extremist ideas and ideologies, which operate at the level of 'common sense', but also the social forces behind them (Gramsci 1996: 48).[15] Melodrama renders history manipulable to the act of constitution. It tends to foreground a single authoritative version of history while open-endedness allows for a multiplicity of responses to co-exist. *Khamosh Pani* finally works as a text that is fraught with ambiguity. It succeeds in creating a space which allows the audience to examine personal histories and 'unheard' stories. Eventually, it functions as a communicative act, which initiates a dialogue with the reader/spectator. Will women like Zubeida get to voice their dilemmas? Or is Ayesha's end the only route to 'freedom'? Will women like Ayesha and Zubeida be able to envisage other alternatives for themselves? These are questions the audience must answer for themselves. Clearly then, both form and content feed into one another in order to make *Khamosh Pani* doubly disruptive, the ideological lynch-pin for buttressing dissenting sentiment. Signification operates through social consensus and the lack of adherence to traditional signification accounts for its 'alternative, liberating newness against the absorptive capacity of ... established discourses' (Terdiman 1985: 13). Deploying images as a principal medium of discursive representation, *Khamosh Pani* offers a powerful visual-auditory account of the trauma that haunts the survivors and descendent generations decades after the political partition of India. The film bespeaks the energies of avant-garde innovation and an enthusiastic embrace of ambiguity, thereby recreating the cinematic edifice to provide the most fitting rendition of the twentieth century experience of the Partition.

## Notes

1. Pacifici 1956: 50–51. Zavattini, a theoretician and screenwriter, was actively involved in the production of Sica's *The Bicycle Thief* and *Umberto D*. He coined the slogan 'today, today, today' and also claimed that the 'true function' of 'cinema [was] not to tell fables' but to 'tell a reality as it were a story', so that there was 'no gap between life and what [was] on the screen'.
2. I will take *Main Hoon Na* as symptomatic of radical and *Gadar* as representative of reactionary melodramatic cinema. While there can be analogies and disanalogies between radical and reactionary melodramatic cinema, it is the commensurabilities I am interested in. Despite the semantic rejection of jingoism, films like *Main Hoon Na* resonate with the power of earlier stereotypes and narrative tropes. The reannexation of tropes leads to syntactic similarity. This, coupled with the representational-compositional context within which the film is produced, allows for a comparison of the two kinds of films.
3. Foucault defines heterotopia as the space which allows for the articulation of counter-hegemonic sentiment. Heterotopias, according to Foucault, are 'something like counter-sites, a kind of effectively enacted utopia in which the real sites, all the other real sites that can be found within the culture, are simultaneously represented, contested, and inverted'.

4. Benjamin proposes a non-teleological reading of history, which can 'blast open the continuum of history'. He insists that this explosion of conventional history is characteristic of all revolutionary classes, irrespective of their spatio-temporal location.

5. The battle of Longewala (5–6 December 1971) was part of the Indo-Pakistan war of 1971, fought between Indian and Pakistani forces in the Thar Desert of Rajasthan (India).

6. In the first chapter of *Mimesis* ('Odysseus' Scar'), Auerbach uses the term 'daily life' to connote realistic depiction as opposed to a sublime style. It is used to compare the Greek and the Hebrew ways of writing.

7. The 'villians' in *Gadar* and *Main Hoon Na*, played by Sakina's father (Amrish Puri) and Raghavan (Sunil Shetty) respectively, serve as points of contrast to Sumar's delineation of Salim (Aamir Ali Malik).

8. *Opsign* refers to the pure optical which breaks the sensory-motor links, overwhelms relations and no longer lets itself be expressed in terms of movement, but opens directly on to time.

9. Steve Neale insists that the radical/reactionary intent of the text is an effect of its aesthetic language and formal features and not simply a matter of narrative.

10. Deleuze uses the phrase while discussing the usage of generic tropes and conventional processes of identification in prototypical Hollywood cinema.

11. Plot is not a structural component of fictional or mythical stories alone; it is crucial to the historical representations of events as well'. White offers a deconstructive approach to history in his books titled *Metahistory* and *Tropics of Discourse*. He believes all histories are embodiments of particular historiographical tropes and insists that a historian answers questions by using three different types of explanations: emplotment, argument and ideological implication.

12. Butalia's project in *The Other Side of Silence*, like Sumar's in *Khamosh Pani*, is to focus on the collection of memories, individual and collective, familial and historical, which, according to her, make up the reality of Partition. Those are, she insists, the history of the event. Similarly, historiographer Gyanendra Pandey's 'fragmentary' approach to writing historical narratives suggests promising ways of recuperating 'truth' from individual rather than grand historical narratives.

13. *Historiophoty* is a neologism coined by Hayden White in response to an essay by Robert Rosenstone to describe the representation of history in filmic discourse.

14. This is evident in the multiple coincidences which colour the plot of *Gadar*—Tara's presence amidst the crazed mob out to kill all Muslims residing in India, Sakina's discovery of her father's musical watch, which convinces her of his death, and Sakina's discovery of her family in Pakistan are all ploys which deploy coincidence to carry the story forward

15. *Common sense* in Gramsci's schema is used to describe the 'natural', taken-for-granted knowledge which protects the interests of the bourgeoisie as natural and inevitable, while the proletariat 'consent' to domination. Internalisation assures that revolution is prevented and the social order is maintained.

# 7

# Partitioned Memories: The Trauma of Partition in Ghatak's Films

Kamayani Kaushiva

*Only through remembrance can painful memories be forgotten*
*—Edward Said*

*The decade of the 1940's was the era of two major historical catastrophes, the Second World War with the Holocaust in Europe and the Partition in India. The experience shaped the consciousness of several generations both in Europe ... and in India.*
*—Margit Koves, 'Telling Stories of Partition and War' 1997.*

$\mathbf{P}$ublic memory is the fundamental mechanism *via* which the collective identity of society is constructed. In India, there is no 'public memory' of Partition, although it survives as private memory in the lives of millions, even decades later. There is no institutional memory of Partition: the state has not seen fit to construct any memorials, to mark any places—unlike in the case of Holocaust memorials or memorials for the Vietnam war. Nothing at the Indo-Pak border marks a place where millions of people crossed borders of newly formed nations, no plaque or memorial at any of the sites of the refugee camps, nothing that marks a particular spot as a place where Partition memories are collected. Rather, the traumatic experience of Partition has been relegated to the realm of collective amnesia. Post-Partition public memory is shaped by a paradoxical dichotomy—the victims are caught between 'Silence and speech. Memory and forgetting. Pain and healing' (Butalia 1998: 356). Any attempt to express the agony of Partition has been so fraught with anxiety: '...is it better to be silent or to speak.?' As Claude Markovits states,

Initially, indeed, a heavy silence prevailed...the violence that went with Partition was largely concealed in public discourse, and its memory remained confined to realms of private pain. (Markovits 2003: 58)

Though historical and literary work on the trauma of Partition gradually emerged, yet cinema, as an important document of cultural memory, was prominent by its absence. Barring a few imaginative endeavours, such as M. S. Sathyu's *Garam Hawa* (Hot Winds, 1973), Partition in cinema seemed to have been avoided rather than confronted. Commenting on the silence that defined post-Partition trauma, Mahey points out:

> If nations could suffer trauma, the Partition certainly ignited one in both India and Pakistan. And, as in some traumata, the victims dissolved into catatonic shock that displayed itself as silence. For a number of years after the event, no writer of any renown on either side of the new border rescued an adequate sense of lucidity to approach the issue. Something had been permanently lost and the inadequacy of mere words was discerned...[as] an understood code of silent mourning. (Mahey 2001: 138)

This 'silent mourning' was, however, broken by the epic vision and sublimity of Ghatak's movies, whose three films—*Meghe Dhaka Tara* (The Cloud-capped Star, 1960), *Subarnarekha* (The Golden Line, also a river in Jharkhand; 1962) and *Komal Gandhar* (E-flat, 1961) unwittingly form a trilogy and are a scathing indictment of the mindless act of Partition. His films address the trauma of Partition from a victim's perspective; they enquire into Partition as a continuing experience, as Butalia views it, the continuing presence of the past in our lives today, a history which refuses to fade away and whose dark shadows of pain and trauma still define our 'present'. It is this sense of hollowness that Ghatak's films strive to portray. Within a rich tapestry of images and motifs, his films encapsulate the intensity of human agony that Partition generated. Ghatak addressed the predicament of homeless refugees for whom Partition did not end in 1947, for whom, rather, its consequences had just begun to shape their lives.

Besides being an event whose consequences had just begun to unfold, Partition was problematic in another respect—it created two flanks, West Pakistan and East Pakistan, which were immensely different in their cultural affinities and orientations. In addition, the impact of Partition on the two regions was drastically different. While, in both cases, Partition generated mass exodus and communal violence, in Punjab the escalation in violence, although grisly and acute, was primarily a one-time affair. It was temporally sealed. After a span of few years, the issue got settled (in terms of exchange of population). However, for Bengal, 'the influx of people brought down to the status of refugees, displaced persons', by the political game, still continues. As has been rightly observed:

> ... the Partition of Punjab was a one time event with mayhem and forced migration restricted primarily to three years (1947–50), the partition of Bengal has turned out to be a continuing process. (Bagchi and Dasgupta 2002)

The exchange of population also differed: while in the context of Punjab it was swifter, in the case of East Pakistan/Bangladesh it is still continuing. Thus, as has been often stated, the story of the Bengali refugee did not end with the 1947 partition. Rather, it continues like an unending tale of long suffering migrants, spanning decades.

This suffering is what Ghatak strove to capture. Fundamentally, his films revolve around two central themes: the trauma of being uprooted from the idyllic milieu of East Bengal and the cultural trauma of the Partition of 1947. Partition was, for Ghatak, a shattering experience because his roots were in that part of Bengal which now fell under foreign territory. Memories of an undivided Bengal pervade his films. He turned a searing gaze at the displaced middle classes. In his vision, elements of grand political tragedy are found in the abject compromises made by decent ordinary people in their desperate search for comfort and security in a profoundly inhospitable world. His innovative films record the trauma of change and the desperation of the rootless and deprived refugees from East Bengal.

After Partition, Ghatak felt both restless and rootless and his films became an expression of his anxiety to find root, to find a refuge: As Ashish Rajadhyaksha points out:

> The initial question of the split of Bengal was to become for him a larger quest—an attempt at portraying the relationships between the new classes formed by the process of urbanization and the machine-revolution and their old traditions. (Rajadhyaksha 1982: 82)

The question led him to take a look at the whole issue of rootlessness afresh, as the search of the refugee for a new identity. For him, this identity had links directly with the past, the centuries old cultural heritage of our ancient societies, wherein lay the unifying forces of the present. As another critic observes:

Ghatak was profoundly affected by the partition of India that came with independence in 1947, ceding the land of his birth to the newly created Pakistan. Indeed, nostalgia for the once undivided Bengal and the traumas emanating out of dislocation and loss of home are basic to almost all his films. (Hood 2000: 20)

Further, the richness of the aesthetic culture of Bengal was lost beyond recovery, the acute loss of which haunts Bengal until date, as Bagchi and Das Gupta write: 'Partition was an ever-unfolding story of the abduction of this young mother from which there was no recovery...' (Bagchi and Dasgupta 2003: 2).

Another point of divergence between the experience of Partition trauma in West and East Pakistan was that while the atrocities that marked Partition in the context of West Pakistan and received (comparatively) ample literary historical documentation, the same is not true for Bengal. As Butalia has stated (during a seminar in 1994): 'A serious gap is the omission of experiences in Bengal and East Pakistan (Bangladesh).'

Ghatak, however, stands apart in his aesthetic attempt to wage a relentless war against a degenerate reality: a reality that severed man's natural roots from his traditional and culturally harmonious past, a reality that pushed people into a politics of destruction and deceit. His films serve as a metaphor for the violent uprooting of the Partition that figuratively crippled and ultimately orphaned a population. He spent his entire artistic life condemning how 'Partition struck at the roots of Bengali culture' (O' Donnell 2005). As Goswami observes, his

> ... was a rare mind. It assimilated the rare spectacle of the partition of Bengal, the bleak memory of refugee camps, the degradation of rootlessnes, the dehumanization of the alienated.... Ghatak externalized his private anguish into a global perspective. This heightening of sensibility annealed his heart into a language which could be understood in distant Punjab and the rest of India, in Poland, Germany, Korea, Vietnam, Palestine, any country which had been sundered by the trauma of separation and the bleeding scar of an overnight border. (*Ibid.*: 86)

## Meghe Dhaka Tara

Ghatak's intense, searing pain found enduring and aesthetically sublime expression in his extremely sensitive film, *Meghe Dhaka Tara*. One of Ghatak's most powerful and innovative melodramas, the film examines the socio-economic implications of Partition, reaching out to the audience with its directness, simplicity, and its unique and stylistic use of melodrama. The film revolves around Nita, a woman who sacrifices her life to rebuild her family shattered by the effects of Partition and the subsequent exodus. Nita's family is a family of refugees from the partition of Bengal; they live in a shanty town near Calcutta, surviving on her meager earnings. Nita is addressed by Sanat (her lover) as 'Meghe Dhaka Tara', an embodiment of perfect woman marred by the dark enveloping clouds of untoward circumstances. Sanat is a scholar in pursuit of higher ideal, who, instead of earning his livelihood, often looks towards Nita for financial assistance. Eventually, however, with the tacit encouragement of Nita's mother, Sanat marries Geeta, a sensuous, selfish woman, a usurper. Nita's acceptance of her fate is remarkable until she falls terminally ill and, after having sacrificed her best years, she finally cries out into the silence of the mountains her will to live. Her cry, 'I want to live', ricochets through the trees as her brother watches helplessly. It is perhaps the most intense moment in the history of Indian cinematic art.

The film opens with an apparently interminable shot of a tree, beneath which we see the protagonist Nita standing. The serenity and compassion that marks Nita's face as she sees her *Dada* (older brother) rehearsing (in pursuit of his dream to become a classical singer, he is oblivious to his duty to provide financial assistance to his family) tells us about the beautiful relationship they share. The next scene reveals the dire economic crisis Nita's family is facing; the grocer accosts Nita, urging her to pay the bill overdue for two months. The scene is very poignant for it serves to highlight the socio-economic plight of Nita's family. The next scene is integral to the film; Nita's sandal breaks and comes undone. This motif, also like that of the tree, runs right through out the film. The resigned, uncomplaining attitude with which Nita accepts her fate, picks up the sandals and walks barefoot on the gravel serves to accentuate the poverty and pathos of her situation as well as her courage and power to endure. This is brought out in stark contrast to the coquettish sister Geeta, whose image is first seen in a mirror against a background of thatched wall, where she is insolently brushing her hair and singing. The image artfully builds upon us the impression of an unscrupulous woman, as she eventually proves to be. Geeta hands over to Nita a letter from Sanat. The scene that ensues shows Nita reading the letter in her room. It is in this letter, Sanat addresses his beloved as Meghe Dhaka Tara. The title of the film echoes the inhospitable economic plight that plagued millions uprooted due to Partition. Parallel to the love theme of Sanat and Nita, Ghatak introduces the beautiful relationship of Nita and her Dada, the only relationship that endures the test of time. While reading Sanat's letter, Nita accidentally strikes against the photograph of her and Dada taken in the hills during one of her childhood visits. She smiles lovingly and longingly as she balances the frame, perhaps, dreaming of her intense desire to return to hills, a desire that the intervention of fate tragically fulfills, as she breathes her last in the sanatorium in the hills. The scene in which Dada comes in and snatches the letter in a playful manner is a parallel to the way in which he will eventually snatch the blood-stained handkerchief from her. Their roles, by that stage, will have undergone a drastic change; Dada, now the butt of bitter diatribes from his mother, the grocer and the world at large, will return to his family after becoming a successful singer, only to find a selfish mother now entreating him to build a two-storey house for her. His beloved sister Nita has, by this time, entered into a self-imposed exile, in an advanced stage of tuberculosis.

The scene where the family learns of Nita's tuberculosis reverberates with intensity. The scream of the father, 'I accuse', without acknowledging his own capability in annihilating the life out of Nita, is remarkable. The disease-ridden body of Nita is now of no use to her parasitic family. The father urges Nita to leave home for her breath now is laden with poison and she is now a burden for the family. Betrayed and forsaken by those very people whom she nurtured and sustained by bartering away her happiness, Nita runs out in the dark night, confronting the storm, clutching to her bosom the photo of her childhood as she runs into Dada who has just returned from making arrangements for her in the sanatorium. The near mad state in which Nita leaves her home is heightened by the song refrain '*Ai go Uma Kole loi*'. (Come to my arms Uma, my child). The refrain moves the film into the realm of myth, where Nita is portrayed as an embodiment of Goddess Durga.

The final dialogue between sister and brother is an intensely poignant scene; ironically, fate has ultimately fulfilled Nita's cherished desire to visit the hills. The scene shows Nita sitting and reading Sanat's letter, as in the first scene when we saw Dada snatching the letter; breathing the last of her life gone waste, she suddenly cries out, with searing and heartrending agony, her will to live: 'I want to live. Tell me just once that I will live.' The cry, along with the helplessness of Dada who knows that it is too late, embraces Nita as the camera pans across the landscape resonating with her endless moaning. Nita's scream is a moment of perfect unity, a moment of complete understanding of all the forces which forged her destiny. The final sequence applies this lesson to the society beyond Nita. She is dead and her sacrifice is over, but its lessons need a final rooting in society to have a real effect. The film ends on the scene where its theme had actually been initiated, the broken sandal which, emphasises Nita's poverty-ridden existence. We see Dada seeing another girl whose profile resembles Nita, who also picks up her broken sandal in her hands and walks on gravel with a stoicism which reminds us of millions of such women whom fate has forsaken. Nita, thus, is an embodiment of the travails and misery that played havoc in the lives of unaccountable millions whose lives changed beyond recognition in the post-Partition scenario. The film elucidates how family mores and ethics are torn to shreds in the face of dire poverty induced by forced migration due to Partition. The mother's anxiety and her dread at becoming homeless yet again drives her insane to the point that she sacrifices Nita's aspirations to fulfill her own selfish ends. The scene wherein the mother asks Dada (whom she earlier used to degrade) to build her a house of two storeys is symbolic of the pain of losing one's home. Ghatak's film reveals how Partition ate into the very entrails of society by the massive dislocation it generated; the economic hardships it sponsored created a society where relationships no longer had any relevance.

## Komal Gandhar

In *Komal Gandhar*, Ghatak addresses the problem of refugeehood, of being torn from one's roots and the pain it incites. The film opens with a play being enacted; the theme of this play is the theme of the film— the protagonist of the play is lamenting the partition of India, expressing his pain at becoming a refugee. The first dialogue uttered in the film is in the play and that sets the tone of the film. 'Why?'—this question echoes the dilemma of millions whose lives were transformed beyond recognition by the politically motivated Partition, leaving them with pain, memories and the eternal quest for a new homeland. The protagonist of the play woefully asks why he should leave the country of his birth. He reiterates, 'Why should I leave this lovely country, my river Padma?' The film is an expression of the horror of being reduced to the status of a refugee, an ignominy borne by millions who had no say in the political game, a game that raped them of their nationality and sense of belonging; the character in the play calls himself 'accursed' for being, 'a homeless refugee'. As Syed Sikander Mehdi writes: 'Once a refugee, always a refugee. Like death, the memory of uprooting, flight, refuge, return....' (Mehdi 2003: 85) are ever-present in refugee consciousness.

> There is no escape from this past, it has to be lived and relived.... Post-partition refugee life for millions of Hindus, Sikhs, and Muslims living in India and Pakistan is no different. They live in memory and memory lives in them. The bitter past is always there with them. In the process the memory of refugeehood has become concretized, structured, and rooted—making healing very difficult. It is, after all, not easy for the victims to forget the bleeding past and forgive those who looted and plundered, committed rape and murder of near and dear ones, and inflicted forced migration. (*Ibid.*)

The film elucidates the bitterness that claimed millions. It enquires into how Partition continued to make its presence felt in innumerable ways.

> [T]he major legacy of Partition was the identity based rift which came about in the lives of millions of individuals suddenly torn from their familiar frame of life, their lands (the majority of displaced persons were peasants), and their ancestral homes in the name of an utterly abstract principle: the principality of nationality.... (Markovits 2003: 56)

When Ghatak started making his films, he did not have a deliberately designed trilogy which dealt with the Partition issue. While in *Meghe Dhaka Tara* and *Subarnarekha* he brings forth the degeneration, in the Partition milieu, of morals and ethics, in *Komal Gandhar* he went further—he enacted the politics of Partition *vis-à-vis* the theatre group that once had been a unified, whole, and eventually became embroiled in ugly politics and faced division and acrimony. As he observes,

> In *Komal Gandhar* I had to face the problem of operating at different levels. I wanted to draw simultaneously on Anasuya's divided mind, the divided leadership of the People Theatre movement of Bengal, and the pain of divided Bengal. (Ghatak 1975)

As the film progresses we see the two rival theatre groups being brought on a common platform by the efforts of Anasuya. This rivalry can be seen as an allegory for the division of India.

The most intense moment of the film is when the rail track is shown and the train running on it abruptly comes to a halt, the track barricaded, for it marks the border. One of the characters remarks that he finds it incomprehensible that trains which are meant to unite are here representing separation. Anasuya's searing cry, imbued with intense and piercing agony, echoes in the background as the train rushes towards the dead end.

The film reverberates with an old folksong—'*Aey paar paddaa o paar paddaa/Moddi khaaney chaur/Tahaar moddeye bosheye/Aachen shibo saudagor*' (On this bank is the river Padma/On the other bank is the Padma too/And an island lies between them/Where lives Lord Shiva/The trader great)—which voices the agony of millions who were perplexed by the division of their land. A heart-searing scene in the film is where Anasuya is looking across the flowing Padma, where she can see her home, which they had to abandon, a hearth now occupied by strangers. The agony of being able to see your *badi* (home) within, and yet out of reach, is beyond our imagination.

The film is also replete with wedding songs from East Bengal—*Aam tolaaye zhumur zhaamur/Kaula tawlaaye biyaa/Aayee lo shundorir zhaamaayee/Mukut maathaye diyaa* (A stirring of breezes cool in the mango grove/A wedding blessed by the auspicious green plantains all around/Comes now the groom for the beauteous bride/Wearing chivalry's glorious crown). The song metaphorically suggests the desirability of a union between separated lands.

As Ghatak himself wrote,

> …wedding songs are profusely scattered throughout *Komal Gandhar*. I desire a reunion of these two Bengals. Hence the film is replete with songs of union. (Ghatak 2000a: 50)

and

> The main note of my *Komal Gandhar* was set on the unification of the two Bengals. Hence, throughout the film we played the tunes of old wedding songs, with the same note of concord playing over the scene of a harsh separation. (Ghatak 2000c: 75)

This pain of partition finds sublime expression in his film *Subarnarekha*, where he expresses the eternal quest for a new homeland, the quest of millions reduced to the status of refugees.

## Subarnarekha

*Subarnarekha* is about rational elements like history, war and its aftermath, mass displacement and loss of an old habitat and hence roots on the one hand, and irrational entities like destiny and fate that are not supposed to but do affect human beings and their conduct to alter their lives irreversibly on the other. (Partha Chatterjee 2003)

One of Ghatak's most impressive and complex films, made in 1962 but released in 1965, *Subarnarekha* tells of Ishwar Chakrobarty and his young sister Seeta, who are living in a refugee camp after Partition. It is a poignant portrayal of the economic and socio-political crisis destroying the very existence of partitioned Bengal. The film opens with a stark portrayal of inhumane socio-economic conditions, amidst which people are struggling to find their moorings in a refugee colony, ironically named 'Navajeevan'—new life—a satire directed upon the hopes of people engaged in the futile pursuit of a new homeland. The hardship thus faced by Ishwar and Seeta is symbolic of the plight of faceless and nameless millions who, like them, became victims of a politically motivated decision to divide the country. The naïve yet persistent manner in which Seeta keeps asking her brother, Ishwar, about her (*nutan badi*) new home, is extremely sensitive and focuses on the problem of rehabilitation being faced by victims of Partition. Ishwar's sole purpose in life is to provide a 'sense of belonging' to his orphaned sister, to provide for her a *nutan badi*. His transition from an intellectual to a factory manager is a comment on the compromise that Partition wrought upon innumerable lives. Harprasad, the schoolmaster who has nurtured the new home of his fellow unfortunates, accuses Ishwar of being a coward and denounces him for thinking only of his own welfare and not that of the others around him. Ishwar meanwhile, adopts Abhiram, a destitute, proving that he is a man of honour; hence the degenerate state to which fate eventually reduces him is extremely poignant.

The film has some extremely beautiful moments with a sensitive portrayal of the relationship between Seeta and Abhiram. Ishwar's refusal to Seeta and Abhiram's marriage is the pivot on which the story now enfolds. Seeta's elopement and her betrayal breaks the spirit of Ishwar, who wanders aimlessly for six years and is on the verge of suicide when the most powerful scene of the film unfolds. Harprasad, whose pursuit of ideals ends in severe disillusionment, returns now, where Ishwar, disillusioned and bordering on insanity, is trying to take his life. Harprasad had, decades earlier, abandoned his friendship with Ishwar; he had seen Ishwar's decision to fulfill his duty towards Seeta rather than fight for the rights of homeless people as a betrayal of the ideal.

Now, upon his return, when he sees Ishwar on the verge of taking his life, he rescues him by quoting from Tagore's *Shishu Tirtha*. He then takes Ishwar to Calcutta where the degeneration of Ishwar begins in earnest. Meanwhile, Seeta has been reduced to prostitution after the tragic demise of Abhiram. The scene where Ishwar enters Seeta's room in a drunken state, taking her to be a prostitute is one of the most powerful scenes in the film. The grotesque manner in which Seeta embraces death and Ishwar's heart-rending cry are haunting. The film concludes with Ishwar, endowed with the responsibility of bringing up the son of Seeta and Abhiram, dreaming, like Seeta, of his *nutan badi*. The final scene, heart-breaking and of immense beauty, focuses on Ishwar and Binu, the orphaned little son of Sita and Abhiram, walking away towards a craggy landscape with the horizon far in the background, accompanied by the choral chanting of the 'Charai betiye' mantra on the soundtrack, in search of a new life. It sums up the forced political displacement of millions, in our own times and earlier, of people whose only crime was that they had sought a little peace, dignity and happiness in their lives.

The film, thus, is a comment on the havoc wrought upon millions; it is a testimony of how an entire culture became victimised because of a political decision to divide a homeland. Ghatak has tried to encapsulate how the partition of India affected the psyche of Bengal and how, though decades have passed since this unfortunate tragedy happened, it continues to cast its dark shadows on the lives of millions in unaccountable ways. Ghatak himself comments on the vision that informs his films:

> We were born into a critical age. In our boyhood we have seen a Bengal, whole and glorious.... This was the world that was shattered by the War, the Famine, and when the Congress and the Muslim League brought disaster to the country and tore it into two to snatch for it a fragmented independence. Communal riots engulfed the country. The waters of the Ganga and the Padma flowed crimson with the blood of warring brothers.... Our dreams faded away. We crashed on our faces, clinging to a crumbling Bengal, divested of all its glory. (Ghatak 2000a: 49)

This trauma informs almost all Ghatak films. He acknowledges that it has been difficult for him to forget the pain of Partition, an enduring trauma which 'cannot be frozen in the past' (*ibid*). This task of acknowledging and chronicling the saga of pain that millions underwent is perhaps best documented through films. Films are akin to memory; as David MacDougall observes, 'Films have a disconcerting resemblance to memory ... an intimation of memory perfected' (Macdougall 1998: 231). Thus films bestow a 'kind of immortality' on a subject. Hence, perhaps, no more suitable medium can be found for articulating the pain of Partition. Indeed, artists and filmmakers have, of late, responded and the last decade has seen several instances of aesthetically powerful films made on the tragedy that defined India in this century—Partition.

# Rapprochement

# 8

# Defining a Non-Pakistan-centric Post-globalisation Self in Hindi Cinema 1996–2006

Sunny Singh

## Studio Logo and Pre-credits

The past decade has seen dizzyingly spectacular changes in Indian society, politics and economy, at a pace that rivals a classic Manmohan Desai production. The key reason for these changes is primarily a demographic transformation which has ensured that over seventy per cent of the Indian population is under the age of forty.[1]

Not only does this demographic transformation impact the country's exploding work force and aspirational challenges, it has also required a colossal shift in the popular national narrative, as can be evinced by the past ten years of Hindi films. While much is made of the 'rise of Hindu nationalism of the early 1990s' in Hindi cinema, less attention has been paid to a generation coming of age in an increasingly maturing democracy, where the one-party rule of generations gave way to a series of coalition governments. The years between 1995 and 2005 have also been marked by a second round of nuclear tests in 1998, a low-intensity border conflict with Pakistan in Kargil in 1999, economic sanctions from the US and EU countries that barely made a dent in the country's growing confidence, and, finally, an increasing economic and international political clout. Since 2001 and the international events following the attacks of 9/11, the country has also benefited from the shifting set of geo-strategic priorities of various global powers.

Set against the backdrop of such rapid historic changes, Hindi cinema has followed its historical role of engaging with events and reflecting as well as anticipating the nation's discontents (Prasad 1998; Vasudevan 2000). In the past decade, the Hindi film industry has attempted to both reflect and construct an adequate, the national self-image as well as an appropriate national discourse for these changes. This process has seen various guises and stages, but this essay will focus on the following:

1. The naming of and focus on Pakistan as a major of source of terrorism and internal unrest, with a simultaneous blaming of a feeble, ineffective or oppressive state.
2. The transformation of India's Muslim minority from apparent susceptibility to Pakistan to citizens of the contemporary nation-state.
3. The construction of contemporary national identity through an 'independence' narrative that sidelines and ignores the Partition of 1947 as a keystone of the formation of national identity.

Drawing on films as different as *Border, The Legend of Bhagat Singh, Gadar, Phir bhi Dil hai Hindustani, Sarfarosh, Lakshya, Main Hoon Na, Rang de Basanti,* and *Fanaa,* among others, this essay explores the above mentioned issues through readings of the film-texts and how they mediate, legitimise or, indeed, subvert entrenched Pakistan-centric political discourse through the use of content, theme, star-power, or indeed *auteur*-intent. I also attempt to demonstrate the gradual but distinct move by Hindi cinema from a Pakistan-centric and Partition-related construct of the national self-image to an increasingly self-reflexive and self-reflective one. These films are not necessarily chosen for their alleged 'quality' or theme, but instead for their self-professed commercial intent.

## Flashback

Representations and constructions of the national identity, as well as representations of Pakistan in Hindi cinema have long been a subject of personal interest, perhaps because my own identity has long been linked to both of the above, and far too often Hindi cinema has been the only medium of constructing and articulating that identity.

The first time I realised I was Indian was in 1980. Before that year, being Indian meant very little more than march-past ceremonies in school on 15 August and 26 January.

In 1980, we moved to Islamabad, Pakistan; the move was linked to my father's job. The Indian government felt that its efforts to promote 'people-to-people' contacts were best served by educating the children of embassy personnel in local schools. That of course meant that we were bussed off to the Rawalpindi cantonment every morning, to attend 'pre-approved' schools. My first experience at the Rawalpindi school was of being abused and beaten up for precisely a part of my identity I had never considered before—my nationality. There was little recourse: the school authorities preferred to ignore what they classified as schoolyard spats and often teachers took a hand in penalising the handful of Indian students. The situation was complicated further with my clear realisation that complaining at home would have meant being sent back to live with relatives in India. The choice—rather heroically conceived with a healthy dose of Amitabh films—was between staying with parents and fighting alone in the schoolyard, or returning to India and losing parental presence.

Little wonder then that those years in Islamabad were marked by obsessively watching Amitabh Bachchan films, partly for moral support and partly to learn the actor's fighting techniques. On the daily drives to school, the popular song from *Lawaaris* (1981): *'Jiska koi nahin uska to khuda hai yaaro'* ('Those who have no-one have God') became an anthem, allowing an identification with the relevant film-text/star-text so painfully acute as to be self-definitive.

In the years following those spent in Islamabad, I have watched the Hindi cinema industry attempt to alternately profess peace that would 'unite' the two countries based on linguistic or ethnic similarities, or pin the blame for all national discontents on our troublesome neighbour. Perhaps the films have merely reflected the Indian polity's own obsession with Pakistan, as well as of the inability of the Cold War-era superpowers to de-hyphenate and de-couple their relationships with the two countries. Simultaneously, an overwhelming nostalgia by filmmakers who came to Mumbai after Partition and a generation of Independence-linked nationalists ensured this Pakistan-focused cinema remained in these two well-established grooves.

## Credits

However, the first clear inkling of change came with the release of *Maachis* (Matchstick) in 1996. Made by the renowned *auteur* Gulzar, the film unflinchingly takes up the issue of Punjab militancy in the 1980s. The film places the responsibility for the 'making of terrorists' squarely on an unjust, corrupt and oppressive state that scapegoats innocent civilians, who are then forced to take up weapons. At the same time, Gulzar also does not flinch from referring to Pakistan's role in supporting the militancy as well as arming the movement. In a telling scene, the militant commander Sanatan (Om Puri) explains that the group must wait for the rocket-shooter (Veeran, played by Tabu) to show up after receiving training across the border. With this throwaway dialogue, Gulzar acknowledges the role played by Pakistan in arming and training militants, without ever removing the focus from the narrative that asserts that internal conflicts are solely responsible for the violence. However, it is important to note that, here, all mention to Pakistan is covert, with Sanatan referring to the shooter as travelling from 'across the border'.

Like many other films that have preceded it, *Maachis* also chooses to leave the neighbouring country unnamed. However, with that film, Hindi cinema takes the first step into simultaneously identifying Pakistan as the source of the weaponisation of militants as well as holding the Indian state responsible for the citizens' discontent that forces them to take up arms. Other films that follow have taken one or both of these trends to their logical conclusion. Further elucidation of the themes outlined for this essay requires some initial discussion of the films that reflect the trends. As mentioned earlier, these films have not been selected for their quality, but for their commercial intent and relative success.

First, the increasing focus on Pakistan as a major of source of terrorism and internal unrest reaches its height in the years of electoral turbulence in India, especially between 1995 and 1999. Among the films discussed as part of an evolving continuum of the Pakistan-centric discourse are *Border* (1997), *Sarfarosh* (The Martyr, 1999), *16 December—All Forces Alert* (2002; henceforth *16 December*), *The Hero* (2003), *Main Hoon Na* (Don't Worry, I'm Here, 2004), and *Lakshya* (The Objective, 2004). They all identify Pakistan overtly as an enemy nation, although the last two begin to move beyond the combative debate to begin reflecting on the national self in relation to the enemy, rather than directing the national gaze solely outwards.[2]

At the same time, Hindi commercial cinema has not minimised the role of the Indian state, often depicted as corrupt and repressive. This facet is most clearly seen in representations of the Muslim minority in cinema. Along with *Sarfarosh*, films such as *Mission Kashmir* (2000), *Fiza* (2000), *Khakee* (Uniform, 2004), and *Fanaa* (Annihilation, 2006) take up the role played by the Indian state that exacerbates the marginalisation of Muslim citizens of the country as well as the violence experienced internally. As Hindi cinema moves away from a primarily Pakistan-centric threat to the national fabric, the films also show a dramatic change in the representation of the Muslim minority in the country.

From a marginalised, supporting role in *Sarfarosh* to the central space in *Fanaa*, the de-centering of Pakistan from the national psyche is accompanied by a transformation in the status of the Muslim characters. The films increasingly reduce their marginalisation and susceptibility to oppression by providing the Muslim characters with agency in the narrative. While a simplistic reading may lead one to assume that the agency can only be exercised for the preservation of the hegemonic state, the recent portrayals of Muslims in commercially successful films seems to signal a move away from the dichotomous Hindu/Muslim and Indo/Pakistan discourse that has plagued the region for the past century.

This marginalisation of Pakistan in the national discourse has also led to a (re)visioning of the independence struggle that allows a view of the colonial past and the freedom struggle that is not hampered by an automatic discussion of the Partition. Films such as *Lagaan* (The Tax, 2001), *The Legend of Bhagat Singh* (2002), *The Rising—Ballad of Mangal Pandey* (2005; henceforth *Mangal Pandey*), and *Rang de Basanti* (Colour Me Saffron, 2006) construct a pluralist, secular vision of colonisation and subsequent decolonisation that seems to signal a trend for future productions.

## Cut to the Present (1996–2006)

The early turbulent years between 1996 and 2006 also saw the first 'war' film hitting the Indian screens in decades, with *Border* raking in record collections in 1997. The film fictionalises the battle of Longewala during the 1971 Indo-Pakistan war along the western border. The historical situating of the film allows director J. P. Dutta to name the 'enemy' state within the film text. However, despite the martial narrative, the director cannot avoid an apologist note by including a final lament against war with the final credits rolling to the tune of the song: *'Mere dushman, mere bhai'* ('My enemy, my brother'). The final shot of the film is a rather artificially inserted image of the flags of India and Pakistan unfurling side-by-side. *Border* is perhaps the only war movie in the world to include the 'enemy' flag as its last visual sequence.

Curiously enough, the 2004 release, *Veer-Zaara*, also reverts to this historical past in order to stage a trans-border love story. The film's romantic narrative is nominally set in the past—ostensibly twenty years before the present—which allows the love to flourish between the Indian air force officer Veer (Shahrukh Khan) and the Pakistani politician's daughter Zaara (Preity Zinta). When the film jumps to the present, despite its ostensible message of 'peace' read out in the courtroom by an emotional Veer, it appears to suggest that cross-border distances are unbridgeable in the present, except by political and human rights-linked actions. There can be no *Veer-Zaara*-style love story for the present generation on the subcontinent, as represented by the young Pakistani lawyer, Saamiya (Rani Mukherjee), whose travels across the border to India have no ostensible impact on her.

If *Border* names Pakistan in the context of the 1971 war, India's unequivocally 'good' war in the national narrative, it requires a film linking the Mumbai underworld, drug and weapons trade, and home-grown militancy to identify Pakistan as a source of continued national instability. *Sarfarosh* is groundbreaking not only for its overt identification of Pakistan, both on maps used in the narrative and in dialogue, it also weaves into the narrative a number of real-life events, including the links between Mumbai underworld dons and Pakistan's ISI, weapons-smuggling and, finally, the complicity—willing or unwilling—of Pakistani artists. Drawing on a host of press, police and intelligence sources, director John Mathew Matthan constructs a complex tale where art, law-enforcement and international crime converge to build a fast-paced action film.

*Sarfarosh*, like many other films before and after, represents the Muslim minority in India through the marginalised figure of Inspector Salim (Mukesh Rishi). His personal isolation is acutely and poignantly highlighted. While the police establishment doubts his honesty in arresting Muslim criminals, the hardline elements within the Muslim community also mock his allegiance to Islam. Salim's character, however, is also representative of the economic underclass, denied access to the higher ranks of the police as represented by the Indian Police Service (IPS) officer, ACP Ajay Singh Rathod (Aamir Khan). At the same time, his class origins allow him access to the underbelly of Mumbai city in a way that his social and professional superiors do not have. Salim's isolation can be interpreted as the general condition of the Muslim minority in the country, which feels its loyalty questioned by the majority community on the one hand and its religious dedication doubted by hardline international and domestic Islamists on the other. At the same time, Salim's own agency in choosing his loyalties can be read symbolically as a choice available to the minority population, complete with the necessary consequences.

The film also tangentially includes a mirror-reflection from across the border, in identifying and discussing the conditions of the *mohajirs*, or those who migrated from India—primarily Uttar Pradesh and Bihar—to Pakistan during Partition. Initially, at least, there seems to be symmetry in Salim's anguish at the doubts regarding his national loyalties with the anger shown by Gulfam Hassan (Naseeruddin Shah), a famed Pakistani *ghazal* singer. The film, in extending the dominant nationalist discourse, shows that Hassan lacks the possibilities of acceptance open to Salim, despite sharing his religion with his compatriots. While Saleem is not only accepted and apologised to by Rathod (as the stand-in for the Indian state), Hassan, in turn, is betrayed and abandoned by the ISI officer. The implicit message, then, is that despite differences in religion, Salim—and therefore the Indian Muslim—has a greater role and choice in the national enterprise than ethnic-minority Muslims across the border.

National passions whipped up by the Kargil war in 1999 seemed to put a temporary freeze on the construction of Pakistan-based debate, as few films addressed the issue during that year. At the same time, the war in the mountains provided India with its first televised war, with the emotional reactions and outpourings giving proof to the power of the cinematic images. However, 2000 marked a clear shift in the Pakistan-centric rhetoric in commercial Hindi cinema, with the release of *Mission Kashmir* and *Fiza* within months of each other. Both films starred the light-eyed, 'foreign-looking' Hrithik Roshan, his exotic looks helping in the construction of the marginalised Muslim youth in both films.[3] While *Fiza* presents the Muslim marginalisation and militarisation within India as being a result of the rise of Hindu nationalism, in specific pinning the blame on the Mumbai riots of 1992–3, *Mission Kashmir* sets its tale in the more complex backdrop of Kashmir militancy in the 1990s, where state oppression—deliberate as well as unwitting—leads a young orphan to militancy.

*Fiza* ends on a tragic note—both narratively, with the protagonist's death, as well as thematically, with the overwhelming message seeming that there is no valuable or positive space for the Muslim minority in India. The film is a complex articulation of Indian-Muslim fears regarding its minority status, which lead Amaan (Hrithik Roshan) to take up arms to 'protect' his people, while his apparently moderate sister, the eponymous Fiza, rejects any possibility of joining the national (Hindu) mainstream by rejecting the marriage proposal from Anirudh (Bikram Saluja). Perhaps unwittingly, the director falls into a trap of his own making when Fiza is shown as incapable of separating the state—ostensibly defined in the film as Hindu and anti-Muslim—from the majority population. Angered by the injustice that she sees meted out to her brother, she rejects her suitor Anirudh, who has remained steadfast, loyal and supportive all along. Her apparently irrational decision, and the director's depiction of it, may also be interpreted as the minority community's capricious exploitation of the majority community's assistance and patience. For the director, the only choices available to India's Muslim minority seem to be death, with a detour through militancy, perpetual marginalisation or, even more frighteningly, absorption into the Hindu majority. Politically and thematically caught in a bind, the director has little recourse but to revert to a reactionary community identity that can only reject contemporary society.

In the same year (2000), *Mission Kashmir*, on the other hand, took up the issue of national identity through the prism of the unrest in Kashmir. Locating the conflict within the family, the film plays out the traditional Hindi cinema tropes of identifying the family as the nation (Gokulsingh and Dissanayake 1998; Virdi 2003, and others), and constructs the ideal Kashmiri (thereby Indian) family, formed by Neelima (Sonali Kulkarni), a Hindu woman married to Inayat Khan (Sanjay Dutt), and a Muslim police officer, whose son is an unwitting casualty of the rising Islamist tensions in the state. In their grief, the couple adopts an orphan, Altaaf (played as an adult by Hrithik Roshan), whose parents have been killed in a police raid led by Inayat Khan. On discovering Inayat's involvement in his family's death, the child runs away and grows up a militant. His attacks against the state pit Altaaf against Inayat, leading up to an action-packed finale, where the father-son pair must confront each other before uniting against the 'enemy'.

The entire family, and thereby the nation, is not only traumatised by nominally religious extremism but also caught in a cycle of reciprocatory violence throughout the film, a situation that must be resolved by uniting in the face of external threats. Not surprisingly, the film relies on the image of the Hindu mother as the symbol for the nation, a fact underlined by Neelima's declaration: 'No matter who fires the shot, the bullet shall only hit my breast.'

However, within the discursive evolution, the film also signals a subtle shift. In a series of references that appear prescient from our perspective today, *Mission Kashmir* includes the shadowy presence of a figure eerily reminiscent of Osama bin Laden. Within the narrative, this figure is the puppet-master, the overlord of the Pakistan's ISI as well as a non-state actor whose loyalties are with no particular nation-state, including the one that temporarily serves his/her interests. With this figure, *Mission Kashmir* heralds the gradual shifting of focus from a Pakistan-centric source of instability to globalised Islamist terrorism as a growing threat to the Indian nation-state, where the country's western neighbour is merely a pawn in the larger geo-strategic game. Moreover, a further shift in the politics of naming the enemy also specifically identifies Pakistan's shadowy ISI as an agent and player in this international federation of destabilising terrorist forces.

The theme of linking Afghanistan-based Islamist terror networks with connections to Pakistan's ISI is furthered with films such as *16 December* and *The Hero—Love Story of a Spy* (henceforth *The Hero*). The former also introduces a new plot element to commercial Hindi cinema—the threat of the use of a nuclear weapon by rogue non-state elements. Curiously enough, as a corollary to the globalisation processes, both films also included NRIs (non-resident Indians) in far corners of the globe as potential patriots whose intrinsic loyalty to the 'homeland' could be counted on for national enterprises. In Hindi cinema then, not only did the terrorist threat go global in the post-9/11 scenario, but so did the country's ability to mobilise its resources transnationally to act against that threat.

Returning however, to the filmic introspection of the nation-state, numerous recent films have dealt with contentious themes like the state's role in marginalising the minority community, and the doubts embedded in the majority community regarding Muslim loyalty to the nation-state. The most obvious amongst these are *Khakee* and *Dev* (2004), dealing with the issue of choices (or the lack thereof) available to the minority community. The issue of the state repressing the population and silencing dissent is reflected clearly in *Khakee*, where an alleged 'ISI-agent' Dr Iqbal Ansari (Atul Kulkarni) is found to be a loyal citizen framed by politicians for his refusal to assist corruption. *Dev*, in turn, explores the role of the state further, setting the narrative in the backdrop of communal riots and increasing intercommunal suspicions. The political establishment is shown to place its own interests above that of the nation, as well as to exploit communal rivalries and suspicions to its own advantage.

However, it is important to note that (re)presentations and (re)visions of the minority community are in flux and new possibilities have been presented by recent releases, most notably by *Fanaa* (2006).

The marginalisation of Pakistan in the discussion of Hindu-Muslim relations within the contemporary nation-state reached a new high with the release of *Fanaa* (2006). Once again set in Kashmir, this film returns to the issue of transnational nuclear terrorism, this time devoid of any real religious grounding and played out entirely by non-state actors with little or no community, religious or national ties. It also revisits the motif of family as nation, this time setting the narrative within an entirely Muslim social and familial context. Referring constantly, visually and thematically, to earlier nationalist cinematic texts such as *Mother India* (1957), the film places the Kashmiri Muslim woman, Zooni (Kajol), at the centre of the narrative. Physically blind from birth, her trip to Delhi brings her in contact with the tour guide/ terrorist Rehaan (Aamir Khan) and, quite literally, 'opens' her eyes. The shot of a terror attack by Rehaan on the President's residence is rapidly cut to a scene of Zooni in the hospital, regaining her eyesight after surgery.

The second half reveals Rehaan's identity as a terrorist on a mission to secure nuclear parts for an unidentified 'Kashmiri liberation' group. Like Radha in *Mother India,* Zooni is ultimately faced with the choice between her nation and her lover, constructed here as the choice between her son and her husband. The last scene also echoes *Mother India* Rehaan; runs with the electronic device he has stolen, reminding the viewer of Birju's riding away with Champa. To allow the men to escape with their 'stolen' prize would mean giving up on the village's honour (*Mother India*) or its safety (*Fanaa*). Like Radha, Zooni too calls out for Rehaan to stop. And like Radha in the earlier movie, Zooni must also shoot and kill Rehaan in order to secure the national narrative. Her physical stance, clutching the pistol in both hands, legs apart, also echoes Nargis's bounty-hunter posture from the earlier film (Chatterjee 2002).

Despite the similarities with the earlier film, *Fanaa* does not shirk from contemporary complexities, either of the nation-state or of the delicate balance needed to place the Kashmiri-Muslim mother at the centre of the national narrative. Immediately following Zooni's first shot, Rehaan turns to fire back, his physical reaction a result of instinct and training. Yet the camera remains on his face as his expression changes from rage to confusion and finally sad acceptance of inevitability. The director then pulls out for a long shot of the two lovers set against each other in a Mexican stand-off, their pistols pointed at each other. It is Zooni who finally pulls the trigger, making her act seem deliberate and considered than that of *Mother India's* Radha, who pulls the trigger in extreme rage. Zooni, after all, is no mother killing her son in an extreme rage. She is a single mother, who has broken earlier taboos to follow her own life, and her decision to kill Rehaan is no less considered or decisive.

Not surprisingly, the final sequence of *Fanaa* also refers to *Mother India*, as Zooni and her son lay flowers on two graves, one possibly of Zooni's father and the other of Rehaan. Yet, this is no enfeebled tragic mother inaugurating a dam that fills the fields with water tinged with metaphoric blood. Zooni's task isn't over as she prompts her young son to offer his respects and then gently guides him away from the graves. The final image is not one of the price of sacrifice but of the continued resilience that allows Zooni to claim her rightful place in the centre of the national narrative.

In stark contrast to *Fiza*, the final frame of *Fanaa* leaves open a multitude of possibilities for the Muslim minority's role in the nation-state, delinked from memories of Partition and of suspected ties to Pakistan. Not surprisingly then, religion has little space in the discourse of *Fanaa*, and Pakistan is merely another nation to be 'informed' of political and military developments. In the film, the Indian defence minister merely informs his Pakistani counterpart of the 'developments'. There is no recrimination, suspicion or even accusation in the discourse. As the Indian Muslim takes centre-stage in the narrative of national identity-building, Pakistan is finally marginalised, and eventually excised from the picture.

Before moving forward to discussions of recent (re)visionings of history and thus (re)definitions of the nation-state, two films deserve a mention in the evolving discourse on Hindi films' representations of national selfhood. *Lakshya* and *Main Hoon Na*, both released in 2004, were works of a new generation of directors. Farhan Akhtar and Farah Khan, their respective directors, represent the generation defined not by memories of colonialism or the Partition, but instead brought up in the 1970s. Not surprisingly, the definition of the nation-state for both these directors is quite startlingly different from that of the earlier generations.

*Lakshya*, ostensibly set in the backdrop of the Kargil war, explores the coming of age of a spoilt young man with no apparent ambition.

Despite the war rhetoric and the spectacularly shot action sequences, the film is relentlessly self-absorbed. The 'enemy' is merely a distant, nameless force whose only role is to function as the opposition against which the nation-state defines itself. The protagonist declares on first looking at the border guarded by Pakistan's outposts, 'For the first time I know what it means to be an Indian.' The borders thus become the defining space for identity, regardless of what lies beyond. Curiously enough, the statement also sets to rest residual nostalgia about re-unification (as was the case, for example, in the films of the 1960s and 1970s, which reached their pinnacle with *Amar Akbar Anthony* (1977). Not surprisingly, the *lakshya* (goal) that the young protagonist finds is achieving control of a ruthless mountain-top, similar to Tiger Hill. The narrative plays itself out by his effacing the 'enemy' and turning the war action into a *bildungsroman* for the protagonist.

The second film, *Main Hoon Na* by Farah Khan, reflects the sensibilities of a generation whose first memory of historical events is the Emergency. Inspired by the Nasir Hussain and Manmohan Desai brand of extravagant spectacle, the film recuperates the lost-and-found metaphor, although this time in order to resolve intranational differences, with the family once again serving as the metaphor for the nation. The brothers, born of different mothers and the same father, must resolve their disagreements overcome, past hurt and injury, in order to face the current destabilising threat. In this case, the threat is from an internal source, from a group of former army officers who can neither forgive past atrocities nor move forward, and therefore will hold the nation hostage to their radical agenda.

The film also marks the completion of the transformation of Shahrukh Khan's star persona, with meta-textual links to Rama, a process that follows the trajectory of the past decade (Singh 2005). If the turbulent 1970s had required a martial narrative of the embattled hero, personified by Amitabh Bachchan's Mahabharata-linked star persona, the post-liberalisation, globalised India identified more closely with the Ramayana narrative, where war must be waged as a necessity, and stability and prosperity are the primary goals. If the earlier generations required change to be brought about by constant strife and cataclysmic violence, the current generation places greater importance on responsible behaviour and change brought about gradually and, if possible, without violence. Not surprisingly, the imaginary Ramarajya, personified by Shahrukh's star persona of the good son (*Dilwale Dulhania Le Jayenge,* 1995 (The One with the Heart will Take the Bride), *Mohabbatein*, 2000 (Love)), the good friend (*Dil to Pagal Hai*, 1997 (The Heart is Crazy)), the good father (*Kuch Kuch Hota Hai*, 1998 (Something Happens)), and the just ruler (*Asoka*, 2001) find their apogee in *Main Hoon Na*. His character is named Ram, the righteous warrior who suffers familial exile, yet makes peace with his stepmother, winning his half-brother's loyalty, and finally rescuing his chosen mate—along with other hostages—from certain death.

Although *Main Hoon Na* contains ostensible references to peace talks with Pakistan, oppositions to the peace negotiations as well as the conflicting views regarding Pakistan are depicted as entirely internal to India. Pakistan's reactions, or indeed actions, are of secondary importance in achieving a national stance.

## Post-interval: (Re)visioning the Past

Perhaps there ought to be no surprise that the marginalisation of Pakistan in popular discourse and imagination has a corollary: a view of the history of decolonisation that takes no cognizance of the rancorous history of events leading upto Partition. In (re)constructing a history that can be entirely self-focussed and reflective, recent cinema has begun reverting to not only pre-Partition figures such as Subhash Chandra Bose, Mangal Pandey and Bhagat Singh, but has also begun imagining (and imaging) a mythical past free of the stain of Partition. In films ranging from *Shaheed Udham Singh* (2000) to *Rang de Basanti* (2006), there is an emerging trend of viewing history as de-coupled from Partition and Pakistan.

One aspect of this trend has focussed on (re)covering and (re)presenting leaders and activists of the independence movement through bio-pics such as *Shaheed Udham Singh*, *The Legend of Bhagat Singh* and *Bose—The Forgotten Hero* (2005) who are represented as more than simply members of the Indian National Congress, and are also removed from the events leading up to Partition in 1947. However, a more interesting trend has been of films depicting both colonial history and resistance through narratives that marginalise the Partition as an event while engaging directly, and without mediation, with the colonial experience. These films include *Lagaan*, *Mangal Pandey* and, far less successfully, *Kisna* (2005). While the trend is still at an early stage, these films have thrown up interesting postcolonial issues: the intersections of gender, race, desire, and power, which indicate a new willingness to engage with the colonial experience, revealing a growing sense of self that allows such a direct engagement with the former coloniser.

*Mangal Pandey* presents a complex vision of the colonial past. However, it also simplifies one aspect of that past: the dissensions and conflicts between Hindu and Muslim communities within the country and the ensuing competition for power. By setting its narrative in 1857, the film attempts to erase the taint of Partition and revert to a mythical past where Indians could join a national cause, regardless of their religious affiliations. This revisiting and revisioning of the colonial past is crucial to the growing national narrative that considers the 1947 borders as the defining boundaries of the modern Indian nation and chooses to ignore and erase narratives that challenge that view. This growing view is linked intimately with the demographic, political and economic changes of the past decade and can be see as a process of constructing a contemporary, self-reflective identity to account for the changes and experiences of the nation.

However, the exigencies of identity-creation mean that (re)visioning history cannot be limited to the distant past. Clear links must be forged to the presence and potential future of the nation. While *Mangal Pandey* and *Lagaan* portray the past in a heroic light, allowing it to function as contemporary national myth, other films have attempted to link the past to the present, articulating popular fears and discontents. Films such as *16 December* and *Tango Charlie* (2005) attempt to apply the post-Independence history of India to contemporary conflicts and thus to threats and challenges facing the nation. However, *Rang de Basanti*, the last film under discussion in this essay, meshes India's colonial memory with contemporary reality to construct a contemporary nationalist discourse. More importantly, perhaps, the film is the first attempt at moving beyond Fanonian ideals of postcolonial relationships to an uncharted space where the former colonised and colonisers may meet in equality, with mutual respect and in recognition of a shared past.

The film brings together Sue (Alice Patton), the granddaughter of a British colonial jailor, James McHeneley (Steven Mackintosh) to India with a group of young university students in Delhi. Sue, a filmmaker, is looking for the 'third kind of man', which her grandfather has described in his diary when referring to the *garam dal* (hot headed) revolutionaries of the Independence movement. She plans to film their story, although her own channel in the UK has cut the budget for such a film, suggesting that she focus instead on Gandhi because 'Gandhi sells'. In India, she begins filming on a shoestring budget and with a group of reluctant actors. Slowly, through shared experiences, the Indians, as represented by the group of students, and the British, as symbolised by Sue, also begin to communicate across the faultlines of history, sharing both guilt and pleasure, and a closely bound past.

More relevant to our discussion is the marginalisation and erasure of memories and discussions of the Partition from the narrative. Although the contentious position of the Muslim minority in India is indicated by the film, with Aslam's father demanding that he retain no contact with the majority population, and his brother hinting at an extremist hate-filled form of Islamism, Aslam's desire to fully participate in the nation is privileged as the dominant image. His talent as a poet and his 'secular' clothing of jeans and loose shirts are indicators of an 'educated' Muslim who can participate fully in the nation's destiny. The contrast is clearly established with his brother and father, who are depicted as 'old-fashioned' or uneducated and, in both cases, marginalised from the destiny of a post-liberalisation, globalised India. Of course, DJ's family is also similarly marginalised, while Ajay's is marked by the absence of a father ostensibly sacrificed at an earlier date for the benefit of the nation-state. This link is not incidental, as the film very clearly centralises and privileges the aspirations and challenges facing a nation where more than half the population is under twenty-five years of age.

However, the film also establishes the idea of national identity as a constantly renewing process rather than a fixed ideal, where all extremes are not only unacceptable but also detrimental to the integrity of the nation. Laxman Pandey (Atul Kulkarni) is initially shown as a passionate Hindu fundamentalist, active in politics and fighting against the apparent 'Western corruption' of Indian values. His devotion to the nation is never in doubt, although his definition of the nation in fanatically narrow terms is posited as dangerous and self-destructive. His increasing awareness of the complexities of politics and his eventual overcoming of hatred for Aslam as a Muslim are at the heart of the self-reflexive national identity offered by the film. Laxman begins by calling Aslam a 'Pakistani', an idea that is echoed by Bismil suggesting that Ashfaqullah would be safer in Afghanistan amongst his 'own people'. The journey of both Laxman and Bismil to finally recognising the Muslim minority— symbolised by Aslam—as an integral part of India's reality and future is foregrounded repeatedly.

The joint deaths of Ashfaq and Bismil by hanging, and of Laxman and Aslam, are crucial to this ideal of a national identity as a constant process requiring joint sacrifices from both majority and minority communities. The director chooses to focus on Laxman's and Aslam's joined hands in the moment of their deaths, reinforcing the sacrifices needed from both communities for the nation's changing needs.

*Rang de Basanti* makes a clear correction between the past and the future, where the two can never be entirely delinked. As DJ says, India's trouble is 'having one foot in the past and the other in the future'. However, (re)visioning and (re)presenting can allow for alternative views of history, and therefore alternative ideals for the future. The future, the film suggests, lies in picking up passions and ideals from the past while adapting them to new realities. The initial shot of Bhagat Singh reading Lenin is cleverly echoed by Karan's disdainful distribution of his father's wealth, just as Bismil's religious fervour is reflected in Laxman's early passionate activism for the Hindu fundamentalist cause. The past shall influence our present, the film asserts, but we can draw what we need from it to shape our own future.

## Closing Credits: Conclusion

Commercial Hindi cinema has long played the role of popular historian and narrator for the country, constructing images that affirm, challenge and subvert hegemonistic discourses offered by the state, the majority community and the socioeconomic-political elite. In negotiating this space, Hindi cinema has attempted to represent and decipher historical changes for the masses, as well as anticipate them. This role has required popular cinema to address issues of internal dissent as well as external threats, especially the historically traumatic and contentious relationship with Pakistan. Over the past sixty years, Hindi cinema has careened between extremes of xenophobic and aggressive nationalism, especially in times of war with that neighbour, and a paternalistic pacifism that appears to deny that neighbour state its validity as a separate nation. Popular Indian discourse on Pakistan has been perceived by that nation as an Indian refusal to accept its identity as a separate state. At the same time, attempts to maintain peace within the borders have meant that all discourse on Hindu-Muslim relations within India have been consistently tainted with memories of the Partition.

Recent cinema, however, reflects a dramatic shift in discourse, reaching instead to an earlier past as well as reflecting upon a post-Independence reality to construct a national identity that does not include references to Pakistan. Thus, Hindu-Muslim relations within the country can be framed in an internal context. The positive aspects of this development are easy to see. However, this trend in popular discourse-making does risk erasing a traumatic element of the country's history.

Yet, perhaps, it is time, sixty years after Partition, to move beyond its imprisoning discourse. With a growing population that has no direct memory of either colonialism or Partition, the needs for national histories and myths have also changed. For identities to be relevant, histories must be (re)covered, revised and (re)presented. At the same time, the process of a constantly self-renewing popular discourse on national identity(-ies) must be considered a maturing, a true coming-of-age for both the nation and popular Hindi cinema.

## Notes

1. Extrapolated from figures at www.cia.gov/publications/factbook/geos/in.html. Accessed 11 June 2006.
2. A corollary of the Pakistan-centric discourse in Hindi cinema has been the Partition-based films, of which *Gadar* (2001) was the most vocal representative. A full discussion of these films is beyond the scope of this essay. However, it must be noted that an ideological shift has also occurred in the (re)presentation and (re)vision of this event in Hindi commercial cinema.
3. Further discussion would be necessary regarding the differences in subjectivities reflected in films made by Muslim filmmakers like Khalid Mohammad (*Fiza*, 2000) and primarily Hindu ones like Vidhu Vinod Chopra (*Mission Kashmir*, 2000).

# 9

# 'Kaisi Sarhaden, Kaisi Majbooriyan':[1] Two Countries, Two Enemies, One Love Story

## Nirmal Kumar

Hindi films are all love stories, especially those made with the box office in mind, so much so that there is a joke going around that even if *Star Wars* or *ET* were to be made in India, they would have love stories along with song and dance injected into them. This idea is most inextricably associated with highly successful filmmakers like Raj Kapoor and Yash Chopra, both masters of their craft, both having defined filmmaking in India. So, when these two filmmakers came to make films on Pakistan, they had to be love stories.

Both filmmakers are Punjabis and had been affected by the partition of India in more than one way. For anyone connected with what is Pakistan today, making a film with Pakistan as the location of the story is not emotionally easy, nor is it easy to get acceptance from the audience. Yet both took calculated risks, both going a step ahead of other filmmakers in not allowing bad political relations between the two countries to affect either the narration or the characterisation. Considering the big names, these films create immense hype even while they are being made. So, while the fact that Raj Kapoor was planning to make a film on Pakistan made great news, his casting Pakistani actor Zeba Bakhtiyar made headlines and received huge media coverage, a successful publicity ploy to lure viewers to cinema halls.

Despite similarities—both films are made by Punjabis, on love stories between Indian and Pakistani protagonists—there are substantial differences in the cinematic handling of the tales, vastly dissimilar style and content. While Kapoor had a background in meaningful cinema, sometimes called parallel cinema, and had been associated with films like *Jaagte Raho* (Keep Awake, 1956), *Jis Des Mein Ganga Bahti Hai* (The Country where the Ganga Flows, 1960) and his most famous film, *Awara* (The Vagabond, 1951), Chopra is an out-and-out commercial filmmaker with a line-up of multi-starrers like *Waqt* (Time, 1965), *Deewar* (The Wall, 1975), *Kabhi Kabhie* (Sometimes, 1976), and *Dil to Pagal Hai* (The Heart is Crazy, 1997). Ultimately, for both Kapoor and Chopra, the prime concern was the commercial success of their films and for this the 'family' as audience had to be kept in mind.

With these credentials, it took great courage to attempt to make a film with Indian and Pakistani romantic protagonists when, after the 1971 war, the relationship between India and Pakistan had taken a turn for the worse. The war had widened the chasm between the two countries because the breaking away of Muslim East Pakistan from Pakistan had effectively negated the viability of the concept of new religious states (Zakaria 2003) and had created unprecedented anti-Pakistan sentiments in India. It was easy to bash Pakistan and meet with box office success. A Pakistan-positive film in India is a commercial risk. Pakistan generates passion, especially in North India where Partition has not been easily forgotten. Of course, love stories per se are market favourites and the surest way to make money. But with so much hatred between the two nations, rapprochement needed both time and great filmmaking. It took the great filmmaker Raj Kapoor to muster the courage, and to combine it with commercial vision and cinematic excellence; to think of a *Henna,* which was finally made by his son in 1991. This gambit was followed years later by Yash Chopra, who made *Veer-Zaara* (2004). Interestingly, the gamble paid off both times and set the cash registers ringing.[2]

Evidently, commercial success has to be seen in the context of social acceptability, the prevalent social values and the political climate. The market reinforces the political discourses but does not create them. They might just reflect the political reality. In a sense, the films in question are verifiable social documents, having passed the crucial test of popular taste and acceptance. In this sense, popular films are affirmations of our beliefs and demands, which then get mass approval. Parashar makes a telling comment on this count: 'On a common playground whose levelling function comes from the screen, the audience for popular Hindi films are carnival goers turned consumers. Here a unified national identity can apparently be represented through synchronization of image and narrative.... Indianness is a constant, is a construction, one of the many we juggle as we absorb our own images from the reflecting pool of popular culture (Parasher 2002: 15).

Moreover, a unique feature of Indian cinema is that the family as an audience has shaped commercial cinema, though, in the West, where the audience comprises individuals, cinema is not a family outing nor the only source of entertainment. In India, and much of South Asia, watching films is a family ritual. This weighs heavily on the minds of filmmakers, financiers and distributors. Post-2000, with the emergence of multiplex cinema, this may be changing, but earlier this was the touchstone of a film, making for commercial successes or failures. Even so, a film's acceptability to the family audience is still the prime market truth. Major filmmakers who have stuck to this formula have tasted unprecedented successes at box office. In this sense, such films become powerful social discourses. To qualify as family films, the films need to follow certain norms: no sex, limited violence, limited political statements, and lots of song and dance and family melodrama.[3] The films under scrutiny here, despite taking the bold step of showing normal human emotions across the line of control, strive to qualify as family films even as they present troubled love stories against the political saga of Partition. Also, both have very popular music to attract this segment of the audience.

In the Punjabi-dominated film industry, any subject with Pakistan as the theme becomes instantly popular. As already stated, making a film 'soft' on the enemy country Pakistan was a great risk in 1991 when relations between the countries were at their worst Somehow, Raj Kapoor knew that the time had come for a thaw (Khubchandani 2002), to talk of love and dialogue between the two countries. By conceptualising this film, he laid the ground rules for making a film with Pakistan as the subject, rules which have been generally followed till now.

This film is a story of an Indian Chander, played by Rishi Kapoor, who falls in love with a Pakistani woman Henna, played by a Pakistani actor Zeba Bakhtiyar. In *Henna* (as in *Veer-Zaara*) the male protagonist is a Hindu, a rich timber merchant of the Baramulla district in Indian Kashmir. He is engaged to a woman whom he loves very much. On his way to his ring ceremony, he has a car accident and is swept across the line of control to the Pakistan side of Kashmir. He loses his memory and the film reinvents him as Chand. In this reinvention is implied a transformation from Hindu to Muslim, from Indian to Pakistani, a possible enemy to a stranger who has lost his memory and needs rest and medical attention.[4] The delicateness of the situation is not lost on the audience. The message is loud and clear: that India occupies the chauvinistic position, while the 'other' nation is the 'junior' and the relationship needs the serious and 'loving' attention of political doctors. The feminine Pakistani hand that cures Chand is the behaviour that dominant India expects from the smaller polity of Pakistan, behaviour of service and servility. This traditional fraternal relationship typical in the South Asian situation is a reminder of the mythical sacrifices of the younger brother Lakshman in the service of his elder brother and lord, Ram. These ideals of brotherhood have inspired many narratives and have influenced the discourse of social and even the political relationship.

It is to be noted that in both films and also others with Pakistan as the theme, the man is always from India and the woman from Pakistan. The underlying discourse is that the Indian-Hindu-male sexuality must appropriate the Pakistani-Muslim-female sexuality. This narrative attempts to echo the military conquest of Pakistan where India came out victorious every time, and such stories thus became an extension of the military engagements between the two countries. Anil Sharma's *Gadar* ('Revolution', 2001) was the crudest and most emphatic assertion of this military-culture continuum. Here, the male Indian protagonist plays the 'macho' lover-rescuer to the beleaguered Pakistani female protagonist.[5] The working assumption is that the predominantly Indian-Hindu audience in India would not be able to accept a story where the Pakistani-Muslim man sexually annexes an Indian woman. Since Hindi films are made primarily for an Indian audience, they can ill afford to reverse this chauvinistic storyline and male-female equation. However, in other significant ways, the two films under review here have refreshingly not taken recourse to prevalent populism. Kapoor and Chopra went ahead of their times when they made these films, foreseeing love and not war between the two nations. When no one could even remotely predict a thaw in India–Pakistan relations, these films predicted just that—one started the trend, the other completed it.

The thirteen-year gap between the two films is also of some interest to both the student of history, and of political science and international studies. The relationship between the two nations underwent tremendous changes in the intervening years. From outright identification as the enemy country in *Henna* in 1991, Pakistan has moved to being seen in a more congenial light. In 2004, both countries were trying to shed the baggage of Partition and the bitter memories of the wars fought, Kargil notwithstanding. This is reflected in *Veer-Zaara*. The film is candid about the antagonistic political reality of the two nations. Yet, through all the formalities of law courts and advocates, the film talks of rapprochements and the need to build bridges, with the younger generation taking charge, represented by the young woman lawyer Saamiya (played by Rani Mukherjee). The onus of bringing change is on the post-Partition generation who is ready to forgive and forget, for whom the Partition is a historical fact and nothing more. Moreover, despite being an Indian Air Force officer, Veer Pratap Singh (Shahrukh Khan) does not talk of war, does not carry weapons, and mouths none of the usual anti-Pakistan slogans. Two recent reinforcements of this argument have come from widely reported media reports: one, from Akshay Kumar, a major Indian male star (also a Punjabi) refusing to mouth anti-Pakistan dialogues in his films, on the grounds that he has fans across the border too; and two, from the portrayal of the two countries in *Main Hoon Na* (I am There for You, 2005), a major box-office success directed by a Muslim. The latter breaks the stereotype of the 'Muslim-terrorist-Pakistani' of Hindi films. Here the terrorist is a Hindu and Pakistan is shown to be keen to take some positive steps towards improving the India-Pakistan relationship. Let us also not lose sight of the fact that the director of the film is a modern, young Muslim woman. Such a development would not have been possible but for the bold step taken by Raj Kapoor in *Henna* in 1991.

## A Pakistan without Terrorism

*Henna* is remarkable on many other counts. Despite having Kashmir as the stage for the story and almost the entire film being based in Pakistan, it has no terrorism in it. Although there is hatred and mistrust between the two nations, they are not engaged in armed hostility. The villain or the bad man is the evil policeman, who could as well be an Indian or a Pakistani, although, in this case, he is Pakistani. There is no AK-47-wielding terrorist waging a war in the name of Islam. *Henna* is a story of simple people divided by Partition. Fate brings the two protagonists together in love, forcing them to confront the fact of politically divided but culturally similar countries. The *jihad* for Kashmir is yet to start, though Henna's brother does use the 'Indian spy' expression for Chand (or Chander); the phrase refers to those Indians who cross the border in a suspicious manner and then feign amnesia to disguise themselves. But there are no cries for *azadi* (freedom). Pakistan Occupied Kashmir (POK) is shown as living a normal peaceful existence. Chander (Rishi Kapoor) is a successful Hindu businessman from Baramulla, living in a palatial house, driving without fear, and openly meeting his beloved in a park. There are no gunshots in the background. Recent films like *Fanaa* (Destruction, 2006) and *Sheen* (2004) show such situations, with Kashmiris having picked up guns and shouting azadi, and Kashmiri Pundits (Hindus) being displaced and brutalised. Gunshots are as much a part of the backdrop as the songs. The Kashmir of *Henna* is nestled in snow, where love songs are not drowned in gunshots and where the simple life of the poor but loving Kashmiris has not been politically loaded with the jihad war cry of the fanatics.

In *Veer-Zaara*, too, Chopra has steered clear of any hate-filled situations; Pakistan is accepted as a legal entity. The male protagonist is a Hindu air force officer from Punjab. Significantly, Chopra relegates the Partition and attendant bitterness to the sideline. He ignores the two decades of violence in Kashmir. When Zaara, a Pakistani Muslim, meets Amitabh Bachchan, a rustic Punjabi farmer, he betrays no bitterness or hatred for the country of her origin and welcomes her warmly. Her Pakistani origin is just a footnote, mentioned but neither despised nor questioned. This acceptance of Pakistan as just another country shows maturity on the part of the Indian filmmaker, who has been able to overcome the phobia of Pakistan. Along with *Main Hoon Na*, which is one of the most positive film on issues related to Pakistan, *Veer-Zaara*, too, shows ungrudging acceptance of Pakistan as a separate entity.

A significant part of *Veer-Zaara* has been shot in a Pakistani jail and law court, both spaces arms of the Pakistani state. While *Henna* is primarily filmed in open landscape *Veer-Zaara* is shot mostly in closed spaces, perhaps emphasising that it is people who make and mark differences. The setting, in *Henna*, of the open fields of POK, with village people referring to religion straight from heart and responding to the state in an unencumbered manner is replaced by the official, urbane, educated, professional characters of *Veer-Zaara*. So, while Khan Baba speaks of Chander's release into India without giving thought to the legality or illegality of such action, Saamiya speaks of freedom for Veer Pratap Singh in terms of rules, constitutional and human rights, and the complex relations between the two states. While, in *Henna*, Henna's brother dies in the process of helping Chander cross the border, in *Veer-Zaara* Saamiya tries the same but through the due process of law.

By 2004, both India and Pakistan are nuclear powers, and have fought three full-scale wars and one minor one in the Kargil sector.

The urban classes of both India and Pakistan have accepted the political reality of two independent nations, as have, in *Veer-Zaara*, the Indian Air Force officer and the rich and powerful Pakistani family of Jahangir Hayaat Khan. Obtaining visas and visiting the other country is no problem. The film highlights the middle-class urban values of state, the political power play and the legal manipulation. State intervention is most visible in *Veer-Zaara* in the shape of police officers who arrest Veer Pratap Singh, the Pakistani jail, the lawyers, and the courts. It is to be noted that the senior advocate Zakir (played by Anupam Kher) defends the constitution and rights of the Pakistani state. The now soft, now hard jail officer is forced to assert and agree with Zakir's contention that the interests of Pakistan are supreme, though the same officer had earlier testified in the case of Veer Pratap and pleaded that he be freed on humanitarian grounds. Interestingly, at the end of the courtroom drama, the Pakistani advocate Zakir admits defeat. He says, 'But now I understand that the future of these countries is in the hands of youngsters like you, who do not measure humans as big and small, man or woman, Hindu or Muslim, who do not rake up bitter memories of the wars of 1947, 1965 and 1999 at every pretext, who wish to address the future with the truth and only the truth. And there is no stopping a country where truth prevails.'

These words are a direct condemnation of the political processes on both sides. The states have failed to measure up to the expectations of the people by forcing Veer Pratap Singh to fight for his identity (Saamiya declares that her legal battle is not to prove or disprove whether Veer Pratap Singh is a spy, but to restore his real identity). Therein, lies the crunch: the political states of the two sides have failed to deliver. The people, who are culturally one, feel cheated by their states. The feeling is echoed in no uncertain terms by Veer Pratap, when asked by Zaara's mother if all sons in Hindustan are like him. Veer replies, 'I don't know, but all mothers are like you', affirming the oneness of the cultural associations with motherhood across the border.

## A Gendered Discourse

Both films have shown women as a strong sex. No doubt the two directors are known to have packaged their women dramatically and sensuously (Dwyer 2000: 143–59). But, at the same time, their women are portrayed as having strong internal convictions. Varsha Joshi has shown that domestic women in royal Rajput houses, though unseen in public, could play very important roles in the public realm (Joshi 1995); the apparently domesticated woman can actually play a very prominent role. Henna decides to tend to an unknown male, even expressing her love for him. Later, when it is discovered that her man is a Hindu and an Indian, she takes the bold step of getting him across the line of control. In 1991 the film was not ready to let her cross the line of control; she dies in the crossfire between Indian and Pakistani armed forces. But, by 2004, much water has flown down the Sutlej and Beas rivers and Chopra is able to make his heroine fairly easily cross the line of control a couple of times. Zaara is made to appear a typical woman from any patriarchal South Asian family, where her destiny is determined by her family. She agrees to all till she discovers herself and her love; then she becomes assertive. Zaara, the caring submissive daughter, effortlessly crosses over to the Indian side to fulfill the wishes of her Sikh nanny and, later, crosses over again to help with the school set up by Veer's uncle in the Indian Punjab village. Her last act of submission to the memory of her love (she does not know that he is alive in a Pakistan jail) is the most courageous assertion of her choice.

This highlights the fact that the major similarity between the two films is the presence of strong women characters who know their minds and who can take decisions despite their oppressive patriarchal families. They dare to think independently, almost rebelliously, such as the characters of Bibi Gul and Henna in *Henna,* and of Zaara, Shabbo and Zaara's mother in *Veer-Zaara.* Exemplary courage and human qualities are shown by some of the lesser characters whom no one expects to stand up for any cause and who are fully domesticated. Bibi Gul (Farida Jalal) makes pots to earn a living and lives all alone, doubling as the village doctor and standing up against all the villagers when the matter of Chander being Indian and Hindu comes to light. Similarly, the remarkable characters of Shabbo and Zaara's mother stand out; Shabbo helps Zaara with money for her to travel to India, then she keeps Veer Pratap in her house in spite of the risks in doing so. Zaara's mother, though fully domesticated, shows her strong will and her streak of independence when she visits Veer Pratap at the bus station on his way back to India, to say that she wishes that Zaara be his in every life, giving him an amulet for protection. For an elite Pakistani woman, whose daughter is engaged and is to marry soon, to support her daughter's relationship with another man, and that too an Indian and a Hindu, is an affirmative action. Her signalled dissent against the will of her patriarchal family is no less than rebellion for her.

Above all, both Henna and Zaara are strong female protagonists. They may not wield guns or utter patriotic dialogues, but they show strength. Women of typical Hindi films are often spoilt rich brats, and are supposed to do nothing more than sing and dance and get married in the end. Here, the two women are strongly domesticated to start with. Henna is illiterate and lives in a family dominated by strong men. Her sole act of independence is when she takes the cattle for grazing and sings in the beautiful POK valley. She wears the *hijab* but no *purdah*. But when she finds Chand (Chander) downstream, she brings him home and nurses him to health. She, her family and her village consider her interaction with a stranger normal.

Zaara too is quite independent, even though she is fully aware of the fact that as a woman she has only one fate: 'To get married and bear children.' Yet, she can take a decision to travel to India, without the permission of her parents, to immerse the ashes of her Bebe. Her behaviour and body language, especially with Veer Pratap, do not betray any subordination. She knows her mind, does not mind the company of a man, has very definite views on women's education, which she articulates to Veer's uncle, ideas that she later makes genuine efforts to realise by running the school in Veer's Indian village for twenty-odd years, leaving behind her family, country and an arranged marriage. Zaara, by the end of the film, appears to be a completely liberated woman, even her love for Veer acquiring a constructive edge.

The fact that Zaara chooses to leave her family and engagement in Pakistan to come to India to run the school for girls set up by Veer's uncle is the filmmaker's attempt to forge an accepted independent sexuality which is yet domesticated and close to the ideal of Indian womanhood—the *adarsh bhartiya naari*—reinforced time and again throughout the film. She allows herself to be dressed for participation in the *Lohri* festival of the village, thus enabling Veer's uncle to conjure an image of her as the (Indian) daughter-in-law, her Pakistani identity notwithstanding. Towards the end, when she finally comes back to India with Veer, Saamiya offers Veer a box of *sindoor* (vermilion powder, applied in the hair parting by Hindu women as a mark of marriage). With that her Hinduisation or appropriation by the subsuming Indian religion is complete. The conquest of a Pakistani sexuality had been accomplished by her Lohri participation and reinforced by her acceptance of sindoor in her hair. If in *Henna* the Muslim-Pakistani female protagonist dies in no-man's land, then the inference is that there was no final conquest of Henna's sexuality, but to do this, death seems to be the only way out. In *Veer-Zaara,* in Zaara's coming to India and her eventual marriage with Veer, the sexual overtones of a political conquest are unmistakable. Like Zaara, Pakistan had to be assimilated and conquered. This may well be one of the reasons that the film was so well accepted in North India.

The subplot in both films is regional nationalism—one about Kashmir and another about Punjab, about Kashmiriyat and Punjabiyat, a regional-cultural discourse about uniqueness, which comprises language-religion-literature-food and a shared historical-cultural complex. Such cultural concepts often help transcend political borders and blur bitter historical memories. They help in creating a wider community with trans-political loyalties and help evolve cultural linearity. The artificial line of control that divided India and Pakistan at the national level, and the irrational partition of Kashmir and Punjab, are transcended by a regrouping of people as one community across two political formations. *Henna* is about the love between two Kashmiris and *Veer-Zaara* between two Punjabis. This makes the Line Of Control (LOC) enigmatic and romantic at the same time. This can be seen in the cultural behaviour of the diaspora trying to connect to their own subnational-regional moorings. The cultural complex, real or imagined, helps foster a sense of community, the shared suffering itself becoming the grounds for a feeling of oneness, enabling divided people to come out of serious social crises. Seen in this light, these films would seem to be creating a borderless community of suffering, longing, love, and shared historicity.

While Chander has no difficulty in understanding the culture, language and songs of Henna's village, Zaara too has no problem participating in Lohri festivities and the culture of *sarhad paar* (across the border), and in later running the girls' school at Veer's village. The underlying strong currents of subnationalism are in the two films help cut across religions and through the fragile political situation. Normally, subnationalism is often to hype negative attributes and is pitted against the idea of nation, but in these films the theme has been used to reinforce nationalism. Kashmiriyat and Punjabiyat are highlighted, without being named as such. The opening songs and scenes extol the beauty of Kashmir and Punjab; this utopian reference helps forge easy bonds among the characters.

Both films have the male Indian Hindu leading men caught in Pakistan and dubbed as 'Indian spies', reflective of the deep mistrust and enmity that had crept into the minds of the people across the border. In *Veer-Zaara*, the court scenes allow the lawyers to foreground serious debates about the discourses of nationalism, patriotism, and so on. Again, though made by Indians, the films, interestingly, reveal good faith in the political and judicial setup of Pakistan. In *Henna,* it is the intervention of a Pakistani senior police officer and the foreign department that helps prove that Chand/er is not a spy but actually an accident victim from India. Likewise, in *Veer-Zaara,* it is the Pakistani court which dispenses justice to the victim, Veer, actually apologising to Veer on the behalf of the Pakistani state.

The filmmakers' faith in the legal and administrative setup is easily explained. First, blaming the lower officials and exonerating the higher ones ensured that the films would not be banned in Pakistan. Also, cinematically, with the creation of a co-operative top bureaucratic and political echelon, there is a reassurance that someday things will be fine again, that order will be restored.

## Conclusion

Thus, the two films, though mainly intended to be love stories, go far beyond the limitation of the rubric. Made by successful filmmakers of Hindi cinema, they are studies in contrast with reference to the trajectory of the India-Pakistan relationship. In this context, the love stories become merely the backdrop. But to my mind, the makers want to make a political statement. In *Henna,* the aim is to highlight the Kashmir before terrorism and to bring people's attention to the region. The second film tries to revisit the partition of Punjab at various levels— of India-Pakistan, of the two Punjabs, of Hindu-Muslim, and of man-woman. The aim is to uncover the underlying Kashmiriyat and Punjabiyat which ties the peoples of the two countries. These two films are potent celebrations of the independent political existences of the two countries, underlining the 'love approach' in smoothing ruffled feathers, even if the cause of bitterness cannot be removed. In this sense, the two films call for a third track of India-Pakistan diplomacy—love between Indian and Pakistani youth, holding out an olive branch, a hope. *Henna* and *Veer-Zaara,* moving away from Pakistan-bashing, can be said to have started a wave of Pakistan-positive films, backed by love and political amnesia. Avoiding divisive memories of Partition, terrorism and the many wars between the two separated and bitter nations, they sugarcoat issues to make films that mend wounds. Sometimes, by ignoring we heal.

## Notes

1. 'Alas, these borders, this helplessness'; phrase from a song in *Veer-Zaara*.
2. These films were not made for the film festivals or the arty circuit. These two films are out-and-out commercial films, both in treatment and in success, made by two commercial directors with the primary aim of raking in money. Naturally, this implies that the themes, the treatment and conclusion were popular in their appeal. While *Henna* made Rs 3,25,00,000, and was declared a hit, *Veer-Zaara* grossed over Rs. 41,00,00,000! Source:Box OfficeIndia. com.
3. Karan Johar used this tag line for his film *Kabhi Khushi Kabhi Gham* (2001).
4. Indian films, and now TV serials, are known to create situations where characters have lapses of memory (*'yaddasht kho gayi hai'*); this is used to make dramatic, even melodramatic twists in the story which otherwise would have been difficult.
5. To quote the maker of Sheen, 'All these...movies are primarily love stories with India-Pakistan thing only as their background. In no way did the movies propagate brotherhood between both the countries. It just so happens that the male and female protagonist happen to be from the two countries. Further, he states, 'In Bollywood, ninety-nine per cent of the movies have a terrorist as the hero and his acts are glorified. In *Sheen* the main protagonist was the victim'. Still, the Pandit does not believe in Pakistan-bashing. My aim was not Pakistan-bashing. *Sheen* highlighted sponsored terrorism and its after-effects on the Kashmiri Pandit. It was not a figment of my imagination.'

# 10

# *My Brother, My Enemy*: Crossing the Line of Control through the Documentary

## Aparna Sharma

### Introduction

The view has considerable currency that at a people-to-people level, the Indo-Pak hostilities fizzle out. On both sides of the India-Pakistan border, people have the urge to reach out and share in the cultures of the two nations. Cinema has been one agency through which this urge has crystallised to an extent and some simmering emotions have acquired utterance. While the determined attempts of mainstream industrial cinemas on either side of the border have been worthy—though often melodramatic and sentimental—they have reduced the complexity embedded in people's experiences and world views. In such representations, the forces and pathways of historical circumstance remain distanced, if not fully abstracted, from the fabric of everyday life. History textbooks are now written and strategic analyses formulated into concrete policy—yet memories, anger, affections, indeed the very materials of the experience of Partition are seldom heard.

The generation that migrated across the newly drawn borders is steadily declining. Three wars and a consistent, cold stand-off, complicated by the distinct approaches to nation-building on both sides, tend to eclipse emerging possibilities with antagonisms and idle jingoism that have proven to be more burdensome than useful during the six decades after Partition. Mainstream cinemas and media generally have often fashioned patriotism by reducing the 'other' across the border to the 'enemy', the object of hostility and hate. Against the backdrop of such highly charged antagonisms, it is hard to revisit history and confront it in all its complexities. *My Brother, My Enemy* (2005) is a rare film by two young filmmakers from the subcontinent, a film that critically revisits pervasive world views, uninterrogated bitterness and resentment, by tracing some uncharted histories.

In this essay, I will closely analyse the ways in which this ethnographic documentary complicates and problematises neat categorisations through engagement with some personal narratives as sites where competing impulses and emotions intersect.

In the subcontinent the term 'documentary' often conjures up an image of the 'real', that which is distinct and opposed to the fantasy play of fictive cinema. Deploying the methods of ethnographic cinema, *My Brother, My Enemy* formulates a more sophisticated conception of the documentary that clearly bears subjective experiences, distinct from any aspirations for objectivity, thereby presenting a sophisticated take on the question of the 'real' as something whose complexity evades rationalisations of any kind.

*My Brother, My Enemy* is a 'border film', in that its 'plot involves significant journeying and border crossing [,] and [the] use of border settings'.[1] The film enables us to confront the borders on humane terms, where the memories, angers and losses of the past co-mingle with the inquisitiveness, biases and a frail, rather vulnerable sense of cohesion performed in the present. In order to exposit this, I will commence by unpacking the film's narrative and settings, through which the film manifests sociocultural intricacies embedded in its encounters that are not structured under the formal aegis of a cultural or peace initiative.

The essay will then engage specifically with the camerawork of this film. The camera's choreography, including its framing of subjects in conversations, expositions of locations, and reliance on the telephoto lens,[2] all contribute in making the film a cinematic intervention whose form actualises its discourse. The visual construction of the film pursues exposition while privileging a deterritorialised haptic and textural experience. A very fluid and fragmentary camera vocabulary features in the film. This fluidity, I posit, becomes a mechanism to counter the identity categorisations and positions in relation to nation and religion that the film is interrogating. So while this film, the testimonial of two youngsters for whom the anxieties of the past are not a first-hand encounter, does not posit any clear reconciliations, what it achieves is a laying bare of existing mindsets that on occasions get reaffirmed and on others, collapse through the encounters that the film sets up.

## Interrogating Borders

*My Brother, My Enemy,* is set against the backdrop of the Samsung India-Pakistan Cricket series of 2004. The film arose from British

Pakistani[3] Masood Khan's instant friendship with Delhi-based cinematographer, Kamaljeet Negi, when the two met while attending film school in London three years ago. In his voiceover, Kamal acknowledges: 'We met at film school in London. We could not have met otherwise....' This serves as a framing device for the film; it is clear that the collaboration of the two filmmakers cannot be separated from the landscape in which they met. In a multi-ethnic and advanced capitalist location outside the subcontinent, more urgent disparities of, say nationality, (here Indian and Pakistani), or religion (here Hindu and Muslim) promptly recede and possibilities of transgressing socially normative behaviour and nationally determined thought materialise.[4] One immediately questions whether and how such a collaboration would have materialised if both filmmakers were still situated in their respective 'nations'. Once Masood and Kamal met, they were keen to extend their friendship into their creative occupations. The cricket series became an occasion and a dramatic background to make a film.

The project marked by uncertainties from the start; Masood and Kamal had no script for this piece, only a general idea of possible scenes. But they knew, no matter what they filmed, it would be historically significant. Masood and Kamal are themselves the characters who the film follows. Their experiences, anxieties, hopes, and expectations are the ingredients for the film's narrative. The decision to locate the filmmakers as the key characters of the film is bold, difficult and, as the film testifies, lends to the piece complex relations and meanings.

Both Masood and Kamal travel to each other's country, interact with each other's families and, under the pretence of the cricket series, conduct spontaneous conversations with common persons such as cricket fans, vendors, shop owners, and rickshaw pullers on the streets of the cities they visit. Most of the film is steered through these conversations and interviews; however, a voiceover narration has been included to more fully exposit the emotions that surface through the various encounters of the film. This voiceover is not used in the conventional documentary modality of the 'voice of God', but is instead personal and conversational.

The film commences with Masood's first trip to India where Kamal's family welcomes him. There are some sensitive and conversations here. A pregnant quietude pervades Masood's first few moments at Kamal's home. The very first meal Masood has at Kamal's, touches upon a tough cultural distinction. Kamal asks his mother if the meat that is being served is '*halaal* or *jhatka*' (different methods, Muslim and Hindu, of killing the animal). Kamal's mother is instantly evasive, though Kamal's incessant probing finally rests the tensions. A few minutes into the film, we are confronted with an issue that evokes a history going back to the mutiny of 1857, when Hindus and Muslims were pitched against each other by the British colonisers, who misinformed both communities that the hand grenades they were going to use in revolt had been conspiratorially lined with the fat of pigs and cows, animals considered sacred by both—Muslims are forbidden to eat pork and Hindus to consume the meat of cows. This moment sets up and indexes the deep-seated and intertwined cultural and historical disparities that are likely to surface during Masood and Kamal's journeys.

The remainder of Masood's interactions with Kamal's family are lighthearted, peppered with humour and familial hospitality. In their conversations, Masood and Kamal's family share their reactions when their teams win and lose; they talk about their homes and how they have been conditioned to perceive the 'enemy'; and they share cultural niceties such as the exchange of sweets and *shagun* (offerings) when they meet and part. This prompts Masood to reflect upon the perceived hostilities he has been warned against by family and friends from Pakistan. This reflection is furthered in a finely designed sequence comprising some evocative locations, when Masood travels through the lanes of the religiously and politically sensitive old Delhi near Jama Masjid. Here, Kamal and Masood find themselves in a neighbourhood where Hindus and Muslims live and exist in close proximity. As they see them 'getting on with their daily lives', both start to transmigrate each other's identities, suggesting that the political borders that supposedly divide them are perhaps not so total.

Masood walks into a horse-shed where he gets into conversation with some 'idle' youth. The ensuing dialogue is rigorous. Though some of the characters here are clearly speaking under a narcotic spell, they are certain that the Indo-Pak issue is the making of politicians seeking an electoral base by deflecting attention away from more urgent issues in their respective countries. The sequence has political implications—these are views from the city streets, of masses who constitute the citizenry, not the analysis of the socially and economically mobile elite, or the English-speaking intelligentsia, including strategic, political and defence analysts. On the whole, the sequence at Jama Masjid bears a sense of movement that arises from the intercutting of hand-held mobile images and static close-ups using the telephoto lens. This sense of movement complements the characters' experience of liminality and crossing between positionalities; it is a formal strategy through which the film starts to indicate its discursive stance that is clearly interrogative of the determinations underpinning 'national' identity as defined in relation to the other, the 'enemy'. Repeatedly, Masood comments in his voiceover, 'There is hardly any difference between here and there.' He is puzzled when he sees a Pakistani national flag atop a residential quarter in the area; and when a rickshaw puller warmly engages with Masood and expresses that his poverty far exceeds his understanding of the hostilities between India and Pakistan, the film starts to inject complexity into the subject of national hostility. The conversations in this entire sequence make for a political intervention as the debate on the Indo-Pak conflict gets democratised, resuscitated from the experts and news media and situated in the ordinary spaces, routines and textures of daily life.

## Reflecting the Self

In cinema historically, self-reflexivity[5] has been a valued mechanism to instil awareness that the film text is constructed through the intricate processes of cinematography, editing and projection, thus countering the effacement of the filmmaker/apparatus and the disavowal of the complex filmmaking processes—an attitude that pervades mainstream cinema. In recent years, there has been dissatisfaction with the physical presence of the filmmaker on the screen as limiting, foreclosing his/her positionality. Unpacking the filmmaker as a subject constructed socio-historically and culturally and linking that definition pertaining to the filmmaker's subjective stance to his/her aesthetic strategies contributes to better identifying and appreciating the ideological positionalities underpinning the work.

This imperative has been particularly pursued and argued within anthropological and ethnographic filmmaking. In these practices, the subjective stance of the filmmaker and his/her relationship with the subjects within the film are deliberated more consciously than in other forms of documentary filmmaking, which, in claiming objectivity, are oblivious to the inescapable implication of the filmmaker within the film. Ethnography, most pronouncedly, problematises the position of the filmmaker, drawing attention to the power equations and transactions between subjects, and between filmmakers and subjects in the process of filmmaking. More recently, as the claims for subjectivity have gained credence within the social sciences, ethnographic and anthropological films have been increasingly drawn towards confronting and confusing the conventional disparity between object/observed and subject/observer, without necessary resolution, and the emphasis has started to shift from films that describe, towards those that make central the very eliciting discourse and exchanges between filmmaker and the film's subjects.

*My Brother, My Enemy* is rich in its attempts to indicate the filmmakers' subjectivities and the relationships they forge through the film. The economic background of the two subjects is apparent—they both belong to urban and educated middle class[6] families with aspirations towards being upwardly mobile. Despite initial hesitation in confronting their families with the camera, hinted at in both filmmakers' conversations with family members, the location and decor of their homes in India and Pakistan, their neighbourhoods, the languages and accents of family members' speech and their codes of dress, become indices through which we are able to position the filmmakers in relation to class and socio-cultural dynamics.

More importantly, history is a key thematic as the film consistently raises the subject of Partition. By doing this, it reveals that the characters we are interacting with in the film do not exist in an ahistoric vacuum, untouched or unmarred by the forces of historical circumstance. History is confronted frontally in the narrative pertaining to Masood. The first reference is made when, from Delhi, Masood travels to Punjab, to the village from where his grandparents hailed prior to Partition. He meets his family's old acquaintances. In this sequence we are witness to a verification process—the persons Masood meets recollect and determine whom, among their peers from a lost era, Masood is related to. Memory and emotion are the principle agents in this scene, the spontaneity and edginess of which could perhaps never be encapsulated in a fictive script. Masood is welcomed, and his grandparents' old acquaintances describe how agonising it was to, first, lose childhood friends and then wait in the hope that they would return some day. Masood even goes to the house where his family had once lived. It is occupied by a Hindu family, one that was ousted from Pakistan during Partition. Masood reflects that theirs is the 'same story' as his family's, 'mirrored', 'reversed'.

All throughout his stay in India, Masood is filmed by Kamal. From Punjab Kamal and Masood travel to Pakistan. The positions of the characters in relation to the camera now switch. Kamal is the subject of the lens, while Masood its operator. There is a visible distinction in how each filmmaker frames the other that is both impulsive, in keeping with the documentary circumstance of the piece, yet subtly subjective, as if, through the camera, the two friends were themselves addressing one another. Masood comes across as an extrovert, informal and conversational. This effect is achieved through very mobile and tentative hand-held camera images that lend him the persona of a face amidst a crowd. Kamal, on the other hand, is mostly seen from a low-angle position. This does not glorify him in any way as authoritative—an understanding commonly linked to the effect of a low-angle image. Rather, the low angles complement his calm and contained persona, testified to in his responses to queries he is confronted with. In this disparity of framing, the camera emerges as a responsive entity, one that is sensitive to spaces and the relations being forged between characters.

Consequently, our awareness of the film/text makers is not purely technical; they are not merely filmmakers operating video equipment. They emerge as agents effected by, and involved in, the process of unpacking socio-historical and cultural intricacies. They surface, as embedded in the filmmaking process, politically and socio-culturally, in a manner wherein they are engaging with and interrogating their identities, which is indicated aesthetically. Since we engage with them on rather emotional terms, their ideological stances too do not command rhetorical authority. This is a rich possibility because we are not situated in or given a predetermined ideological position within the text; rather, we participate in the evolution of the filmmakers' stances through the course of the film.

## 'Being with': The Scope of Camera Choreography

Throughout the film, the camera is largely hand-held. This makes it a fluid presence and through it the screenplay assumes a strong tendency for spontaneity. The shakiness and tentativeness of the hand-held camera parallels the film's approach towards its subjects. The film is a not a meta-commentary on Indo-Pak relations. It is not a conventional documentary that seeks exposition or argument through the triadic structure of 'for', 'against' and the detached/objective commentator, a structure that pervades broadcast journalism and sections of television documentary. The filmmakers have not engaged with experts, activists or commentators of any kind. This is the film's mechanism for resisting, indeed undermining any totalising or authoritative perspectives that would, by their nature, be partial and reductive. The innocuous experience of everyday life—where it is difficult to disentangle past and present—is the richly textured backdrop for the film.

The only opinions we engage with, besides family, are in impulsive conversations with ordinary persons on streets, in market places and shopping malls, and outside venues where a game of cricket is being played. The result is a variegated palette of people's sentiments and biases in the social psyche start to surface. What is most lasting through these conversations is the volatility of human sentiment. Also, the filmmakers are not overly concerned with displaying political correctness while editing some of the comments they have garnered.

After India wins a match during the series that Masood has been watching in a plush shopping mall on the outskirts of Delhi, he is cornered by a crowd that stresses, in rather aggressively celebratory terms, how India has defeated Pakistan. When Masood reveals he is Pakistani, the aggressive and jingoistic stance almost melts, making way for apologies that very soon crystallise into a moment for a nostalgic snapshot. Masood is given reassurances by members of the crowd that he should not feel alienated or isolated, and is invited to feel at home. In this shot that lasts nearly a minute (fifty seconds approximately) the camera first follows Masood. Then, as Masood is joined by youngsters drawn towards him being a Pakistani, the camera retreats to accommodate more members of the crowd, until finally, Masood with Kamal facing him are both encircled by a huge crowd. At this moment, Kamal lifts the camera, losing Masood in the frame, and makes a circular panning movement to reveal all faces that have suddenly been provoked by the presence of the camera. This is a very hypnotic movement, as the camera 'becomes' an entity both provocative and responsive in the scenario: characters within this image are drawn towards the filmmakers, while the camera's movement itself acknowledges the crowd that has formed in response to it. As everybody breaks into celebratory cheering and laughter, it becomes apparent that it does not matter to the crowd what the film is about. The camera is a magnetic pull for the crowd and its concerns matter little.

Kamal's experience in Pakistan is distinct and the camera emulates this. On the occasions when he is cornered after a game, the conversations are more politically sensitive, often slipping into the subject of Kashmir. He acknowledges that he feels confronted on the subject of Kashmir and has to, without his wanting to, defend his posture as an Indian. While all conversations are polite, some are clearly underpinned by the mechanisms of blame and confrontation. Some of Kamal's roadside interactions also reveal how much India impregnates the Pakistani imagination. In some, vox-pops the fascination with Bollywood is revealed, in some, anger towards the Gujarat riots, and in yet others, a sense of appreciation towards India's rising economic status in Asia and the global economy generally. Throughout, the interviewees furnish uneasy differences and disparities between the economic and socio-cultural fabrics of the two nations.

On these occasions, the camera remains largely static, facing the interviewees from a frontal position. This static and frontal address corresponds with the confrontational and fixed positionalities the filmmakers encounter as subjects express rather rigid and antagonistic mindsets. The stasis of the camera on these instances contrasts with the largely fluid movement in the remainder of the film. It parallels the frustrations that Kamal expresses in his voiceover and further, though subtly, reinforces the distinction between the worldviews of the filmmakers, who are engaging with identity as being constructed, as they collide with the identities of their subjects.

Kamal and Masood have very clearly derived from the traditions of *cinema verite*.[7] The 'normal' domestic spaces of both their homes have been accessed; family members interact not in formal interview situations but amidst their day-to-day activities. The framing of each person within the domestic spaces complements their characters. This aspect is crucial. The camera has here not positioned itself directly as if adopting a questioning stance in relation to the subjects. Neither is it trying to empathise with them, by replicating their point of view[8] or by developing a viewing position proximate to theirs. What the camera is seeking is to get 'near' the interviewees. At no instance do we have a full view of any member. Their bodies are fragmented and the families are never encountered as collectives. Through this attempt at nearness and fragmentation, the camera is acknowledging the disparities between the subjects such that the impossibility of a coherent communitarian stance is indicated, but without undermining particular subjectivities.

Further, the nearness of the camera is a double articulation of subjectivities, that of the characters and subjects within the frame and those behind the lens. This nearness evokes the 'being-with' that French philosopher Giles Deleuze has indicated with relation to the perception image.[9] Deleuze develops his discussion from Jean Mitry's text, *Esthetique et psychologie du cinema*, II. 'Being-with': [The camera] no longer mingles with the character, nor is it outside: it is with him (Deleuze 1986: 72).

Deleuze explains 'being-with' in relation to how such a camera attends to the enunciation of subjects within and without the frame, deriving from linguist Bakhtin's conceptions in *Marxism and the Philosophy of Language* (1973). Deleuze (1986: 73) states:

> There is not a simple combination of two fully-constituted subjects of enunciation, one of which would be reporter, the other reported. It is rather a case of an assemblage of enunciation, carrying out two inseparable acts of subjectivation simultaneously, one of which constitutes a character in the first person, and the other which is present at his birth and brings him to the scene. There is no mixture or average of two subjects....

The most poignant and enduring impression arises in Masood's conversation with his grandmother in her kitchen. She is cooking *chapatti*s (unleavened bread) for dinner. Between attending to the stove and rolling the chapattis, she recalls with an anger that exceeds yet maintains her consciousness towards the camera, the bloody and horrific murders of her relatives during Partition. Her comments include recollections of the bloodshed and horror when neither man nor animal were spared in the violence. She wishes Allah never shows those times to anyone ever again. The antagonism in her voice contrasts sharply with the action of domesticity we find her engaged in. In this instance, the camera is static and placed low, viewing Masood's grandmother from a side angle; she references both the camera and Masood, who, it appears, is not positioned directly behind the camera. The static camera contributes to the catharsis in this sequence and facilitates in revealing fully the ironies that impregnate the scenario. Masood indicates that this narrative has never been shared with him before; and even though he has returned from India questioning the antagonisms and enmity at home, he too feels, as his grandmother speaks, an anger raging within him. In textual terms, this sequence is tough because it is allows us a dialogue between the subjects within the frame and behind the lens, a dialogue that is emotionally charged and full of with contrary feelings. The intensity of Masood's grandmother's account aside, the self-referencing within the sequence by acknowledging the complex imbrication of past and present by Masood problematises any prompt resolution within the film and thereby within the discussion of Indo-Pak ties.

This sequence is a close record of history in the voice of a subject who has participated in its movement. Masood's expression of his discomfort upon hearing his grandmother sets up the cinematic apparatus as attempting nearness with the subject without fully attempting her viewpoint in a manner that echoes the discursive stance of anthropological filmmaker, Trin T. Minh-Ha in her 1982 film, *Reassemblage,* which arose from her ethnographic field research in Senegal. In the voiceover to the film, Minh-Ha (1992: 96) states:

> Scarcely twenty years were enough to make two billion people define themselves as underdeveloped.
>
> I do not intend to speak about
>
> Just speak near by

Minh-Ha has been one of the key figures in recent discussion surrounding the scope and extent of ethnographic documentation. In her practice, we encounter a profound muddying of the categories of the 'observer' and 'observed'. She has critiqued conventional ethnographic film practice in terms of the 'division of the world into those 'out there' (the subjects of ethnography) and those 'in here' (in the theatre, looking at them) (Russell 1999: 4). She asserts a more fluid conception of ethnographic practice that assumes particular significance with respect to third world subjects, for her intervention initiates the scope of engaging on more competing and problematising terms that both confront and endanger perceived power equations and stereotypes.

In this respect, there are two other sequences within *My Brother, My Enemy* that furnish a complexity in the experiences of the film's principal characters, the filmmakers. The first involves Kamal's meeting with Masood's family; the second is an earlier sequence when the filmmakers cross the Indo-Pak border at Wagah, Punjab. Masood tells us in his voiceover that he had not informed his family he would be accompanied by Kamal on his return from India. In a very lucidly edited segment of the film towards the close, we see Masood informing his grandparents he would like them to meet Kamal. Masood's grandfather is unwelcoming and assertive in his rejection of Hindus. Meanwhile, we follow Kamal through the streets of Lahore and Rawalpindi, receiving that warm hospitality Pakistan is known for. The drama peaks as Kamal arrives at Masood's home. There is a tension at this moment, for we are aware of Masood's grandparents' animosity. Kamal is welcomed into the family. We see this in the very subtle body gestures and demeanour of all characters within the scene. As a mark of respect, Kamal touches Masood's grandfather's feet. In return, he receives warm blessings. This is perhaps the most moving moment of the film. Masood, in his reminiscent voiceover, says that something 'had changed' at that moment. As these words arise, the camera recedes from the scene, as if acknowledging the emotional intensity of the moment and according it a dignity that the camera's presence and literal visualisation would shatter.

Throughout the film, we have found Kamal and Masood accessing liminal spaces, where the antagonisms and disparities between India and Pakistan seem challenged if not fully overcome. The sequence in Old Delhi and the domestic spaces of both filmmakers's homes are key in this respect. Towards the middle of the film, when the filmmakers cross the Indo-Pak border to enter Pakistan, we are transported to the flag changing ceremony at the Wagah border. The filmmakers cross the border—this is depicted through a brief fade to a black screen, after which the colour palette on the screen is visibly distinct. In place of the Indian tricolour, we see the green Pakistani flag being hurled in celebration. On the soundtrack the music pitches high and the sloganeering from the crowds at the ceremony includes cheering for the Pakistani nation. Just as we are absorbing the disparity between the two tightly defined and culturally inscribed landscapes, Masood critiques the absent-minded jingoism displayed at this scene. This is the most critical and direct address within the film. At this instant, the film fully articulates and delivers its position with relation to the border and Indo-Pak hostility. The filmmakers belong to a generation that is sensitive to the concerns and experiences of the generations before them, but through this sequence both filmmakers, indeed as the ideological apparatus, exhibit their dissatisfaction with the summarily reductionist propaganda their nations and communities adopt and exhibit in relation to one another.

## Through the Telephoto Lens

Throughout the film, both filmmakers have consistently used the telephoto lens[10] on the digital video camera. This facilitates their complex take on national identity. The premise of the film, the encounters it conjures and the worldviews it exposits have all been edited in a fashion that suggests an interrogative stance towards defining national identity in opposition to the 'enemy'. The suggestion is clear: such a reductive take on a perceived enemy is oversimplified. This understanding situates the filmmakers' experiences beyond national or spatial definition. They have attempted to unpack identity as fluid, volatile and complex, operating within history, politics, propaganda, and memory, and certainly not limited within jingoistic nationalist sentiment.

The liminality and fluidity that the filmmakers have encountered deterritorialises the filmmakers. Imagery arising from the telephoto lens serves to deterritorialise viewing positions within the film, departing from a naturalist perception that obscures depth of field, and often fragments subjects, lending a softness in focus to them. Thus, the imagery, in its form, parallels the filmmakers' stance. It manifests fragmentation, exaggerated camera movements and close texture. It provides an advanced perceptual experience wherein our engagement with the image does not pertain to it being visual evidence that solely corroborates the film's encounters.

The camera provides us with candid images of subjects, haptic reflections of locations, surface textures, and mobile encounters that lend a sense of rhythm to the piece. The editing of the film, which finely mixes the telephoto images with wide-angle long and medium shots, makes our engagement with the film visually lyrical and rhythmic. In this sense, the camera choreography assumes a poetic dimension and the apparatus emerges as not subservient to the film's occupation, verifying and thereby reinforcing the confrontations encountered. Our engagement is extended to another realm, beyond political argument and towards a perceptual dimension.

Though the two filmmakers are never revealed engaged in cinematography, their presence in aesthetic terms cannot be evaded. The film surfaces as not only articulating subject positions but, as ideology and aesthetic coincide, the film itself is pushed away from a purely content-based occupation, towards form. This is useful cinematically, for now the camera apparatus is not simply a means of recording or visualising; rather, is an entity in itself. This stance towards form, whereby the work emphasises the apparatus, parallels the conception of the 'free indirect subjective' that Deleuze evokes in relation to Italian filmmaker Pier Pao Pasolini's cinema, where he notes that the camera:

> does not simply give us the vision of the character and of his world; it imposes another vision in which the first is transformed and reflected. This subdivision is what Pasolini calls free indirect subjective…it is a case of going beyond the subjective and the objective towards a Pure Form…. It is a very special kind of cinema which has acquired a taste for 'making the camera felt. (Deleuze 1986: 74)

The telephoto lens within *My Brother, My Enemy* has been specifically employed to develop close-ups and proximate imagery. The close-ups themselves are deterritorialising for they serve in abstracting the subjects from any space or time coordinates. Bela Balazs, deriving from Henri Bergson's analysis of time and duration, has noted that the close-up serves in opening up the experience of film viewing into more dimensions:

> The facial expression on a face is complete and comprehensible in itself and therefore we need not think of existing in space and time. Even if we had just seen the same face in the middle of a crowd and the close-up merely separated it from the others, we would still feel that we have suddenly been left alone with this one face to the exclusion of the rest of the world…the expression and significance of the face has no relation to space and no connection with it. Facing an isolated face takes us out of space, our consciousness out of space is cut out and we find ourselves in another dimension. (Braudy and Cohen 2004: 316)[11]

Long and medium shots have been injected to not only contribute towards orientation within space and contextualisation,[12] but also as a mechanism to create breathing space in the consistently close imagery, engaging with which can turn visually straining, and to insert a subtle lyricism in the visual assembly of images. In this, the filmmakers have attempted to inject dynamism by exploring disparate heights and angles that result in variegated positions of viewing. The camerawork emerges as not approximating the perspective or position of viewing of the/any human eye. In this way, the film averts a naturalist-humanist representation, even though it is engaging with some very close human encounters. The departure from a naturalist perception brings the work very close to the constructivist discourse within film theory and the constructionist discourse within social anthropology. The multiple positions of viewing within the film remind us of Soviet filmmaker, Dziga Vertov's declaration that the *kino-eye* (camera eye) is distinct from the human eye.[13] Further, in anthropological terms, we are able to view identity and subjectivity as being constructed, formulated in historical encounters and not innate or given. The constructivist and constructionist stances within the film help undermine the tendency to equate distinctions between India and Pakistan in reductivist terms based on originary notions pertaining to religious and racial opposition, which posit Hindus and Muslims as eternally antagonistic.

## Conclusion

*My Brother, My Enemy* provides us with some complex moments that reveal the volatility of identity. While the film does not arrive at a resolution, it leaves us with a people-to-people encounter, wherein national identity and its claims in relation to a perceived enemy are complicated, if not totally collapsed.

In the last scene of the film, we see Kamal leaving on the train back for India. When the credits roll later, there seems no certainty gathered from the film. With the injection of the filmmakers as the key characters of the film we are, in any case, aware that the film is from a subjective position. The camera choreography, its spontaneity and impulsiveness complement only the subjectivities we are engaging with. The film has attempted to contextualise the filmmakers for us without resolving their subject positions in any conclusive or assertive terms; at the same time, we are aware that their subjectivity is not uninterrogated or a randomly constructed personal narrative. The two filmmakers express their dissatisfaction with the borders between the peoples of the two nations. At the same time, they return to their respective spaces. Consequently, the film steers away from any rhetoric or assertion.

The camerawork within the film is responsive to space and relation dynamics. This, in itself, re-situates the camera as more than merely an expository device, thus questioning the view of the documentary image as objective, as evidence. The deterritorialisation of viewing positions complements the film's attempt at confusing the fixed positionalities pertaining to nationality and religion evoked through borders. The film starts with the two filmmakers stating they belong on either side of a border. Through the film, that border is repeatedly crossed and rendered unclear. Though the film does not have a conclusive resolution, it provides us with a richly textured view, and sentiments that indicate how difficult it is to disentangle politics, propaganda and history, indeed, the past and the present.

## Notes

1.  Hamid Naficy uses Norma Iglesias's formulation that he has 'modified considerably'. (Naficy 2001: 313, endnote 10.)
2.  The specifics of this lens are discussed later, in the concerned section of the essay.
3.  The film does not provide us with any indication that Masood is British Pakistani. In a conversation with the author, Masood stated that it was a deliberate decision

not to include that information, for with that definition the film's claims might have been readily challenged.

4. This instance in the film reminds one of Vijay Mishra's discussion surrounding the use of foreign landscapes in Bollywood cinema. Mishra, through textual analysis, observes how diasporic spaces and foreign landscapes are generally complex locations for transgressing social norm, performed in Bollywood with relation to romance. (For a detailed discussion see, Mishra 2002: 235–69). *My Brother, My Enemy* posits the friendship between the filmmakers as both problematical in India, which can be appreciated in view of their social and cultural background as discussed below, and as a transgression, given the memories and experiences of Masood's family from the Partition.

5. Self-reflexivity is the technique of acknowledging the nature of the filmmaking process. It often involves the presence of crew and camera within the image. 'This style of filmmaking which draws attention to its own process is often termed "self-reflexive"' (Nelmes 2003: 414).

6. Masood is British Pakistani; it was his parents who migrated to the United Kingdom. Through interaction with his family in Pakistan, it can be gauged that his family belongs to the middle class of Pakistan.

7. The origins of *cinema verite* are in the Soviet documentary style that emerged after the Revolution in the 1920s, exemplified in the work of Dziga Vertov. Vertov was the documentarist for the Soviet newspaper, *Pravda* (truth). The filmed edition of the paper, which Vertov developed, was termed *Kino-Pravda* (film-truth). Vertov characterised his cinema as one where 'there were no actors, no decors, no script and no acting'. The style later influenced French cinema, particularly the cinema of Jean Luc Godard in the 1970s, and ethnographic filmmakers Jean Rouch (Dixon 1997). Susan Hayward notes that Rouch initially termed his 'objective' style as 'cinema direct', where there was 'no staging, no mise-en-scene and no editing'. In the 1960s he shifted away from this purist style towards 'a more sociological investigation' where he staged shots and edited his footage. This style he termed as *cinema verite*. 'Less objective, but no less real, *cinema verite* attempted to catch reality on film. Ordinary people testified to their experiences, answered questions put by Rouch or his colleagues.' (Hayward 2001: 58–59) The earliest and most poignant remains Rouch's *Chronique d'un Été*. In *My Brother, My Enemy,* all conversations are completely spontaneous.

8. The point-of-view in cinema is related to the notion of the subjective camera. It is usually a shot that represents the point of view of a character, looking at what the character sees (Dick 2002: 61).

9. As the term indicates, the perception image pertains to perception. However, Deleuze discusses the perception image as being distinct from the 'nominal definition of "subjective" and "objective"'. He holds the perception-image as being 'semi-subjective', in which camera-consciousness takes an extremely formal determination (1986: 76).

10. The telephoto lens magnifies distant objects and has a narrow angle of view. In this measure its mechanism is often compared to that of a telescope. Unlike the wide-angle lens that emphasises perception of depth and often distorts linear perception, the telephoto lens suppresses depth perception. Masood and Kamal used a Panasonic DVX 100, a digital video camera with a zoom lens that has a variable length, ranging from wide-angle to the telephoto (Monaco 2000: 80).

11. While Balazs concentrates on the face in close-up, Deleuze has stated that the affect of a close-up need not be limited to the face only. 'And why would a part of the body, chin, stomach or chest be more partial, more spatio-temporal and less expressive than an intensive feature of faceicity or a reflexive whole face?' (1986: 97).
12. For a detailed discussion of the long shot in terms of its anthropological qualities of establishing relationships with and within space, see Collier and Collier 1948.
13. For Dziga Vertov, the camera, which he termed *kino-eye,* was distinct from the human eye. It could move freely and access that which was not readily available or could be missed by the human eye. In *WE: Variant of a Manifesto,* the *kino-eye* is defined thus: 'I am kino-eye, I am a mechanical eye. I, a machine, show you the world as only I can see it. Now and forever, I free myself of human immobility, I am in constant motion, I draw near, then away from objects, I crawl under, soldiers, I fall on my back, I ascend with an airplane, I plunge and soar together with plunging and soaring bodies. Now I, a camera, fling myself along their resultant, manoeuvering in the chaos of movement, recording movement, starting with movements composed of the most complex combinations.... Within the chaos of movements, running past, away, running into and colliding—the eye, all by itself, enters life. I climb onto them. I move apace with the muzzle of a galloping horse, I plunge fullspeed into a crowd, I outstrip running (1984: 17).

# 11

# Fascist Imaginaries and Clandestine Critiques: Young Hindi Film Viewers Respond to Violence, Xenophobia and Love in Cross-border Romances

## Shakuntala Banaji

Tarang (twenty-two, a Hindu assistant pharmacist, London, 2005): I've watched Hindi films all my life. My mom and *nani* [grandmother] made me when I was little, to learn Hindi. I saw all the old films with the Kapoors and Mr Bachchan, and all Shahrukh-Kajol, Aamir-Juhi love stories, but I never watched the ones on India-Pakistan. I mean I liked them very much for the songs, but that is all.

Shaku: The songs? Are there any in particular?

Tarang: So many! (Pause.) Every song in the film *Main Hoon Na* is just great! But that isn't truly one of 'those' films. Few years back we watched *Gadar*—maybe a movie not many people here would see. I cried in front of my mom when they are driving in the truck, you know? He is taking her to the border. It was so sad, like when my mom takes my nani to the airport and we all feel we may not see her again. The songs were sad, colourful and...er...full of passion. But the film was bad. It really made me angry. Stirring up bad feelings on all sides like Fox News! Just ridiculous.

Shaku: Where are your parents from, actually?

Tarang: They were from Pune, you know. But before that my mom came from Lucknow and that's where my nani lives.

*The most disturbing fragments are those that resist the hegemony of any clearly articulated text.*

*—Bharucha, The Politics of Cultural Practice, 2001*

## Introduction

In relation to the line running between India and Pakistan, Hindi films have, for decades, been dipping first their toes and more recently their entire limbs into imaginary waters on the other side of the border. Hindi film critics have long complained that many films appear to do this explicitly to bolster a sense of (fictional) patriotic Indian identity in opposition to that which is Pakistani and 'other', and that they do so in the service of a xenophobic ruling ideology that serves the interest of a corrupt and highly authoritarian political elite (see Prasad 1998; Vitali 2000). However, do such critiques—however powerful and legitimate—actually reflect the ways in which viewers 'read' and respond to the invitations of these films? What kinds of satisfactions and anxieties might the films speak to that are not articulated in day-to-day life? And, equally significantly, if there are some viewers who are prone to respond to certain filmic invitations more powerfully than to others because of their experiences and backgrounds, how do these responses tie in with existing politics and political situations in South Asia and the diaspora? Using a case-study approach, *via* young people's comments as well as through existing critical literature, this essay articulates some controversies surrounding the films *Gadar* (Tumult, 2001) and *Veer-Zaara* (2004), which take as their subject matter cross-religious or cross-border romances set against the backdrop of a fragmented and fictionalised history of the relationship between India and Pakistan. I will especially look at the way in which issues of social class, national identity, diaspora, and religious affiliations in the films resonate differently with viewers from different backgrounds and locations in India and the diaspora.

## Hindi Film Studies: Questioning Theoretical Borders

Concern with the possible negative 'effects' of Hindi films on audiences is not new: in fact it continues to haunt those writing on the subject (see Chatterji 2003; Dasgupta 1993; Mathur 2002). In one example, Srividya Ramasubramaniam and Mary Beth Oliver argue that 'the idea that heroes would be shown engaging in sexual violence is cause for concern, as social learning perspectives suggest that when likable, attractive characters such as heroes perpetrate sexual violence on screen they are more likely to be imitated by viewers' (2003: 334). In another instance, Arti Shukla (2005), discussing films that invoke images of the Indian nation in contrast to Pakistan, refers continually to what the populace might be making of these films. She argues: 'These films…provide not only entertainment, they also satisfy the audience's moral and political desires by providing a tool to make sense of what is going on and understand the actions of the governments of the two countries.' Fareed Kazmi's Gramscian conclusions quite moderately sum up a number of anxieties about the 'dangers' of Hindi films:

> Conventional films do not simply reflect the social world, but actually construct a coherent version of social reality within which ideological tensions can be contained and resolved…. In other words, through highly complex and devious means, it [the conventional film] privileges 'preferred' meanings over 'excluded' meanings, thereby reinforcing the 'given' of the system, and absorbing or referencing out all potentially oppositional connotations. (Kazmi 1999: 215–16)

In all these examples, connections between viewers' actions and film narratives are drawn hypothetically, based not on actual instances or accounts but on perspectives from social psychology and textual analysis. Despite a few studies of Hindi film audiences (Bhattacharya 2004; Derné 2000; Dudrah 2002), there are a number of reasons why the view of Hindi films as a closed and coherent system of representation and reception has remained prevalent. Quite particularly, growing unease about the increase in religious fascism and xenophobic nationalism in India (Bharucha 1998; Bhatt 2001; Mankekar 2000), its witting (or unwitting) support from the diaspora (Bahri 2001; Mishra 2002; Rajagopal 2001) and horror at the social practices of religious, gender and sexual violence (Pushkarna 2001; Sarkar 2002) appear to emphasise the need for an understanding of links between viewers' national, gender and ethnic identities, and their spectatorship. In the opinion of numerous critics, (Kazmi 1998; Valicha 1988; Vishwanath 2002), viewers uncritically watch films that seem at best to ignore and at worst to encourage authoritarian beliefs and circumstances, such as the xenophobic hatred between India and Pakistan. Of course, some textual theorists discussing Hindi films have summarised their assumptions about audiences in relation to the pleasures of spectacle and emotional excess, an avowed 'need' for tradition in a threateningly modern world, and the potential of films to shore up a sense of personal and group identity. As with all primarily theoretical accounts of film, this collective picture tells, however, far from the whole story.

While, superficially, each of the textual accounts of Hindi films appears accurately to encompass some aspects of the films, the nature of the assumptions about *audiences* raises a series of problematic questions. Are all the narratives, romantic sequences, music, costumes, dialogues, lyrics, and other aspects of Hindi films equally ideologically 'suspect' and the pleasures they bring to viewers morally 'dubious' by virtue of their connection to an authoritarian ideology and an oppressive society? What of viewers such as Tarang, quoted at the beginning of this chapter, who find pleasure in films, aspects of whose narratives they clearly despise? Just how *do* young viewers interpret the visual and verbal discourses of gender, nation and ethnicity in commercial Hindi films in the light of their perceptions of their own national, ethnic, gender, and sexual identities? If a viewer's identity may be shaped by intersecting, and contingent, aspects of history and experience (Ghosh 2002; Staiger 2003), then to what extent do varying class, religious, geographic, national, community, and home environments alter, influence and/or counterbalance conceptions of gender and national identity read into Hindi films?

## Methodology

My fieldwork comprised mixed methods and a wide variety of data which was analysed both individually and comparatively. I carried out much of the fieldwork in London and Bombay over a period of two and a half years, between 2000 and 2003, during which I took extensive notes on the home lives, cinema environment and popular film consumption of young Hindi film viewers. The bulk of the data in this chapter is based on extended in-depth interviews with forty viewers between the ages of sixteen and twenty-five. The interviews were constructed in a semi-structured manner, lasting between one and four hours, which were then analysed thematically in the light of forms of discourse analysis stemming from social psychology (Hollway 1989; Potter and Wetherell 1987). Thus, although aspects of viewer identity such as class, gender and religion are seen as being significant in shaping experiences of life and film, interviewees' accounts are presented as part of a snapshot of Hindi film viewing rather than as being representative of entire communities' viewing positions.

A participant observer at over eighty Hindi film showings, I kept a field diary and took dozens of photographs of cinema halls and viewers; I visited some of my interviewees at home or college, went shopping with others, or to the cinema, and discussed Hindi films extensively, all activities which I recorded in the field diary. In addition, I examined articles on Hindi films and stars, sexuality, ethnicity, gender and race from popular film magazines, newspapers and the internet, and watched Hindi films on DVD and VHS, which formed part of the context for film appreciation and consumption amongst my sample. An additional two months of interviewing in 2005 in both cities for a related project enabled me to revisit some of the issues raised by interviewees in my initial sample, with a new set of viewers and some more recent films, of which *Veer-Zaara* was one. Rather than coming from a selected list, all the films discussed either happened to be showing when I undertook the research or were specifically chosen for consideration by the young people I interviewed.

## Forced Crossings and Techno-memories?: *Gadar* and its Mixed Reception

In this section, through a case study of responses to the film *Gadar: Ek Prem Katha* (Tumult—A Love Story, 2001) I examine the notion, put forward by Sumita Chakravarty (2002: 224) that 'the institution of narrative cinema in its mainstream forms may actually be resistant to nationalist imaginings, given that the nation is always mediated by its fragments, that is by individuals whose particularities of dress, speech and life-style locate them within specific regional, social and cultural configurations'. Of course, this notion does not exist in isolation or simply in relation to the 'imagined communities' of cinema and fiction put forward by Benedict Anderson (1983). Its context is, in fact, far more mundane and can be summed up in the twin concerns of critics: a) the images of Hindi cinema articulate and encourage widespread jingoism amongst the Indian populace and in the diaspora; and b) such film propaganda has actual psychic and social consequences, from the masking of opportunist anti-Pakistani stances taken by the government when they wish to start a war or encourage ethnic and religious violence, to the promotion of smug self-satisfaction on the part of the Indian viewer and government and, ultimately, the deepening of divisions in South Asia, which have long-lasting effects on the life of the region.[1]

Opening to an extended and brutal sequence of post-Partition violence by Muslims against Sikhs in India, *Gadar* purportedly tells the story of a Sikh truck driver who saves a middle-class Muslim girl from gang-rape and death after her family flee to Pakistan. He waits until she has fallen in love with him to marry her and start a family with her, only to have his idyllic life thrown into a maelstrom of angst when she visits her family in Pakistan and is held prisoner by them. The hero's trip with his little boy to Paksitan to 'recover' his wife takes up the second half of the film, which depicts Pakistan as highly repressive, fundamentalist and full of hatred for India, and most Pakistanis as pawns in the hands of their evil leaders. The brief happy ending, in which all are reconciled, only follows an extended sequence in which the hero single-handedly destroys swathes of the Pakistani army.

At the time I was conducting out initial interviews, *Gadar* was sweeping across belts of India, to all intents and purposes a 'super-hit', but struggling and failing to emulate success of *Lagaan* (The Tax, 2001) in other countries. Both were, avowedly, 'fictions' of history; but in the press, much was made of the fact that one (*Lagaan*) harked back to a utopian pre-Independence arena in which a nationalist message had the power to unify people across class, gender, caste, and religion, while the other (*Gadar*) was causing actual fracas between sections of the populace (see 'Sena terms Muslim protestors of *Gadar* anti-national', 2001; and 'Storm over partition love story', 2001). Young people I interviewed outside cinemas were fiercely divided in their assessment of the film; some thought it was a splendid romance or reminder of history; others asserted that they simply didn't care what the film was about, it was a must-see because it 'looked big'; yet others asserted categorically that they had no wish to see a film that 'caused religious divisions'. During private in-depth interviews, however, a number of more detailed and clearcut viewing positions were clarified.

Bhiku was one of the first viewers I spoke to, who consciously constructed himself not as a fan of Hindi films but as a 'thinking viewer', someone who wanted to know more about the world. In this sense, his commentary on *Gadar* is crucial, because it shows just how far the blurred boundaries between fiction and history appeal to those who most wish to distance themselves from what they see as the romanticism or escapism of Hindi films.

> Bhiku (a twenty-three year old Hindu shop assistant, Bombay): In *Gadar* they show people's anger towards Pakistan. After many years all the anger is in the people's minds and some of the dialogues pinch Pakistan, so people—the audience—get happy.

Shaku: So, in the theatre where you saw it, people liked those anti-Pakistan speeches?

Bhiku: Yes. Because people feel helpless to do anything against Pakistan, but when this dialogue is delivered they are showing what is there inside.

Shaku: Do you think similar things are shown in Pakistan?

Bhiku: Yes, why not? On both the sides the media has put a lot of anger in people's minds. Common people should have common sense.

Shaku: But do they? (*Both laugh. Long pause.*)

Bhiku: One thing I like in *Gadar* is that it has at least shown the pain that people face when leaving their roots, the trouble they would have faced in leaving that place. The cruelty which both sides committed...they have tried to show the pain...I couldn't even imagine the pain, that of people who lose their relatives at that time. Their Muslim priests are publishing it more as Muslims versus other communities. Some of the acts of some Muslims that have made the majority (*Pause.*) and the government's acts also—the government has tried to be neutral, to show themselves neutral, but they have done injustice to the other—the Hindu community.

In analysing a piece of talk such as this and the ones which follow, it is important to chart the shifts and movements, the withdrawals, emphases and patterns in the context of other information about the intersecting identifications and experiences of the speakers (Barker and Galasinski 2001; Potter and Wetherell 1987). In the first section of this segment, Bhiku speaks first of the film as a text, albeit one with a popular edge, showing this awareness in his mention of 'dialogues' that self-consciously 'pinch' Pakistan. Later he moves to his sense of the film as a political vehicle for supposedly 'authentic' frustrations about 'political/religious favouritism',[2] which to him explain the popularity of the film with Hindu audiences in India and of films similar to this with Muslim audiences in Pakistan. Bhiku's expression of his enjoyment of the film as turning on a need to be *informed* about the brutal realities of Partition and of finding such information in the film, are a worrying confirmation of the fact that such films do get used, in some viewers' minds, as replacements for 'real' histories of Partition. As psychoanalytic theorist Sudhir Kakar explains, 'Cultural psychology in India must necessarily include the study of the psychic representations of collective pasts, the ways the past is used as a receptacle for projections from the present' (1996: 12–13). Bhiku moves from speaking of his enjoyment of *Gadar*, and that of others in the theatre where he viewed it, to the brutality and violence of Partition, to the inflammatory speeches of 'their' 'Muslim' priests (on both sides of the border). This process strikes me as extremely political and far from disinterested. As I have argued elsewhere (Banaji 2006), this can be read in the light of a trend towards the *erasure* of secular histories of India in the past decade and their *replacement* by fictions of Hindu fascist provenance (Bhatt 2001: 92–94, 206–207; Butalia 1995: 58–81; Sarkar 2001: 268–88).

Yet a range of different existential and political frameworks do exist amongst viewers, and these appear to alter the reading of meaning radically, intriguingly suggesting, perhaps, that where Hindi films attempt to be most didactic, they may fail most consistently with a whole range of viewers who do not already share their primary ideological outlook. Ismail, a young working-class Muslim in Bombay and Jatin, a middle-class Hindu in London, both exemplify this notion, while Neetu and Neha engage with other aspects of the film, suggesting that even strongly nationalist films leave room for multiple readings. I quote at length to give a sense of these viewers' differing contexts and concerns.

Ismail (a nineteen year old Muslim sales representative, Bombay): (*Unclear sentence*). You know the disturbing things, like the Shiv Sena Chief, Bal Thakaray.

Shaku: Yes?

Ismail: So many of his statements are against Muslims. But the government can do nothing to him. Why can't they? He should be in jail. This is what you have to ask. He has had case after case made against him, but nothing touches him. And, with such anti-Muslim sentiments around, how do people expect the Muslims in this country to feel that India is our country?...And then, the dissatisfaction [of a few Indian Muslims, regarding their status in India] being expressed by the gesture of supporting the Pakistan cricket team is interpreted by most Hindus as a signal of allegiance to Pakistan.[...]You have all sorts of communication technologies at your command, like internet and computer and phone. But if you had *nothing* then the films would be the best way for you to find out what is going on in the city next to yours. It may be a one-sided picture, but who says you have to accept only that picture? At least it is some sort of news. People have to think for themselves, whether something is right or wrong[....] And films like *Gadar, Border* [1997]—the film producer is just trying to make money so in India he will praise India and elsewhere—well (pause) have you seen the VCD version? They've cut out many of the anti-Pakistani dialogues because they want to be financially successful overseas, even in Pakistan. So they'll do that. Again, take the movie *Sarfarosh* (The Martyr, 1999), they showed the whole of it on

*Zee* but on the VCD they simply cut out the bits that made sense in the plot. So as not to offend certain groups....

Ismail uses *Gadar*, *Mission Kashmir* (2000) and *Border*, which he has been describing to me prior to this point, to springboard into a discussion of his feelings about being a working-class Muslim in India. His comments detail and challenge the supposedly commonsense insistence—among the middle-class Hindu public and implicit in films such as *Sarfarosh*—that all those *within* the nation must prove their loyalty to India in overt ways in order to retain the right to remain on national soil. In doing so, Ismail constructs national identity both on and off-screen as far more a matter of justice and dialogic loyalty than birth or ethnicity—the Indian nation must include, acknowledge and protect Muslims, both psychologically and legally, if it is to receive the 'love' demanded. Towards the end of the discussion, however, he returns to the issue of films as a means of 'information', but with a twist. Rather than seeing them as wholly retrograde *fictions of history* that inflame anti-Muslim and anti-Pakistani feelings, he explains that, for viewers like himself, particularly those unlike me '(you have all sorts of communications technologies at your command...'), such films are necessary interventions, a means of tracking changes in the public sphere, or finding out about a 'neighbouring city'.

As if exemplifying Ismail's point that having access to a range of communication technologies allows one the luxury to view such films as *fiction rather than as information*, Jatin, a highly educated viewer, draws on his knowledge of history and of film to critique *Gadar*:

Jatin (a twenty-four year old Hindu trainee professional, London): ...I actually got irritated with *Gadar*. That Sunny Deol film.

Shaku: Why was that?

Jatin: Well, he's Sikh, but he calls himself a Hindu all the time. And I thought—'He says, 'We Hindus, we don't buckle down to you Muslim people', and it's just basically him destroying Pakistan on his own. (*Laughs.*) And it's like a Sikh marrying a Muslim, but it's like she becomes virtually a Hindu! So you can see the BJP funda values coming out there. (*Laughs.*) It's set in 1947 and they've got these Apache helicopters coming down on this train and Sunny Deol just gets his gun out and shoots it down. It's very over the top....

Shaku: If you had a choice, where would you live?

Jatin: I wouldn't go back to India—I wouldn't fit in there...I think of myself as Asian, not completely British, maybe, British Asian.

Obviously, the fact that some people do not have access to trustworthy information about history and politics does not excuse directors who deliberately misrepresent swathes of history in the service of fascist ideologies and militaristic policies. However, for those interested in the cultural aspects of media viewing, one has to ask what censorship of such films would actually achieve. Regardless of the intentions plausibly attributed to the directors (Chatterjee 2003; Gahlot 2001; Prasad 1998), it is obviously not the case that all viewers come away from these films spouting jingoistic rhetoric. Could it not be the case that debate and critique may, in fact, be opened up by the most apparently 'closed' films? For instance, focusing on the romance that twines itself around politics throughout *Gadar*, Neetu, a school, girl discusses her belief in the 'power of love' to bring forth the humanity in people who are otherwise divided by their religious or national affiliations:

> Neetu (a sixteen year old Sikh, Bombay): The main thing I don't like in India and in Pakistan is that they are very religious and they say you have to follow this religion only…. Here there are many people who are very close-minded…. Now Hindi films are pushing towards an open-minded point of view… and *Gadar*, even though that is an action movie, it is very touching how she comes into his religion and all, like how she follows it and how she sacrifices and how Sunny Deol is going to sacrifice and even he is ready to take over the Islam religion. That is a good thing that even he is willing to take on her religion. I think such relationships can work across religions. That was very touching to me.

> Shaku: Oh Yes?

> Neetu: Yes. Because nowadays there are many Hindus marrying Muslims and Muslims marrying Christians and all. It can work. (*Very vehement.*) I agree with those things. I believe in those things because I believe in love. Even we have to sacrifice and even they have to sacrifice.

Ignoring completely many of the sequences in the film that appear to denigrate Pakistan and Pakistanis, Neetu emphasises the importance of the scenes where the heroine 'becomes' Sikh and the hero agrees to become a Muslim, if this will allow him to live peacefully with his wife and child in Pakistan. Herself from an immensely restrictive family, and engaged in a clandestine relationship with a man from another community, Neetu interprets the film as encouraging gender equity in terms of the construction of cross-religious relationships. While this is hardly the most apparent reading of the film, it is obviously significant for some viewers and should not be dismissed out of hand.

One of the only viewers I spoke to in London to mention *Gadar* in a positive light, Kalpesh echoes both Bhiku's sense of the film as a reminder of 'history' and Neetu's pleasure in it as a romance that challenges religious prejudices.

> Kalpesh (an eighteen year old Hindu, London): I like those sorts of [realistic] stories where there's a Hindu and a Muslim and they fall in love, you know? Because that's what's actually happening in our real life. The communities are mixing. And, umm, the thing that I don't understand, yeah, is that our parents love these movies, and yet they don't let us do it. (*Emphatic.*) When it comes to the crunch they wouldn't let us do anything like that. No way.

Like Jatin, Neha critiques the modality of the violence depicted in *Gadar,* refusing the film's framing of the Indian hero versus the Pakistanis on these grounds, but, like Kalpesh and Neetu, she accepts the romance as psychologically compelling:

> Neha (a twenty-three year old Jain housewife, Bombay): ...In this *Gadar*, there is this hero who can kill so many people at a time. (*Laughs.*) This is not possible. After watching this we say, 'Let Bobby Deol, Dharmendra and Sunny Deol go to the border and border forces come home. (*Laughs.*) These three could protect the whole border!'
>
> Shaku: Yes, I see what you're getting at.
>
> Neha: At least in English movies, with Arnold and all, we can see their muscles and at least we can see the reality in it.... (*Laughs.*)
>
> Shaku: So which do you prefer?
>
> Neha: Fights, violence in Hollywood films.
>
> Shaku: But?
>
> Neha: The romance, in Hindi films. Without doubt.

Clearly, even if one accedes to the view of a film as something that contains 'messages', rather than as a multilayered audiovisual representational medium with all kinds of possibilities for pleasure and communication, film 'messages' are not as straightforward as some textual accounts (see Nandy 1996; Valicha 1988) might suggest. While the young people in these interviews overtly invoke understandings of modality and experiences of ethnicity as their grounds for rejecting some of the xenophobic politics they read into *Gadar* and other films like it, their comments imply that they see these films as playing a range of social and economic roles on both sides of the border that are not always coherently linked to their ideological frameworks. The same film that, for Bhiku and Jatin, is primarily about the wrongs—in one case imaginary—done to the Hindu populace and the nature of Pakistani/Indian nationalism, it can also be read as providing the spur for debate in an information-deprived populace, affirming a belief in love and friendship between communities, and asserting the need for men and women who marry into a different community or nation to make equal sacrifices in terms of their identity. It is interesting that the very textual accounts that most poignantly show films such as *Gadar* 'othering' Muslims or Pakistanis, are systematically 'othering' the people who watch these films, constructing them as absolutely different, unsecular, xenophobic and vulnerable to the films' supposed effects, thus decreasing the potential for constructing bridges across various divides. However, could it be possible that, as Ismail explains, when it comes to films, just as with news programmes, viewers who do not already arrogantly believe that they know the 'truth' have to be given a chance to make up their own minds, to sort right from wrong?[3] The following section examines the narratives of viewers who have watched a number of cross-border romances, and explores their changing feelings for Pakistan and India based on their responses to some of these films, notably *Veer-Zaara*, which tells the story of an Indian man and a Pakistani woman who fall in love when she is on a trip to India, and when denied a chance to marry by the girl's politician father, they first agree to sacrifice their love and then, betrayed by the 'villain', they endure decades of personal suffering, exile and loss of identity in order to remain true to each other and themselves.

## *Veer-Zaara*: Bollywood Sentiments or a Political Change of Heart?

Engaging with the convoluted interstices of communal subjectivity in the Indian subcontinent (Kakar 1996; Sarkar 2002), and with the increasingly opaque and fragmentary responses these have engendered across theatre and popular culture in India, Rustom Bharucha asks whether 'the construction of somebody's other [can] be dismantled through a blurring, if not dissolution, of its polarities' (Bharucha 2001: 131). With precisely the question of such a 'dismantling' and 'blurring' of oppositions in mind, this section investigates the possibility that Hindi films dealing with cross-border romances contribute not to a static and fixed nationalist ideology but to a range of meanings with regard to borders and belonging, the national self and the 'other'. Much of the press coverage of Yash Chopra's latest hit *Veer-Zaara* centred both on the love story between the protagonists and on the fact that half of it was set across the border in Pakistan. Generally this film was viewed as representing Pakistanis in a slightly more balanced light than a number of other recent films (see Deshmukh 2004; Hoffheimer 2005). Discussions with viewers in Bombay and London aimed to assess the actual ways in which the film was perceived.

Kumkum, a nineteen year old UP-born Hindu check-out assistant in Bombay, gives an account that segues into this discussion of *Veer-Zaara* because it suggests answers to a number of questions about the connections between audience politics and film discourses:

> Kumkum (Bombay, 2005; in Hindi): I love Preity in *Veer-Zaara*, how she does care about the honour of her family but puts her honesty and love above religion and above her country, Pakistan. Shahrukh also puts his love above India.... They have sacrificed for each other and they have been like heroes for others to see this is what matters, not the land or the border. You know I listen to the songs and I feel, '*Haan, woh bhi hamara desh hai, yahan bhi unka desh hai*' (Yes, that is our country too, this is their country too).

> Shaku: Do you know many people who believe this, the way you think?

> Kumkum: Why not? All my friends. Even my brothers and my parents. Only media and governments create divisions in India-Pakistan. *Veer-Zaara* is only speaking what is in many people's hearts.

> Shaku: Earlier you told me you enjoyed watching *Sarfarosh* and also *Gadar*. Aren't those films strengthening the divisions you dislike?

> Kumkum: So? You must have also enjoyed those movies—the songs are very good, the story is surprising, the acting is nice...I did not watch them and think '*Haan, woh log Pakistani hain, hum log Indian hain*' (Yes, those people are Pakistani, we are Indian); I thought about the choices that humans come face to face with in our life. *Gadar* is only just one film. But it has many different messages for many different people. If another *Gadar* is made, I will still go to watch. Yes.

Kumkum eschews patriotism in favour of romantic and personal loyalty. She praises *Veer-Zaara* for its egalitarian gender relationships and emphasises its (didactic and sentimental but humane) penultimate message, which is one that encourages the breakdown of cross-border suspicion and the acceptance of the 'other' as akin to the 'self'. Most saliently, Kumkum's response to my question about the politics of

*Sarfarosh* and *Gadar*, two films she mentioned liking, confirms the notion outlined in the previous section that even films with apparently tightly closed ideological frameworks do hold a—albeit limited— number of *alternative* viewing positions that are not rejected by all viewers. Openly anti-xenophobic, Kumkum's insistence that she will continue to watch apparently propagandist Indian films precisely because these are media texts with pleasurable storylines, actors and songs serves as a corrective to the view that such films are enjoyed or act merely as vehicles for particular partisan messages. Kumkum clearly resents the notion that she can't make up her own mind. But what of viewers who do appear to accept the politics of such films as a basis for their view of Pakistan?

Neela, a seventeen year old, lower middle-class Hindu schoolgirl befriended me outside a cinema hall in Bombay at the showing of another movie and was eager to discuss her interest in romantic films, an interest that also had a political edge.

> Neela (in English): When I was little my feelings were all against Pakistan. No doubt. (*Pause.*) Mummy-Papa felt very strongly on the terrorism issue. They felt Pakistan was a place where it is one way only, the Koran and all that is being put forward. You must be knowing this? (*Pause.*) Even in the last few years I had seen many Hindi movies that show Pakistan as such a place, where you do not dare to say anything against your father or your country or your religion; even love is not accepted.

> Shaku: Really? (*Pause.*) Such as?

> Neela: *Pukar* [The Call, 2000], *Sarfarosh*, you must be knowing.... In *Gadar* it ends with a happy story. After all villains... Pakistani villains get killed by the hero, even India is happy and even Pakistan. I mean the families. Other films, I remember the stories and sometimes not the names. But in last two years my feeling has started to change towards Pakistan. (Long pause.)

> Shaku: You changed your mind after...?

> Neela: ...Just a few months back I watched *Veer-Zaara* in the theatre with my friends and I was crying so much. Boman Irani was a strong character. Priety was a strong character. Shahrukh was a strong character. Watching them I understood that India-Pakistan are like two friends who have quarrelled for so many years. Both will not bow the head. But the children have decided, *'Dosti karenge, pyaar karenge'* (We will be friends, we will love one another). This war must end. When Shahrukh was speaking in the court, everyone in my group clapped. If Mummy-Daddy came with me, I could not be clapping! (*Laughs.*)

Neela is a viewer who openly discusses her family's politics *vis-à-vis* Pakistan in relation to Hindi films. Unprompted by me—and unaware of my political views—she introduces the films that she has watched over the years and charts her changing feelings on the subject of India's relationship with Pakistan. She speaks of 'war' and cross-border 'terrorism', although *Veer-Zaara* is overtly about no such thing, and her commentary suggests that media products such as films, while also reinforcing some of the beliefs she has acquired from her parents, are the means by which she ultimately comes to question those beliefs. As such, sequences in these films provide her with alternative imaginaries to those she might otherwise inhabit. From her testimony it is possible to conjecture that censorship of particular films might be both futile and potentially dangerous in that, on the one hand, it would fail to deal with the context producing the representations and, on the other, it would provide an authoritarian solution to an authoritarian problem. Having discussed this issue with various respected secular and gender activists, I am aware that this will not be a popular view. However, based not only on Neela's description of her own and her friends' reactions to Shahrukh's speech at the end of the film but also on her humorous assertion that had her parents been there she would have had to censor her response—'I could not be clapping'—it is worth recollecting that while we continue to call for censorship in situations such as violent ethnic conflict, more often than not media censorship serves the interests of those who do not wish to break down barriers, engage in self-critique or blur boundaries.

It cannot be forgotten, however, that assertions about audiences and their meaning-making may prove contradictory. An interview with Sheba, a twenty year old British-Pakistani teaching assistant whom I met through my work in London, illustrates that, even in contexts other than the already ethnically charged and xenophobic atmosphere of urban Indian in the last decade, the rhetorical construction of Pakistan as 'other'/'enemy' can hold damaging and hurtful meanings that don't necessarily result in a rejection of the films *per se*:

Sheba (in English): Even though we enjoy all Pakistani serials, Hindi films not Lahore films have always been very special for me and my mother and my sisters. But sometimes we did get the feeling that it was like a crime to be Pakistani.... I mean! You've seen the way they suggest things, I mean, like in that old movie *Border*, the absurd things they tell us, 'It is okay to help a Pakistani.' In *Gadar*, maybe one or two Pakistanis might friendly but the others are just thick and act like dogs and they get chopped by the hero. Remember that scene with the water pipe?

Shaku: The pump? Yes. (*Pause.*) Have you seen any films that do not make you feel like this?

Sheba: No, not really. *Pinjar* [The Skeleton, 2003], that was interesting. Maybe a more neutral film. But (*pause*) it had this atmosphere that most Pakistanis are cruel, not having compassion, except maybe one or two. (*Pause.*) *Veer-Zaara* is the only one I can think of that made me feel that actually Pakistanis, Indians, these are the same blood, and in both places you can have bad people and good people. It was simple. But it was powerful for us. I enjoyed so many scenes in that film, not just because of the India-Pakistan friendship message....

Shaku: You say it wasn't 'just because of the message'. Why, then?

Sheba: Because it is a beautiful romance. I mean, it shows that passion and love can start in a few days and can last a lifetime. It shows the strength of women, how they work together, how men should take them more seriously. And it allows you to feel the dignity of people in Pakistan; that is rare. Compare it to the family scenes in *Gadar* and you know what I mean.

Sheba, who has grown up in London in a Pakistani family watching Hindi films, deliberately uses the language of 'self' and 'other' in her discussion of films about Pakistan and, not necessarily as consciously, discusses the films as interventions in subcontinental political mindsets. Her memory of the scene in *Gadar* where the hero massacres scores of unknown Pakistani 'aggressors' may be in contrast to her use of the word 'neutral' about *Pinjar*, but her sense of the overwhelming narrative construction of Pakistan as a horrible place to be and Pakistanis as generally 'cruel, not having compassion' tie in with many critical readings of these films (Fazila-Yacoobali 2002; Sethi 2002; Vasudevan 2000). Sheba confirms that simple assertions about viewers 'making up their own minds' are inadequate in discussions of media representation. Clearly, viewers may well make up their own minds in the end, but what about the psychological damage that occurs when those being 'othered' watch this process day after day? And equally pertinently, given various concatenations of history and politics, when does textual propaganda, however diversely framed and interpreted, count as incitement to communal hatred?

Sheba articulates her critique of propagandist cross-border films in media terms, comparing sequences of Pakistani family life in *Gadar*, where evil is basically motiveless, with those in *Veer-Zaara*, where even unjust family authority in Pakistan is given emotional and psychological depth and rationale. However, the fact that one major depiction is better than the other should not prevent one from asking questions about other representations in *Veer-Zaara*. Mohsin, a fifteen year old British-Asian student in London says, 'Why is the Indian family in *Veer-Zaara* so much fun and so loving and the Pakistani one so strict and unhappy? Who causes all the problems in the film?' So, one is prompted to ask, when will we see a Hindi blockbuster where the secular, modern hero's family is Pakistani and Muslim, and the loyal heroine a devout Hindu girl from this side of the border resisting her authoritarian village?

However, in honour of the melodramatic and sentimental pleasures made possible by these films, I close this section with a brief quote from Firdos, a twenty-one year old rickshaw driver in Bombay, with whom I got chatting as we listened to film music. It is fitting that in his last sentence he conflates the actors and their characters, implying perhaps that by playing characters who blur exclusive nationalist constructions, these two stars contribute to changes in off-screen politics:

> Firdos (in Hindi): It was all about humanity [*insaaniyat*]. For me the best films, like *Veer-Zaara*, they tell something not about men or women, not about money, but about humanity. After I watch such a film, I do not feel inferior that I never went to school. I do not cry everyday because my mother and my father are dead. I feel like any person can make a difference in this world, like Shahrukh and Priety.

## Conclusion

Nations and boundaries dominate the imagination, even the modern, supposedly globalised imagination of the 'transnational' intelligentsia. For some, thinking of themselves as belonging not to a tribe or a territory, a religion or a nation can be destabilising—even impossible. For others, the mention of borders, whether real or symbolic, always conjures an urge to step across and explore. This is as much the case with sexual and ethnic identity as it is with national identity and films may provide a safe yet exciting mechanism for such imaginary journeys. Viewers responding to *Veer-Zaara* and *Gadar* don't simply move backwards and forwards along a spectrum in terms of their thinking about themselves and the 'other', Indians and Pakistanis, 'back home' and the UK, but actually move unexpectedly and tangentially as if in a web of ideas, constructing as well as expressing their identities through talk. Within this context of constant positioning and repositioning *vis-à-vis* the interviewer and the films, many associations made by viewers do appear, as Chakravarty conjectures, to use the films as imaginary contexts or pretexts in ways that resist, ironise or deconstruct as much as they acknowledge, and shore up 'nationalist imaginings'. As usual, however, there appear to be some aspects of these films that do not yield themselves up easily to playful deconstruction.

At a *textual level,* it should be noted that, even at their best, *certain sequence*s in a number of Hindi films dealing with India and Pakistan invite some viewers to think of themselves as 'other' in order to keep watching with pleasure; while, at their worst, they have to be understood, among other things, as contributions to authoritarian or ethnic supremacist ideologies which, off-screen, have resulted in violence and death. Nevertheless, all the viewers interviewed negotiate meaning from an intersection of identity positions, *via* myths and experiences, calling on their own knowledge, beliefs, understanding of family or community opinion, and media consumption. Some of them do use Hindi film imaginaries as invitations to nationalist, fascist or humanitarian sentiment. As such, they use them as a means for shoring up pre-existing beliefs and worldviews, confirming or undermining suspicions about 'the other'. Other viewers use these same sequences as a means for critiquing and challenging current social norms and contexts, and therein lies much of their enjoyment as fans. Yet others engage pleasurably in multimodal aspects of films such as music, dance and romance, while remaining aloof from narratives that implicitly construct some religions or nations as 'other'. In this context, it is important to ask what censorship or banning of these films hope to achieve, and whether censorship is indeed the right path to take.

Finally, then, following the questioning of the theorising of meaning as transparent, unitary and immanent in cross-border Hindi romances, some tentative answers have been offered. Contradicting a view of the cinema-going public as basically apolitical and interested in 'mindless entertainment', *Veer-Zaara, Gadar,* and other films on terrorism or national security such as *Sarfarosh, Mission Kashmir* and *Border,* are frequently introduced by young viewers *in the context of* discussions of modern politics. Based on evidence gathered through extended conversations and interviews with viewers of these films in two countries, this chapter has argued the need for an understanding of Hindi film spectatorship as being heterogeneous, psychologically contradictory and always emotionally engaged—whether through individual or altruistic fantasies and critiques. Such spectatorship is also always built around the potential of texts to be read as fragmentary and internally divergent, articulating radical positions at odds with their own (frequently socially retrograde) dominant discourses but also inviting complex—and threatening—pleasures through fleeting or more extended participation in compelling 'reactionary' ideological positions and equally compelling 'anti-authoritarian' personal ones. Nevertheless, just because restricted textual representations and discourses do not force or entail psychic closure for audiences does not mean that we should not call for meanings to be more open, for commercial Hindi films to cover a greater range of imaginaries and possibilities, and for them to incorporate the critiques of viewers from a range of perspectives.

## Notes

1. *In The Hindustan Times* (20 November 2003) Saibal Chatterjee writes, 'It is no coincidence that all these films deal...with the perfidies of Pakistan while singing paeans to the courage and commitment of India's brave young soldiers.... A pliant mass media is exactly what the purveyors of Hindutva [the then BJP government and their allied organisations] or an intolerant, exclusivist line of thinking—need, to propagate their world view and keep hatred and distrust of Pakistan on the boil.'
2. This notion that the government 'favours minorities' is a common complaint made by 'common-sense' sympathisers of the Hindu right with regard to Muslims and the lower castes in India.
3. However naïve it may be to imagine that all viewers struggle to find balanced political outlooks and information about society from the films they watch, it is equally absurd and politically reactionary to think that a majority simply acquiesce to propaganda without questioning it. Scepticism may not lead to radical political action, but my research suggests that amongst working-class viewers, as Ismail implies, it is at least as prevalent as jingoistic patriotism.

# Interviews

# 12

# Aijaz Gul on Cinema in Pakistan: History, Present Scenario and Future Prospects

## Interviewed by Arshad Amanullah*

*[Hailing from a family of film exhibitors, Aijaz Gul is the leading film critic and historian of Pakistan. He has been writing on films for the last eighteen years in the Pakistani as well as foreign media, and has three books on cinema to his credit. Gul was the last managing director of the now defunct government-run National Film Development Corporation of Pakistan. The interview took place on the sidelines of the recently concluded Osian-Cinefan Film Festival, and has been edited for the purposes of this book.]*

**A**rshad Amanullah: Why is Lollywood, Pakistan's once thriving film industry, now in terminal decline?

Aijaz Gul: Well, the Pakistani film industry has enjoyed a boom after Independence. The fact is that the film industry in Lahore didn't come into being in 1947. Lahore was a thriving capital of films, especially Punjabi films, and many notable filmmakers were working there before 1947. Pakistan's first film, *Teri Yaad*, actually started before Independence but was released in 1948. It was directed by Dawood. It was a very bad film but it made the beginning. There were so many people who sacrificed their glowing careers in Mumbai in late forties and migrated to Pakistan. Some of the notable people who came from Mumbai to Lahore were Noorjahan, Shaukat Hussain Rizvi, Sohan Lata, Nazeer, and Nisar Bazmi. Likewise, many people left Lahore for Mumbai. So, that was the eventuality of Partition. After the independence of Bangladesh in 1971, cinemas that were in what we used to call East Pakistan are of course not with us anymore. Cinemas in Pakistan, at least in metros, are located at the very choicest places.

So, with the passage of years, the value of property has increased. And with alternatives like cable, DVDs, CDs, and amusement parks, people now have other options. So cinema-going is facing a crisis. We now have about 500 cinemas and almost half of them are not working regularly. Piracy has no limits. Indian films are sometimes available here even prior to their release in India. You know, today's Hindi is very close to Urdu. So when you have so many Indian films in a language that is spoken in Pakistan, Urdu films have suffered. But interestingly, twenty-five Pashto films were produced last year, more than the average of ten to twelve earlier. Maybe the reason is that India [*laughs*] has not produced Pashto films. There is a saying that if Americans spoke Spanish, Britain would have a film industry, and I say, if India spoke Persian, Pakistan would have a film industry.

AA: Why does Lollywood, in terms of technology and expertise, lag behind Bollywood?

AG: When the times were good, people invested in film-related activities. Now, when we are facing a lean time, obviously the people who are in the film trade have shied away. The tragic part is that all those people who took the industry across decades after Independence have passed away. So when the production rate is not very high and the box-office ratio is very poor, then, of course, there is no investment in equipment.

AA: But where is the new generation?

AG: The new generation is definitely there but I just want to mention some very notable directors like Anwar Kamal Pasha, who was a total filmmaker. He was the first filmmaker in the early fifties who directed, produced and scripted films like *Do Aansu*, *Gumnam*, *Qatil*, and *Anarkali*. He was, in a way, the first Pakistani director. Then, there were rebellious filmmakers like Riaz Shahid and Khalil Qaisar, who made films against British imperialism.

AA: Rebellious in what sense?

AG: Khalil Qaisar was rebellious because he was against corruption in the political system, whether it was the British Raj or the Pakistani government. Riaz Shahid was a writer and also became a director but essentially he was collaborating with director Khalil Qaisar. Tanveer Naqvi was their lyricist, Faiz Ahmed Faiz their poet and Rasheed Attre their music composer. So it was a whole team. Riaz Shahid kept on writing against the vices of the system and the curruption in the establishment.

AA: They used different countries as the background of their films?

AG: Yes. They took the subject of Palestine, Andalus, Kashmir. *Shaheed* deals with British corruption in the Middle East. Khalil Qaisar did not live long. He made *Shaheed*, *Farangi*, *Nagan*, *Haveli*, and two or three more films, and passed away in a very tragic way. So, Riaz Shahid took over and did continue with his revolutionary scripts and films. His film *Zarqa* deals with the independence of Palestine, *Gharnata* with Muslims in Spain and *Yeh Amn* with Kashmir. He died in 1972. As he had to face serious problems with the censor board, many people think that he died becaue of the system. His son Shaan, who is now a leading man in films, says: '*Mere baap ko cancer ne nahin, censor ne maara*' (My father was killed not by cancer but by the censor).

AA: Would you say that they wanted to glorify the Muslim past?

AG: In a way, yes. Riaz Shahid wanted to do that time and again. But he also made films like *Gunahgaar*, which takes place in Pakistan. It deals with treason and corruption.

AA: How did he deal with ordinary people, the masses of Pakistan?

AG: Well, *Clerk* would be a good example of a film that deals with the poverty of an ordinary clerk who resists corruption, bribery and palm-greasing, and who lives by his own rules. But he is consistently bugged by his wife who wants more and more material goods; eventually he develops tuberculosis. That was a good subject, but didn't do very well at the box-office because it was very sad and grim.

AA: How did the ban on Hindi films in Pakistan affect Lollywood?

AG: There was a time when over a hundred films were produced in Pakistan and were doing very well. Indian films were being released every month. Cinemas in Pakistan were enjoying the boom in the sixties. Shortly after the second Indo-Pak war, Indian films were banned in Pakistan. Cinema owners didn't raise their voices against the ban because they benifitted economically and Pakistani films were doing very well then. All the filmmakers who had laid the foundation of Pakistani cinema, and their patrons, have now passed away, the number of films has reduced and the quality has gone down. Only twenty-five Urdu and Pujabi films were produced last year; so the cinemas are falling short of films. Thus, the exhibitors are right in asking to lift the ban. I think umbrella protection has had its ill-effects.

AA: There is tremendous demand for Indian films in Pakistan. So why does the government of Pakistan not lift the ban?

AG: You do know that filmmaking is not just art and technology. It's also a big business. The government of Pakistan knows this, and wants to make it as a part of trade or maybe is waiting for still better times when people are even closer.

AA: Is there any chance of collaboration between Bollywood and Lollywood?

AG: The prime minister of Pakistan met the members of the film industry on 13 June and said that he was all for collaboration between India, Pakistan, Bangladesh, Iran, Nepal, and Sri Lanka. I think India and Pakistan are joining hands indirectly. Some of the good Pakistani films that have been produced in recent years have collaborated with India for their production and post-production. They have used Indian singers: Udit Narayan, Kumar Shanu, and Kavita Krishnamurthy. For choreography, Indian art directors have been hired. So I think co-production, collaboration, is already taking place.

AA: What similarity do you find in the cinemas of India and Pakistan?

AG: In India, there are Hindi films and there are regional films. I've been enjoying art films by directors like Shyam Benegal and Satyajit Ray. But films which are being produced today in Mumbai, many of them are banal: they lack subtlety and common sense, their scripts are weak, so is their imagination and their aesthetic values. An educated and intelligent person looks for these things in a good film. However, Bollywood movies are rich in music, production values, cinematography, and editing. They are big in terms of budgeting and casting. because superstars have their own appeal. Average viewers are carried away by all these gimmicks. They do not go into the *script ki baarikiyaan* (nuances of the script), but just enjoy the music, the actresses and the witty dialogues, and like to forget their troubles for those two and a half hours. Interestingly, Bollywood flicks are more popular in Pakistan than Lollywood productions, because Hindi films are technically superior to their Lollywood counterparts. Another reason is that cinemas of both countries have the same ingredients of dance and song, comedy, marriage, parents, the system, and the police. So, like an Indian viewer, an average Pakistani also gets pleasure from these melodramatic contents.

AA: How will the exchange of artists shape the film industries of both countries?

AG: There is a fear in Pakistan that if Pakistani artists go to work in Bollywood, they will be swallowed by the industry and will lose their identity, their star value, and hence their bargaining power. But I don't subscribe to the opinion, because, for one thing, its true that Sawan Kumar gave a very small role to Talat Hussain in *Sautan Ki Beti*. Likewise, Manoj Kumar invited Zeba and Muhammad Ali to Mumbai to work in his production *Clerk*, and their roles were very brief. But these are petty matters and we should not be talking about them. Hats off to Mahesh Bhatt because Meera is seen in *Nazar* from beginning to end. In fact, I would say [*laughs*] Mahesh Bhatt should have reduced her role. However, it's a very average film and the subject is not very original. I think nobody should worry about small roles or insignificant contributions. Let's make a beginning.

AA: How has Lahore reacted to the anti-Pakistan films churned out by Bollywood?

AG: Well, this reminds me of President Musharraf, who, in one of his interactions with journalists from India and Pakistan, said [*laughs*]: 'No more entire Pakistani films. I expect that you would not make those films anymore.' But India, as an independent country, has the right to make the kinds of films the filmmakers want to make. However, they should care about their customers and audiences in Pakistan, and they should start making films differently from what they have done in *LOC—Kargil*, *Gadar*, *Maa Tujhe Salaam*, etc. Pakistan has also made India-negative films like *Tere Pyar Mein*, *Ghar Kab Aaoge* and *Ladki Punjaban*. Neighbouring country bashing might momentarily get cheap claps from the front-benchers but it's friendship which helps in long run. We have to live together as the former prime minister Vajpayee said; you can change friends but you can't change neighbours. So, we must work together into the future.

AA: What are the stereotypes generally seen in Pakistani cinema?

AG: There are many hackneyed characters. There are stereotypical mothers, fathers and dialogues, also found in Indian films, like:

'*Ye shaadi nahin ho sakti* (This wedding cannot take place).' There are stereotypical, formulaic situations. Stereotypical lawyers, judges and courts. I was impressed by Yash Chopra in *Veer-Zaara*. I applaud him for making this film, the right move at the right time. But there were certain things, especially the climax sequence which unfolds in the court, which could have been done differently.

AA: Does Lollywood have stereotypes along ethnic lines?

AG: Yes, speaking of the North-west Frontier Province, there is an actor called Badar Muneer who has been working in films since 1970; he just could not step out of what he has been doing for the last thirty-five years. Sometimes he is brought into Urdu films as a Pathan who speaks Urdu and, of course, with his own accent and delivery. So we have those stereotypes.

AA: To what extent can the Kara International Film Festival, which has already seen four successful years, contribute in creating a quality film culture in Pakistan?

AG: There are upcoming filmmakers who are making films on digitals. Hassan Zaidi, Bilal Minto, Faisal Rehman, and Mehjabeen Jabbar are just a few names. Their works *Javed Champu, Raat Chali Jhum Ke, Beauty Parlour*, etc., stand testimony to the fact that these new filmmakers, are the future assets for Pakistan. n spite of having budget restraints, they are making good films. The Kara Film Festival, Which has been held every December for the last four years, has been providing them a platform to show their work, and let me tell you that the Festival has been making maximum efforts to bring in Bollywood celebrities. In future, it would be a joint launching pad for Indian and Pakistani filmmakers.

AA: Do you have magazines that publish serious stuff about cinema?

AG: Yes, we have specific film magazines and we also have film editions in very distinguished national dailies. *Dawn*, *News* and *Nation* have weekly film supplements. All major Urdu dailies like *Nawa-e-Waqt* and *Jung*, and then weeklies like *Akhbar-e-Jahan* have film sections. *Noor Jahan* and *Nigar*, both from Karachi and *Filmi Parcha* edited by Tariq Lodhi from Lahore are weekly magazines that deal exclusively with films. But serious film criticism is lacking and we need to work on that. Just anyone with a degree in journalism is not necessarily qualified to write on films. I think you should be thoroughly trained in film history and film appreciation and only then should you write on films.

AA: What concerted efforts are being made to promote a vibrant film culture in Pakistan?

AG: Well, in the last three years, there has been a revolution in the media. New TV channels and radio stations are coming up in the private sector. There is a mass communication department in Fatima Jinnah University for women. These young ladies are making short films on very challeging subjects as part of their curriculum. Geo Television of Jung Group, the National College of Arts and many other institutes are coming up in Lahore and Karachi, with courses in films. So a beginning has already been made. Students are already making films with very modest budgets. Hopefully, in two or three years, they will be in the market and will be shown in festivals.

* This is an edited version of the interview. For the original, see http://osdir.com/ml/ culture.india.sarai.reader/2005–08/msg 00112.html

# 13

# Guftagu:
# M.S. Sathyu, Javed Akhtar, Mahesh Bhatt

## Interviewed by Tavishi Alagh

*[Tavishi Alagh, a young filmmaker who has recently made a film on Bombay cinema, the critically acclaimed Bollywood Crossings, met three of the most significant names in Hindi cinema who have been associated with the country across the LOC. M. S. Sathyu, the maker of the poignant Partition film, Garam Hawa; Javed Akhtar, articulate scriptwriter and lyricist for many a 'border' film; and Mahesh Bhatt, filmmaker with ties of blood and soul with Pakistan, all come out with their innermost responses to the issue of 'Pakistan' in Indian films.]*

## M. S. Sathyu

Tavishi Alagh: How has the presence of Pakistan changed in Hindi films? Is it typically a backdrop?

M. S. Sathyu: Minorities in Hindi films are caricatured, be they Marwaris, Sindhis, Muslims, Christians, Parsees, foreigners, Pakistanis. Very occasionally, we do have films that look at minority communities in a real and holistic way, treating them as normal people—good and bad with their own distinct customs and culture, but typically they are caricatured. There is some attempt to change this attitude, let's see what happens....

In the nineties, when the communal party was in power [the BJP], there were a series of disturbing films. Films like *Gadar, Border, Refugee,* and *Sarfarosh* were highly prejudiced and especially disturbing because, in the guise of being patriotic, they were anti-Pakistan. In the process they also become anti-Muslim. This is a big distortion being purported by these films. They condemn Muslims.

There is a large communal element in our film industry, even though it may not seem so outwardly. People see that so many big heroes are Khans, many of the big Muslim stars are married to Hindu girls or Hindu stars married to Muslim girls. So while it's great that there is an acceptance of all of that, that fact is not enough in itself. Sometime back someone wrote that they were disturbed by the name Gauri Khan. Nowadays, due to the open communal agenda, Muslims are also becoming more fundamentalist even in India. The Hindu majority is a reality. We have to learn to live together, minorities cannot stay aloof and apart from the majority; we must live together in mutual respect and our films should reflect that.

The largest population of Muslims in the world lives in India, over thirteen crores. India was ruled by the Mughals for over six generations. Many Hindus converted because it was politically expedient and beneficial to do so. In Kerala, the population is equally divided between Hindus, Muslims and Christians. Traders brought Islam to Kerala but it came in a peaceful way.

TA: Are you saying there is another reality that is not being exploited?

MSS: Yes. There is a people-to-people reality. In Madras, there was an India Pakistan match. Pakistan won the match. One Pakistani player broke a cricketing record—the entire stadium stood up, to applaud him. This is also a reality. Why don't people talk about this? To me, Pakistan is a very friendly nation. I only wish sometime India-Pakistan-Bangladesh are re-united. I know it's a dream, but then we would be the most powerful country in Asia.

TA: I think that the Pakistanis see it differently...

MSS: Well it's a nation without democracy, where you have the rule of the army. They have not grown, we have, they are not self reliant, we are. We are an indigenous economy...

TA: Which is changing...

MSS: Yes, the politicians today are without any imagination. We became a nation because of the vision of leaders like Jawaharlal Nehru, who thought thirty years ahead and focused on self-reliance. We have taken to the American way of hire-purchase—you pay but you don't own. You buy without cash in hand. We have not put in money into public transport, into infrastructure to support these cars that it's become easy to buy. I remember in Mysore, when I was growing up; apart from the king, three families owned cars.

TA: Tell me about *Garam Hawa*. What was the journey you were trying to weave? The fact that there is a political impact to your work? Does it change your journey?

MSS: Since 1947, for almost twenty-five years, no one attempted a movie on this subject. There were people in the film industry, refugees who were rehabilitated in India, but they did not make any film or Partition, probably because it hit a raw nerve.

Partition did not touch my life. I was a student in Mysore at the time, I had just finished school. I had no idea of the widespread trauma. Partition was an artificial division, a few feudals and some misguided leaders took this decision. It was a theoretical division of India, it did not take into account real human beings, families whose lives changed radically due to this division. The Muslim family in my film is shown to have been destroyed through Partition.

Earlier films located themselves in the world of the aristocracy, with Mughal kings or feudal landlords. Ordinary Muslim reality was not represented. As a community in a democracy, Muslims have their own way of living. Some of our best craftsmen are Muslim, some of our best mechanics are Muslims from Hyderabad.

I do attribute a lot to a certain political philosophy. I have been with the left movement in India, with the Indian People's Theatre Association for over thirty years. I am a Hindu by birth, my wife is a Muslim by birth and, though I am an atheist, we celebrate all festivals equally, Diwali, Eid or Christmas.

Shama[1] wrote the screenplay for the film. However, Kaifi Saab[2] made a vital change, he introduced the whole business of shoemaking. In the state of Uttar Pradesh, in towns like Agra and Kanpur, Muslims ran a flourishing leather industry, pre-Independence. Hindus wouldn't trade in leather, only untouchable Hindus would work with leather, so the protagonist's business was shoes. Kaifi Saab had worked with labour unions in Kanpur and he gave another dimension to the whole story. Balraj Sahni was so enthused by the end of the film that at the conclusion of shooting he organised a strike among the shoe factory workers of Agra demanding better wages.

I made the film accidentally. I did not make the film with a target audience in mind. I had given in another idea that was rejected. However, NFDC agreed to this idea. I made the film with 2.5 lacs. It was hard shooting the film in UP, the atmosphere there is very volatile and the crowds disturb you very easily. This is as true today as it was then. Look at what happened to Deepa Mehta's film *Water*. Today, when the nation is so confused, people get swayed by elements that create mass hysteria. When shooting on location in Agra, we were so harassed by bystanders, we had to divert them with a fake second unit using an unloaded camera!

We shot the film in a Hindu house but we changed it into a Muslim house.

TA: Talking about changes, could you tell me a little about them?

MSS: A lot had to be changed to create the ambience of a Muslim home. The colours that are used are brighter, the vessels are made of aluminium as opposed to brass, the shapes are different, the sheets have different designs, the colours are different, and wooden chics are used—that little bit of *purdah*. Also Muslim homes have a *paandaan* and *ughaal daan*.[3] With actors, I underplay, I try to see each character inwardly, and my actors are never loud. So, I believe, they are more effective emotionally.

TA: How was the film received?

MSS: The film was held up at the censors for eight months due to its politically sensitive theme. Then the film was first released in the South. Indira Gandhi [the prime minister of India in 1974], said let the opposition not think that we are trying to influence the Muslim vote, so we delayed the release of the film in the North. It was received very well. It got great reviews and was a commercial success at the box office. A lot of people from Pakistan also really appreciated the film, and it was often invited overseas as well. I travelled with it to France, twice. It was also nominated for an Oscar, but I couldn't go as I did not think it right to approach Air India again for a third free ticket.

## Javed Akhtar

Tavishi Alagh: Do you feel the representation of Pakistan has changed in Hindi films?

Javed Akhtar: I think *Prem Pujari*[4] (1970) is the first film that touched the subject but it did not go down well with the audiences. People associated with the film needed to pin down a reason for the failure of the film and they wrongly attributed it to Indian Muslims not liking Pakistan-bashing! This was an incorrect analysis; and this was proven by the success of *Haqeeqat* and, more recently, *Border*. It takes more than the subject of a film to dictate its success or failure. The treatment of that subject, good music, good acting, a good screenplay is what determines its success. However, that unfortunate overlap started way back then. I never felt the slightest resentment in the Muslim audience after *Prem Pujari*.

In some films, Pakistan and Muslim identity do overlap. *Gadar* (2001) is a good example of that. Implicitly, Hindu identity and Indian identity are seen as one and the same thing. That is a very limited articulation of Indian Identity. In the nineties, a difficult time communally, some films were very careless, and preached a wrong morality. Three things were happening: some filmmakers were making mistakes—unintentionally. Some were very careful about the times and took care not to step into areas that could create trouble, and then there were others who were deliberately stoking a certain kind of religious/jingoistic passion.

Today, our audiences have matured. Today, you cannot win an election based on people's religious affiliations. Indians do not want their sentiments to be exploited for communal gain.

TA: In what ways do your personal experience, your identity and your artistry overlap?

JA: Language is very powerful in creating an identity, more so than religion, because while religious identity may define you when you are awake, language stays with you in your dreams; it defines your unconscious, stays with you even when you are sleep. I would say language is a defining marker for a writer, a poet. However, you are always a collage of different identities. Loyalties are very interesting in that way, they have layers. You might criticize your city amongst your own, but if an outsider says something about Mumbai it hurts. You have multiple affiliations, no one has a single-point identity. I am from Lucknow, I am Urdu-speaking, I am writer, I am an Indian, I am Muslim, I am from Bombay. As a North Indian Muslim, an Urdu-speaking writer from Lucknow, I identify more closely with an Urdu-speaking person from that region, say, a Ramesh Srivastava, a Hindu from Awadh than with a Muslim from Tamil Nadu or an Arab Muslim.

Ironically, riots take place because there is not enough communalism, in that there is not enough of a sense of difference between people, so riots are engineered, to create that sense of difference and bracket people. It's an attempt at a narrower recasting. When there is a threat of violence against you because you belong to one or the other community, then in sharing the same threat an identity is engineered and created. In that moment of experiencing a threat, you become limited to a single identity.

Over the last sixty years, we have created an Indian identity. I feel proud when someone from Bengal or Assam gets the Nobel Prize. If a person from India is put down in a foreign country I feel angry. Ultimately, it's because we have internalised this identity. I was in Pakistan in 1999 and I met with a Mr Bhagawandas, a member of the national assembly there. And it's strange but I felt very protective and concerned about him, I sought him out, feeling, 'I hope he is doing well, I hope he is all right over there.' So it's complicated.

In *Lakshya* we had the character of Major Jalal Akbar, an Indian Muslim officer who intercepts a call by a Pakistani officer who tries to get friendly with him through their shared religious identity; and the Major responds with '*Tumhare liye main sirf ek hindustani hoon*'. (*For you, I am only an Indian*).

TA: Would you speak more about *Lakshya*?

JA: When I went to Ladakh and Bada Ladakh, I met the soldiers on the front and I was moved by their experiences. I found powerful stories, real life stories of courage and human endeavour. I was really very impressed by the dedication and focus of the men and women on the front. Then, I would see upper-middle-class youth in the metros, are they aware that there are duties, responsibilities as citizens? Through the film I wanted to bring them face to face with the soldier on the front. Why should we not tell the stories of our brave young men and women who retrieved a stolen front by making themselves cannon fodder because the enemy is Pakistan? You should not have to doctor a true story in order to be politically correct.

In the army they say if the enemy is at a height then the advantage is completely with the enemy. It was a vast open landscape with no cover. A soldier is visible from four miles. Our soldiers could be successfully shot at from a distance of two miles. In that situation how do you retrieve lost ground? Kargil is a true story, it happened, bunkers were captured, we did find artillery and weapons. It's also a fact that the bodies found there, were disowned by the neighbouring country.

Writers and poets are inspired by the world around them. War is a part of history and as such finds reflection in art and literature. Sadat Hassan Manto wrote a lot of short stories about prostitutes and a few times they brought him up on charges of spreading immoral writing...he said why don't you eradicate prostitution. So if people don't approve of war stories, eradicate war. When there is even a remote hope of reconciliation, common markets and open borders, such films are not made. Cease hostilities, and the treatment of Pakistan in our films changes.

TA: Does the language change when you write for Pakistani characters?

JA: The Pakistani characters in *Lakshya* were supposed to be mainly from Punjab, so they speak Urdu with a Punjabi accent. I am familiar with that Urdu, and so I maintained that diction. I did not use the Urdu spoken in Lucknow, which is distinct and different in terms of accent and the usage of certain words.

TA: Tell me a little about the experience of writing for a film like *Veer-Zaara*.

JA: If you write for Yash Chopra then that is a different experience because he has an ear for poetry and a sense for Urdu and language. So whether it was *Veer-Zaara* or *Silsila*, the songs were more poetic than what I would have written for the average Hindi film. After all, you must remember, Mr Chopra is also from Lahore. (*Laughs.*)

## Mahesh Bhatt

Tavishi Alagh: How has the treatment of Pakistan changed in Hindi films? Is Pakistan merely the Other in Hindi cinema?

Mahesh Bhatt: We are trying our best to call them the Other but in fact there is no dissimilarity between us. We belong to the same racial stock, we are the same people—it was just a family quarrel that turned into a bloodbath of gigantic proportions. Fifty-nine years, maps are redrawn, the Line of Control is lit up, you have demonised the neighbour, and the war industry is flourishing, yet in spite of the incessant war-mongering, you have failed to create distance of the heart, the people on both sides have the yearning to drop their guard. Some Pakistani films demonised us as well, but then some people love Indian products; their songs—their music—becomes more successful when routed through India. My film *Zakhm* was hugely popular there. Our stars like Shah Rukh Khan are hugely popular. The twenty-eight-year-old Pakistani TV icon, Ali Begum Nawazish, says he owes everything to Bollywood films. All their entertainment inputs are from India. Our cultural products have saturated their terrain, including our television. And this is because they relate easier to our TV products. So entertainment products reveal much more, they articulate the aspirations of the people.

Today, it's not possible to go back to some unbroken time in the past, but while maintaining a separation, we should stress on our similarities. When a Hindu classical '*raag*' is sung by a Pakistani singer, it sounds the same. When Indian actors portray Pakistani characters you cannot tell the difference, and that is because the differences are cosmetic. There have been some associations that are limiting and faulty. For example, India/Bharat is equal to Hindu is equal to Hindi. Or that Pakistan is equal to Islam is equal to Urdu.

TA: Is their any slippage between your personal experience and your artistry?

MB: I went to Pakistan post-9/11, and post-Godhra and the Gujarat riots. I found it an exhilarating experience, as I was able to connect with a part of myself. I guess I have always been more of a mother's child, so my Muslim self found an Islamic resonance, so that I truly got to enjoy in Pakistan. The Muslim, the world over, is stifled. The Indian Muslim was living frightened, terrorised deep within himself after Godhra. There [in Pakistan] he is a man in his own home. You can tell from the body language. It is different. We are an aspiring secular country. They are an aspiring Islamic country. Pakistan is still struggling to be born. It is the cursed child. [In India,] we do not have inclusive growth. Muslim identity cannot be severed from India; they scream out, we want our share of the sun, we want representation. The government has failed the Muslims. It hasn't delivered what was promised. Muslims need to be given what was promised.

I love Karachi; I felt a great sense of ease, an extraordinary emotional high. One cannot claim the whole of oneself while denying a part of oneself. There is a Hindu in every Muslim and a Muslim in every Hindu. This region has been a melting pot through time so there is a mimetic learning, and it shows in the similar body language and nuances. I have great personal friends there, Hamid Haroun, the CEO of *Dawn,* is a great friend. A part of me that is stunted and stifled here is in full bloom there, yet that part of the whole is poorer for it doesn't have the presence of Hindu cultural influences. My Muslim part is impoverished over here.

TA: What are you doing to bridge this gap?

MB: We are trying to create a mood, an environment for people to step forward, I spur people to change. We need a private *moksha* [spiritual liberation], we need Buddhist ideology, we need social concern, a concern for social suffering. I am doing a lot of work with Pakistan. I am a regular visitor to the Kara film festival, I think of myself as a self appointed ambassador. I want to work with like-minded people, to help people in Pakistan who have talent to access larger markets, education, and infrastructure.

The intellectual community in Pakistan is ready for a major leap. I am working on a film with all Pakistani actors and technicians, to give a voice to Pakistan in the world!

# Notes

1. Shama Zaidi, noted screenplay writer, is also married to the filmmaker. They have two daughters.
2. Kaifi Azmi, the poet and lyricist. Father of well known actor Shabana Azmi.
3. Spitoons
4. Dev Anand's directorial debut, the film shows Dev Anand as a man who abhors violence and initially refuses to join the armed forces, but has to bow to his father's wishes. He finds himself in the thick of things, when he sees the enemy working against the country's interests. Leaving his beloved, Waheeda Rehman, behind, he goes abroad, to unveil the conspiracy and befriends Zahida, the enemy's moll. Waheeda follows him but is dejected seeing him with Zahida. In time, Dev also comes back and is engulfed in a full scale war to defeat the enemy.

# Filmography

*16 December—All Forces Alert* (2002)
Producers: Anjali Joshi and Arunima Roy; Director: Mani Shankar; Cast: Danny Denzongpa, Gulshan Grover, Milind Soman, Dipannita Sharma, Shushant Singh, Aditi Gowitrikar.

A couple of Indian military officers are removed from service for killing a corrupt officer among them. They are later requisitioned by the Indian army to trace the transfer of millions of dollars with security implications. It comes to light that the money is being transferred to a terrorist organisation which is helping Pakistani officers who were unhappy with Pakistan's decision to surrender in 1971, and who are now plotting revenge by exploding an atom bomb. The Indian military officers (the protagonists) work overtime to save India from that catastrophe.

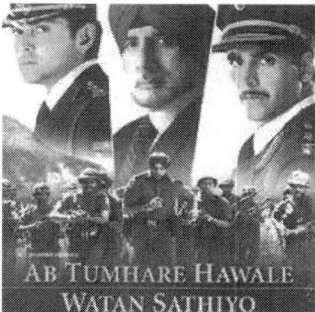

*Ab Tumhare Hawale Watan Sathiyo* (The Nation in Your Hands) (2004)
Producer and Director: Anil Sharma; Cast: Amitabh Bachchan, Akshaye Kumar, Bobby Deol, Divya Khosla, Sandali Sinha.

The film is about Kunal (Bobby Deol), the grandson of Amitabh Bachchan, an army officer whose son (again, Bobby Deol) had died fighting in the Indian army. When Kunal wants to leave the army to go abroad and earn lots of money, his father is disheartened. Kunal falls in love with a woman who is already married to an army officer missing in action and held in Pakistan as a prisoner of war (Akshaye Kumar). The story then moves towards Kunal's heroic efforts to get Rajeev (Akshaye Kumar) back to his wife.

### *Amar Akbar Anthony* (1977)

Producer and director: Manmohan Desai; Cast: Amitabh Bachchan, Vinod Khanna, Rishi Kapoor, Parveen Babi, Shabana Azmi, Neetu Singh.

A typical Manmohan Desai film, with a lost-and-found plot. A criminal on the run is separated from his wife (who becomes blind); their three sons are adopted and reared separately by a Hindu, Muslim and Catholic Christian. They meet as adults after a series of incredible plot twists.

### *Asoka* (2001)

Producers: Shahrukh Khan and Juhi Chawla; Director: Santosh Sivan; Cast: Shahrukh Khan, Juhi Chawla, Kareena Kapoor, Milind Soman.

A fictional story of Asoka, a great Mauryan ruler of ancient India. In the film, Asoka falls in love with Princess Kaurwaki. When he believes her dead, he goes on a bloodthirsty rampage, becoming a brutal conqueror. Around the same time, he has married a Buddhist healer, who plants in his mind the seeds of his eventual conversion to Buddhism.

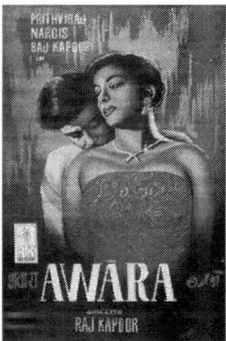

### *Awara* (The Vagabond) (1951)

Producer and director: Raj Kapoor; Cast: Raj Kapoor, Nargis, Prithviraj Kapoor, K. N. Singh, Leela Chitnis, Shashi Kapoor.

The first Raj Kapoor film to feature his trademark Chaplinesque persona, to be repeated in almost all his subsequent films. Raj (the protagonist) has grown up on the streets. His mother was evicted from her home (on mistaken suspicion of infidelity) by her rich and short-tempered judge husband (played by

Prithviraj Kapoor, who is also Raj Kapoor's real-life father). Raj falls in love with his childhood sweetheart who is now under the legal guardianship of his own father, who does all to separate the lovers. Roaming the streets like a vagabond, he finds shelter with a criminal (K. N. Singh), who he later discovers is responsible for his mother's misfortune. So Kapoor kills him and (booked for murder) is produced in his own father's court. His love interest Rita (played by Nargis) defends him as his lawyer. Raj is sent to jail and Rita decides to wait for him.

### *Border* (1997)

Producer and director: J. P. Dutta; Cast: Sunny Deol, Jackie Shroff, Akshaye Khanna, Kulbhushan Kharbanda, Pooja Bhatt, Tabu.

The film focuses on the Battle of Longewala on the Indo-Pak border in Rajasthan, during the India–Pakistan war of 1971. A small contingent of 120 troops, led by Sunny Deol, guards the Indian border against the mighty Pakistani attack led by tanks. The emphasis in the film is on the futility of war.

*Bose—The Forgotten Hero*. See *Netaji Subhas Chandra Bose—The Forgotten Hero*.

### *Chameli* (2004)

Producer: Pritish Nandy Communications; Director: Sudhir Mishra; Cast: Kareena Kapoor, Rahul Bose.

When Rahul Bose loses his pregnant wife in a car crash, he gets depressed and resorts to smoking and drinking. One night he meets a hardened and wronged prostitute Chameli, and they make efforts to help each other recover from the mess they are in.

*Deewaar* (The Wall) (1975)

Producer: Gulshan Rai; Director: Yash Chopra; Cast: Amitabh Bachchan, Shashi Kapoor, Parveen Babi, Neetu Singh, Nirupa Roy.

This iconic film is about two brothers, one a smuggler and another a police officer, who clash because of they are on opposing sides of the law. While the smuggler (played by Amitabh Bachchan) is fighting to avenge the humiliation suffered by his trade-unionist father, the police officer brother (played by Shashi Kapoor) bats for morality. It is the access to their mother that is hyped in the film and the fact that, despite being wronged, the mother sides with the law-abiding son.

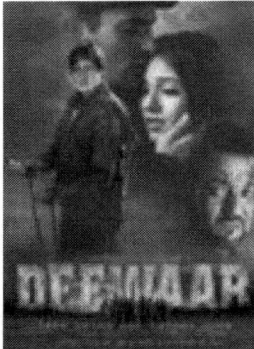

*Deewaar* (The Wall) (2004)

Producer: Gaurang Doshi; Director: Milan Luthria; Cast: Amitabh Bachchan, Akshaye Khanna, Sanjay Dutt, Amrita Rao.

Thirty Indian POWs (prisoners of war, along with their commanding officer Amitabh Bachchan) are in a Pakistani jail since the 1971 war. Some thirty-three years later, Amitabh's son Akshaye Khanna decides to rescue his father and the others. He goes to Pakistan and is helped in this mission by Khan, an ex-prisoner, played by Sanjay Dutt.

*Dev* (2004)

Producer and director: Govind Nihalani; Cast: Amitabh Bachchan, Om Puri, Kareena Kapoor, Fardeen Khan.

Based during the Gujarat riots, this film is about the exploitation of Muslims at the hands of politicians and police officers, who are shown either casual or communal. When Fardeen Khan's liberal Muslim father and believer in non-violence is killed by police officer Dev (Amitabh Bachchan), Fardeen is goaded by a corrupt minister to incite communal violence. A love story with Kareena also unfolds alongside.

***Dil Chahta Hai*** (The Heart Desires) (2001)

Producers: Javed Akhtar and Chandan Sindwani; Director: Farhan Akhtar; Cast: Aamir Khan, Saif Ali Khan, Akshaye Khanna, Priety Zinta, Sonali Kulkarni, Dimple Kapadia.

A film that is unapologetic about the wealth and upscale lifestyle of India's upwardly mobile business class. Three guys have fun and live life to the fullest. Saif plays a character who falls in love with every girl he meets, Aamir believes in changing girlfriends every two weeks or so, and Akshaye does not believe in love. Eventually, all fall in love and how! One of the love stories in the film is very rare in Hindi films—a younger man falls in love with an older woman.

***Dil to Pagal Hai*** (The Heart is Crazy) (1997)

Producers: Yash Chopra and Mahen Vakil; Director: Yash Chopra; Cast: Shahrukh Khan, Madhuri Dixit, Karisma Kapoor, Akshaye Kumar.

A dance extravaganza and love story woven together. Dancer and choreographer Rahul (played by Shahrukh Khan) considers Nisha (Karisma Kapoor) to be the best dancer of his troupe and they are preparing for a great show. It is then that Nisha injures herself and Rahul has to look for another girl dancer. In the process, he finds Pooja (Madhuri Dixit). While Nisha secretly loves Rahul, he and Pooja fall in love during the rehearsals. Unfortunately, Pooja is engaged to Ajay (Akshaye Kumar), whose loving family had given her shelter when her parents had died in a car crash. Finally, Nisha and Ajay gracefully withdraw in order that Rahul and Pooja can become a couple.

***Dilwale Dulhania Le Jayenge*** (The One with the Heart will Take the Bride) (1995)

Producer: Yash Chopra; Director: Aditya Chopra; Cast: Shahrukh Khan, Kajol, Amrish Puri, Anupam Kher, Farida Jalal, Himani Shivpuri, Mandira Bedi, Parmeet Sethi.

This film started what we call now NRI (Non-Resident Indian) films, made to appeal to the nostalgia of Punjabi NRIs. It is the stuff peppy romances are made of. Raj (played by Shahrukh Khan) and Simran (played by Kajol) are Indians living in UK; they go separately on a Europe tour by rail, meet on the way and fall in love. But Simran's conservative father has already fixed her marriage to a village lad in Punjab; he insists on her travelling to Punjab with the family, so that the wedding can take place there. Raj too reaches the Punjab village and manages to win her father over by his charming ways.

*Earth 1947* (1988)

Producer: Anne Mason and Deepa Mehta; Director: Deepa Mehta; Cast: Aamir Khan, Rahul Khanna, Nandita Das, Shabana Azmi, Maia Sethna.

Based on an English-language novel (*Ice-Candy-Man*) written by Pakistani woman writer Bapsi Sidhwa, this film looks at Partition and religious fanaticism through the eyes of an eight year old Parsi girl, Lenny. Two Muslim boys, Dil Nawaz (played by Aamir Khan) and Hasan (played by Rahul Khanna) love Shanta, a Hindu woman who works as an *ayah* in Lenny's household, but the Partition and the bitter and violent Hindu–Muslim riots shatter all that. The film focuses on the way in which ordinary people can be transformed by brutal historical events.

*Fanaa* (Annihilation) (2006)

Producer: Yash Raj Films; Director: Kunal Kohli; Cast: Aamir Khan, Kajol, Rishi Kapoor, Kirron Kher, Jaspal Bhatti.

A hard-hitting film about a hardcore terrorist assigned to create trouble in India by his Pakistani masters. The film highlights the clash between his allegiance to the cause of Kashmiri separatism, and his love for his wife and son. The film directly mentions Pakistan as the country sponsoring terrorism in India

*Fire* (1996)

Producers: Bobby Bedi and Deepa Mehta; Director: Deepa Mehta; Cast: Shabana Azmi, Nandita Das, Kulbhushan Kharbanda, Ram Gopal Bajaj, Ranjit Chaudhary.

A strong cinematic statement in favour of women's right to express their sexuality, through the story of two women and their covert subversion of an orthodox Hindu family structure. Sita (played by Nandita Das) is married to a person who is in love with another woman and does not care for her. In the same family, the elder brother's wife, Radha (played by Shabana Azmi) is childless and feels sexually irrelevant after her husband loses interest in sex. The two female protagonists become attracted towards each other, get sexually involved and have to leave the family when their relationship is discovered.

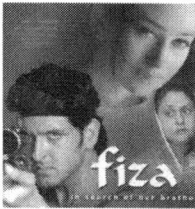

*Fiza* (2000)

Producers: Anjan Ghosh, Sanjay Bhattacharji, Pradeep Guha; Director: Khalid Mohamed; Cast: Hrithik Roshan, Karisma Kapoor, Neha, Asha Sachdev, Bikram Saluja, Isha Koppikar, Dinesh Thakur, Johnny Lever.

The film talks about the alienation of the average Muslim youth, who takes to the gun to snatch justice from the Indian state. Taken to be killed in the Mumbai riots of 1993, the young man's sister, after six years, suddenly sights him alive. She sets out in search of him, only to realise that he has become deeply involved in Pakistan-backed militant activities.

*Gadar—Ek Prem Katha* (Tumult—A Love Story) (2001)

Producer: Nitin Keni; Director: Anil Sharma; Cast: Sunny Deol, Ameesha Patel, Amrish Puri.

A major hit, this film is very loud in its opposition to the creation of Pakistan. This is the story of the love between a Sikh–Indian man and a Muslim–Pakistani girl. It highlights the problems faced by the couple when they meet with active opposition from the girl's father. This film is loaded with anti-Pakistan dialogue.

*Garam Hawa* (Hot Winds) (1973)

Producers: Ishan Arya, M. S. Sathyu and Abu Siwani; Director: M. S. Sathyu; Cast: Balraj Sahni, Farooq Shaikh, A. K. Hangal, Gita Siddharth, Shaukat Azmi, Jalal Agha.

One of the most poignant films to be made on India's partition, and perhaps the first Hindi film to tackle this sensitive subject in a direct and

realistic manner. It portrays the effects of Partition on an ordinary Muslim family—the family of a middle-aged shoe manufacturer in Agra, whose family, like many other Muslim families, has been in the leather business for generations. This is set against the background of the socio-economic changes that are the outcome of the division of the country. It highlights the emotional trauma of losing one's roots and also the complete social and economic devastation that follows.

***Ghulami*** (Slavery) (1985)

Producer: Sajid Nadiadwala; Director: J. P. Datta; Cast: Mithun Chakravorty, Dharmendra, Mazhar Khan, Bharat Kapoor, Kulbhushan Kharbanda, Smita Patil, Raza Murad, Reena Roy, Anita Raj, Naseerudin Khan, Om Shivpuri.

A story of a low-caste man, cruelly treated by the village *zamindar* (landlord) and divested of his land. He returns to team up with Kulbhushan Kharbanda and Mithun Chakravorty (an ex-army man) to fight a fatal but successful battle against the zamindar. A saga of caste, untouchability and the marginalisation of the underprivileged, set in rural India.

***Haqeeqat*** (Reality) (1964)

Producer and director: Chetan Anand; Cast: Balraj Sahni, Vijay Anand, Dharmendra, Priya Rajvansh.

Widely acknowledged as the first war film in Hindi, set against the backdrop of the 1962 India–China conflict. It talks of the brave sacrifice of a small army contingent, led by Dharmendra, surrounded by the Chinese army.

***Henna*** (1991)

Producer: R. K. Films; Director: Randhir Kapoor; Cast: Rishi Kapoor, Zeba Bakhtiyar, Ashwini Bhave, Farida Jalal, Kiran Kumar.

The film highlights the artificiality of the division brought about by the line of control between the people of India and Pakistan, emphasising that people on both sides of the line are really one. It tells the story of an Indian man who accidentally crosses into Pakistan-occupied Kashmir and then falls in love with a Muslim girl there.

***Hero***. See *The Hero*.

### *Hindustan Ki Kasam* (Swear by India) (1973)

Producer: Ravi Anand; Director: Chetan Anand; Cast: Raj Kumar, Chetan Anand, Priya Rajvansh, Balraj Sahni, Parikshit Sahni, Vijay Anand, Padma Khanna, Amjad Khan.

Made in the aftermath of the India–Pakistan war of 1971, it tells the story of one battle where the Indian Air Force (IAF) scored over the Pakistani Air Force. When an IAF air base is raided and lives are lost, a pilot, played by Raj Kumar, swears revenge. The film is about the superior air-strike force of India, and has some commendable dogfights by real IAF pilots. It was the first film made in Hindi that talked of Pakistan by name; until then, naming Pakistan as the enemy nation was not allowed by law in India.

### *Jaagte Raho* (Keep Awake) (1956)

Producer: Raj Kapoor; Directors: Amit Mitra and Sombhu Mitra; Cast: Raj Kapoor, Nargis, Motilal, Pradeep Kumar, Daisy Irani, Sumitra Devi, Sulochana Chatterji, Smriti Biswas.

The story of a peasant who comes to a big town and is thirsty. When searching for water, he unwittingly enters an apartment and is taken to be a thief. On the run from one house to another, he comes across many vices that rather respectable people commit at night.

### *Jhankaar Beats* (Musical Beats) (2003)

Producer: Pritish Nandy Communications; Director: Sujoy Ghosh; Cast: Juhi Chawla, Sanjay Suri, Rahul Bose, Rinke Khanna, Shayan Munshi.

Two friends work for an advertising agency and share a passion for music. They participate in an R. D. Burman competition for two years and fail. One's wife is pregnant and another's has started a divorce petition. It is then that the advertising agency entrusts them with the job of coming up with catchy lines for a condom ad. A modern day musical with new trends in marriage and family thrown in.

***Jis Desh Mein Ganga Behti Hai*** (The Country where the Ganga Flows) (1960)

Producer: R. K. Films; Director: Radhu Karmakar; Cast: Raj Kapoor, Padmini, Pran, Lalita Pawar, Tiwari, Sulochana.

Raj Kapoor produced the film for his longstanding cameraman Radhu Karmakar, who made a poignant film about violence in society, arguing that people on both side of the law can be either good or ruthless and society must be reformed to solve the problems. Raj Kapoor plays a poor musician who gets trapped among *daku*s (dacoits) and is made to believe that dakus were fighting for socialist ideals. But then Raj Kapoor sees the violent side of the dakus and the police alike and decides to set the world right.

***Kabhi Kabhie*** (Sometimes) (1976)

Producer and director: Yash Chopra; Cast: Amitabh Bachchan, Shashi Kapoor, Rakhee, Neetu Singh, Rishi Kapoor, Waheeda Rehman.

The story of the love between the poet Amit (Amitabh Bachchan) and his female fan Pooja (Rakhee). But through a fateful turn of events, she gets married to Vijay (Shashi Kapoor). Amit then marries Anjali (Waheeda Rehman) and turns a successful builder. Anjali had a daughter from her earlier boyfriend; the girl has been brought up in another family. When the daughter (Neetu Singh) discovers that she has another birth mother, she sets out to search for her. In the process, the older generation revisits their wounds and love. Amit meets Pooja and Vijay suspects them to be in love. Vijay and Pooja's only son (Rishi Kapoor) goes to be with his beloved (Neetu Singh), when, in a fire, both families save each others' kin and live happily ever after.

***Kabhi Khushi Kabhi Gham*** (Sometimes Happiness, Sometimes Sorrow) (2001)

Producer: Dharma Productions; Director: Karan Johar; Cast: Amitabh Bachchan, Shahrukh Khan, Jaya Bachchan, Kajol, Hrithik Roshan, Kareena Kapoor.

This is a film mounted on a massive scale by director Karan Johar. It is about a family where the patriarch, Amitabh

Bachchan who adopts Shahrukh Khan as a son and then has a biological son (Hrithik Roshan). But when the grown-up Shahrukh falls in love with a middle-class girl (Kajol), the father throws him out of his rich household. Later, the second son grows up and decides to locate his elder brother and his family.

***Khakee*** (Uniform) (2004)

Producer: D. M. S. Films; Director: Raj Kumar Santoshi; Cast: Amitabh Bachchan, Aishwarya Rai, Akshaye Kumar, Ajay Devgan, Tusshar Kapoor, Tanuja, Jaya Prada, Atul Kulkarni.

Amitabh Bachchan plays DCP (Deputy Commissioner of Police) Anant Srivastava who has been assigned the task of escorting a dreaded terrorist from Chandigarh to Mumbai; he sets up a team of officers comprising Shekhar Sachdev (Akshaye Kumar) and recent recruit Ashwin Gupte (Tusshar Kapoor). Yashvant Angre (played by Ajay Devgan) is leading a team of terrorists to free the terrorist. The terrorists set a mole in the shape of Mahalakshmi (Aishwarya Rai), but Yashwant Angre is arrested, sentenced and, later in a staged encounter, shot dead.

***Khamosh Pani*** (Silent Waters) (2003)

Producer: Vidhi Films; Director: Sabiha Sumar; Cast: Kirron Kher, Amir Ali Malik, Arshad Mahmud, Salman Shahid.

Made by a Pakistani woman director, the film tells the story of a Sikh woman who defies death at Partition, marries a Muslim, practises Islam, and settles down to an outwardly contented existence in what becomes Pakistan. Her past and present collide in tragedy when her brother comes looking for her and her son takes to Islamic fundamentalism.

***Kisna*** (2005)

Producer and director: Subhash Ghai (Mukta Arts); Cast: Vivek Oberoi, Antonia Bernath, Isha Sharvani, Amrish Puri, Om Puri, Harshita Bhatt.

In the late colonial period, that is the 1930s, a young woman Catherine, daughter of the ruthless British Collector meets and falls in love with an Indian village lad Kisna, but the girl's parents are vehemently against the match. The situation turns ugly and she is sent to England. Years later, she comes back again and both have not forgotten each other. But this time, Kisna's uncle and brother oppose the match. To complicate the matter, Kisna is now engaged to an Indian woman and one wily Indian prince has taken a liking to Catherine. Kisna manages to rescue her and reach her to the safety of the British High Commission.

***Komal Gandhar*** (E-flat) (1961)
Producer: Chitrakalpa; Director: Ritwik Ghatak; Cast: Abinash Bannerji, Abhi Bhattacharya, Bijon Bhattacharya, Satindra Bhattacharya, Debabrata Biswas, Salil Choudhuri, Supriya Chaudhury.

The film questions the logic of Partition and expresses a burning desire for reunification. Its abundant songs are replete with the nostalgia for the past, pervaded with memories of undivided Bengal. The most intense scene in the film is the rail track that ends abruptly at the border, symbolising the rupture and the pain for those who can see their homes across the border but can no longer return to them.

***Kuch Kuch Hota Hai*** (Something Happens) (1998) Producer: Dharma Productions; Director: Karan Johar; Cast: Shahrukh Khan, Kajol, Rani Mukherjee, Anupam Kher, Himani Shivpuri, Farida Jalal.

Rahul (Shahrukh Khan) is best friends with the tomboyish Anjali (Kajol). Enter Tina (Rani Mukherjee); Rahul falls in love with her and Anjali (who secretly loves Rahul) is shattered. She leaves town and Rahul and Tina marry. Tina dies soon after childbirth, but before that, has written several letters to her newborn child, to be opened on each of her birthdays until she is eight. She tells her daughter about Anjali and asks her to help Rahul reunite with Anjali. The little girl creates situations which enable the two to meet again. But Anjali is already engaged to Aman (Salman Khan). However, Aman soon realises the love between Anjali and Rahul and sets up their marriage.

### *Lagaan* (The Tax) (2001)

Producer: Aamir Khan Productions; Director: Ashutosh Gowarikar; Cast: Aamir Khan, Gracy Singh, Rachel Shelley.

Set in colonial times, the film tells the story of a poor village which is not doing well, because its colonial masters have doubled the village tax (*lagaan*). When the villagers learn of this they are devastated. Accidentally, the villagers get to glimpse a cricket match being played by the British officers; the nasty British officer offers to waive the village tax for three years if the villagers defeat the British team in a cricket match. Bhuvan (Aamir Khan) accepts the wager, much to the disapproval of the village, whose residents have never played cricket. The British officer's gentle-hearted sister, who loves Bhuvan, helps the villagers learn the game of cricket. Bhuvan conjures up a team with most unlikely players, who eventually win the match.

### *Lakshya* (The Objective) (2004)

Producer: Javed Akhtar; Director: Farhan Akhtar; Cast: Amitabh Bachchan, Hrithik Roshan, Preity Zinta, Om Puri, Sharad Kapoor, Sushant Singh.

A film about a confused rich young man who has no goal in life. He decides to join the army, but soon runs away from training. Taunted by his girlfriend, he joins back and becomes a brave officer who tastes war in the India–Pakistan conflict in the Kargil sector.

### *LOC—Kargil* (2003)

Producer and director: J. P. Dutta; Cast: Sanjay Dutt, Ajay Devgan, Saif Ali Khan, Suniel Shetty.

Made by war film veteran J. P. Dutta, the film is based on the 1999 war in the Kargil sector between India and Pakistan, which saw the two nations come close to nuclear war. As is usual with Dutta, the film has many big stars and good music.

***Maa Tujhe Salaam*** (Salute to My Motherland) (2006)
Producer: Mahendra Dhariwal; Director: Tinnu Verma; Cast: Sunny Deol, Shilpa Shetty, Tinnu Verma, Arbaaz Khan.
A story of illegal infiltration from Pakistan, from the hilly and snow-bound region called Zohanabad. When army intelligence officer Shilpa Shetty comes to know of it, Sunny Deol, an army officer, is sent to deal with Lala (Tinnu Verma), who is the kingpin of the whole immigration racket.

***Maachis*** (Matchstick) (1996)
Producer: R. V. Pandit; Director: Gulzar; Cast: Tabu, Chandrachur Singh, Om Puri, Kanwaljit Singh, Kulbhushan Kharbanda, Jimmy Shergill.
The film traces the rise of Sikh militancy in India, after the storming of the Golden Temple, the assassination of Indira Gandhi and the ensuing anti-Sikh riots. It also talks of the Pakistan link with the Sikh militant movement in India. The story is about the co-option of innocent individuals into terrorist cadres in retaliation to police atrocities in rural Punjab.

***Main Hoon Na*** (Don't Worry, I'm Here) (2004)
Producer: Red Chillies Entertainment; Director: Farah Khan; Cast: Shahrukh Khan, Sushmita Sen, Suniel Shetty, Kirron Kher, Zayed Khan, Amrita Rao, Nasiruddin Shah, Kabir Bedi, Bindu, Satish Shah.
A 1970s style story of an army major who goes to a residential college to protect the daughter of an army general, combining it with his search for his long-lost step-brother. With the enunciation of a political idea such as 'Project Milap', it is probably the most positive film made till date about the changing attitude to Pakistan.

***Mammo*** (1994)
Producer: NFDC; Director: Shyam Benegal; Cast: Farida Jalal, Surekha Sikri, Amit Phalke.
A story of two sisters divided by the line of control. The film follows the travails of the sister on the Pakistani side who has no one to stay with and decides to come to India and stay with the Indian sister and her son. This story about the needless

partition of families shows how Partition continues even decades after the event.

*Mangal Pandey* (full title: *The Rising—Ballad of Mangal Pandey*) (2005)

Producer: Bobby Bedi (Kaleidoscope Entertainment Pvt. Ltd); Director: Ketan Mehta; Cast: Aamir Khan, Rani Mukherjee, Ameesha Patel, Toby Stephens, Kirron Kher.

The story of an army mutineer in 1857 called Mangal Pandey, who led the revolt that shook the British Empire for a few months. The film begins with the friendship between Mangal Pandey (Aamir Khan) and Gordon (Toby Stephens), a friendship that cuts across rank and race. But soon the introduction of a new cartridge laced with pork and beef angers both Hindus and Muslim soldiers, and a revolt follows. Woven into the story is Gordon's rescue of a widow from the funeral pyre, with whom he falls in love, and Mangal Pandey falls for a prostitute Hira (Rani Mukherjee). But the revolt is suppressed and all mutineers, including Mangal, are either gunned down or sentenced to death.

*Meghe Dhaka Tara* (The Cloud-capped Star) (1960)

Producer: Chitrakalpa/Ritwik Ghatak; Director: Ritwik Ghatak; Cast: Supriya Choudhury, Anil Chatterji, Niranjan Ray, Gita Ghatak, Bijon Bhattacharya.

The film exposes the economic upheaval caused by Partition, which subsumes the morality and ethics of a middle-class family. Neeta, the sole earner in a refugee family, eventually becomes a victim of the gnawing lust of a family driven to poverty.

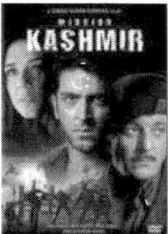

*Mission Kashmir* (2000)

Producer and director: Vidhu Vinod Chopra; Cast: Sanjay Dutt, Sonali Kulkarni, Hrithik Roshan, Preity Zinta, Jackie Shroff, Puru Rajkumar.

The story of a young Kashmiri–Muslim boy Altaf, who sees his parents and family being killed by a masked police officer. Ironically, he is adopted by the same police officer, who is also Kashmiri–

Muslim, married to a Hindu. When Altaf (Hrithik Roshan) comes to know the identity of his adopted father, he runs away and joins the militant rank to take revenge on the killers of his family. The film clearly identifies Pakistani agents as inciting innocent but disgruntled Indian–Muslim youth to the path of militancy.

### *Mohabbatein* (Love) (2000)

Producer: Yash Chopra (Yashraj Films); Director: Aditya Chopra; Cast: Amitabh Bachchan, Shahrukh Khan, Aishwarya Rai, Uday Chopra, Kim Sharma, Jugal Hansraj, Preeti Jhangiani, Shamita Shetty, Jimmy Shergill, Anupam Kher.

Narayan Shankar (played by Amitabh Bachchan) runs his residential college named Gurukul with an iron hand and forbids any show of love or affection on his campus. His own daughter had loved Raj (Shahrukh Khan) and was denied permission to marry him. She committed suicide. The same Raj joins the college as Aryan, a music teacher. He encourages three young students to love. Dramatic conflict is created when Narayan Shankar's anti-love principles clash with Raj's romantic ones. In the end Aryan has his way.

### *Mother India* (1957)

Producer and director: Mehboob Khan; Cast: Nargis, Sunil Dutt, Rajendra Kumar, Raj Kumar.

A rural classic which depicts the vicious cycle of debt and poverty in Indian villages. When Radha (played by Nargis) marries Shamu (played by Raj Kumar), his mother takes a loan of Rs. 500 for the ceremony, and the film shows the crushing effect of the machinations of village moneylenders on poor farmer families. Raj's hands are crushed under a stone boulder and, unable to earn, he runs away. Radha is shown toiling to raise her three sons, while fending off the sexual advances of the moneylender. Her youngest son Birju (played by Sunil Dutt) grows up to be an angry young man, because of the injustice he sees around him. He kidnaps the moneylender's daughter to avenge his poverty. Radha protests against what she sees as an injustice against a woman, and in the confrontation with her son, shoots him dead to rescue the kidnapped girl.

*My Brother, My Enemy* (2005)
Documentary. Producers and directors: Kamal Negi and Masood Khan. No poster available.

A short ethnographic documentary in which two young filmmakers, one from India and one from Pakistan, visit each other's countries and homes. The journeys they undertake reveal old memories and existing mindsets of hate amongst the two nations. The filmmakers question these and hope that with their generation, those antagonisms will reduce.

*Netaji Subhas Chandra Bose—The Forgotemten Hero* (2005)
Producer: Raj Pius; Director: Shyam Benegal; Cast: Sachin Khadekar, Kulbhushan Kharbanda, Rajit Kapoor.

The film deals with the last five years of the Congress leader and freedom fighter Bose, the enigmatic leader whose death is a mystery India still engages with.

*Phir Bhi Dil Hai Hindustani* (Yet the Heart is Indian) (2000)
Producer: Dreamz Unlimited; Director: Aziz Mirza; Cast: Shahrukh Khan, Juhi Chawla, Paresh Rawal, Johnny Lever.

The film is centred around the TV rivalry between two news channels. One has a celebrity reporter Ajay (Shahrukh Khan) and another has Riya Bannerji (played by Juhi Chawla). The story takes a turn when Mohan Joshi (played by Paresh Rawal) is arrested for murder. He escapes and is branded a terrorist. In hiding, he meets the two reporters and tells them that the man he killed had raped and killed his teenage daughter. The confession is taped but vested interests put all kinds of hurdles in its airing and Joshi is sentenced to death. On the day of the hanging, thousands of people, led by the two reporters, march to the jail and rescue Joshi.

*Pinjar* (The Skeleton) (2003)
Producer: Lucky Star Entertainment; Director: Chandra Parakash Dwivedi; Cast: Urmila Matondkar, Manoj Bajpai, Sanjay Suri, Sandali Sinha, Isha Koppikar, Lillete Dubey, Kulbhushan Kharbanda, Priyanshu Chatterji.

A story set against the Partition, about a Hindu woman Puro forced into marriage by a Muslim man Rashid. She finally accepts him when her own family deserts her. She retains a soft corner for her family and her erstwhile fiancé. After Partition, she risks her own and Rashid's life trying to rescue her fiancé's sister from the clutches of a Muslim family.

*Prem Pujari* (Priest of Love) (1970)
Producer: Navketan Films; Director: Dev Anand; Cast: Dev Anand, Waheeda Rahman, Shatrughan Sinha, Zahida, Prem Chopra, Sajjan, Madan Puri.

The film traces the story of a young man, played by Dev Anand, whose father wants him to join the army. He is not keen on this because he is against violence, but finally he is forced to join it. Later, he gets involved in foiling a plot by the enemy against India in the course of which he has to befriend Zahida, an enemy moll. This creates a misunderstanding with his girlfriend. Ultimately, he succeeds in defeating the enemy and regains her affections.

*Pukar* (The Call) (2000)
Producer: S. K. Films Enterprises; Director: Raj Kumar Santoshi; Cast: Anil Kapoor, Madhuri Dixit, Namrata Shirodkar, Om Puri, Rohini Hattangadi, Farida Jalal, Danny.

Two army men rescue a politician from a dreaded terrorist. Interwoven with this plot is the love triangle between Anil Kapoor, Madhuri Dixit and Namrata Shirodkar. Madhuri loves Anil and Anil loves Namrata; fuelled by jealousy, Madhuri conspires to make trouble for Anil Kapoor, and inadvertently facilitates his being branded as a traitor, court-martialled and dismissed from the army. Anil Kapoor fights back to save his honour.

*Rang De Basanti* (Colour Me Saffron) (2006)
Producer: Flicks Motion Pictures Co. Pvt. Ltd.; Director: Rakeysh Omprakash Mehra; Cast: Aamir Khan, Soha Ali Khan, Sharman Joshi, Atul Kulkarni, Alice Patten, Madhavan, Waheeda Rehman, Kirron Kher, Om Puri, Lekh Tandon.

A British filmmaker Sue (Alice Patten) comes to India to make a film on the lives of revolutionary leaders of the Indian freedom struggle, like Bhagat Singh, Chandrashekhar, Rajguru, and Ashfaqullah, and in her search for suitable actors, meets a bunch of aimless guys led by DJ (Aamir Khan). While they research and rehearse for their roles, they begin to understand and internalise the commitment and passion of those historical characters. So, when air force officer Ajay Rathod (Soha's fiancé) dies in the crash of a defective MIG war plane, the four protest against the political corruption that has led to his death. Vested interests amongst politicians unleash violence on them. Finding no legal redressal, the young men kill the defence minister and take over a radio station to publicise the injustices in the system. The state shoots them dead; in this way the film links the stories of the freedom fighters with the modern tale of the young martyrs.

### *Refugee* (2000)

Producer and director: J. P. Dutta; Cast: Abhishek Bachchan, Kareena Kapoor, Suniel Shetty, Saif Ali Khan, Pooja Bhatt.

Probably the only film that talks of the lives of people living close to the border, and their having to eke out a living even if it means helping illegals to cross into the country across the border from Pakistan. The storyline revolves around a Bihari Muslim family, abandoned by all states, wanting to go to a 'Muslim' homeland but forced to attempt it illegally since they are officially refused asylum.

### *Roja* (1992)

Producers: Mani Ratnam and K. Balchander; Director: Mani Ratnam; Cast: Arvind Swamy, Madhoo, Pankaj Kapur.

This film is about newlyweds Arvind Swamy and Madhoo, who go to Kashmir after their wedding. The husband is kidnapped by Pakistani terrorists and Madhoo goads the system to work for his release. The film highlights the direct involvement of Pakistan in the terrorism in Kashmir. By making the story revolve around a South Indian couple, the film brings home the fact that terrorism is a pan-Indian problem.

### *Sarfarosh* (The Martyr) (1999)

Producer: Cinematt Pictures; Director: John Mathew Matthan; Cast: Aamir Khan, Nasiruddin Khan, Sonali Bendre, Mukesh Rishi.

A story of Pakistan-sponsored terrorism and a young police officer's efforts to wipe it out. The film talks about Pak infiltrators, the illegal arms sale, and the problematic relationship amongst the Muslims themselves, the *mohajirs* and the Pakistani Muslims, and between Muslims and Hindus, in a patriotic face-off in favour of the Indian nation.

### *Sarhad Paar* (Across the Border) (2006)

Producer: Nimbus Motion Pictures; Director: Raman Kumar; Cast: Sanjay Dutt, Tabu, Mahima Chaudhary, Rahul Dev.

When an army man Ranjit Singh (Sanjay Dutt) comes back from Pakistani captivity after years of having been taken for dead, the lives of his wife and sister change. Ranjit has no memory save that of one face, the face of terrorist Bakhtawar (played by Rahul Dev). All try to bring him back to normal but in vain. Meanwhile, Bakhtawar plots revenge.

### *Shaheed Udham Singh* (2000)

Producer: Surjit Movies; Director: Chitrath; Cast: Raj Babbar, Gurdas Mann, Shatrughan Sinha, Amrish Puri, Tom Alter, Barry John, Juhi Chawla.

It tells the story of Udham Singh who, during the British Raj, had shot dead General Dyer, the man who had ordered the killing of thousands of men at Jallianwallah Bagh at Amritsar.

### *Sheen* (2004)

Producer and director: Ashok V. Pandit; Cast: Raj Babbar, Sheen, Tarun Arora.

A film about the forced eviction of Kashmiri Hindu Pundits by Pakistan-supported Muslim terrorists of Kashmir. The film was sold with the cover write-up, 'A refugee in my own country'.

### Silsila (Continuity) (1981)

Producer: Yashraj Films; Director: Yash Chopra; Cast: Amitabh Bachchan, Shashi Kapoor, Rekha, Jaya Bachchan, Sanjeev Kumar.

Amitabh Bachchan is compelled to marry his brother's fiancée (Jaya) because of his brother's (Shashi Kapoor, an air force officer) death in a crash. But he cannot get his ex-lover (Rekha, now married to Sanjeev Kumar) out of his life and mind. The ex-lovers meet again and old love is rekindled creating problems in their relationships.

### Subarnarekha (The Golden, Line; also the name of a river in Jharkand) (1962)

Producer: J. J. Films; Director: Ritwik Ghatak; Cast: Abhi Bhattacharya, Madhabi Mukherjee, Satindra Bhattacharya, Gita De.

The film enquires into the far-reaching consequences of Partition. Its theme—the search for a *nutan badi* (new home) highlights the pain of having been uprooted, of being doomed to the status of a refugee in perpetual search of a homeland. Extreme poverty, a consequence of Partition, forces Seeta into prostitution, while Ishwar's tragic encounter with Seeta towards the end is Ghatak's comment on the degeneration of scruples, an enduring legacy of partition which, for him, ate into the very entrails of our society.

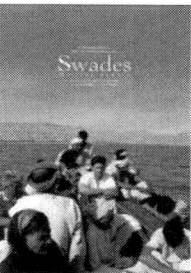

### Swades (Homeland) (2004)

Producer: Ashutosh Gowariker Productions; Director: Ashutosh Gowariker; Cast: Shahrukh Khan, Gayatri Joshi, Vishwa Badola, Kishori Ballal, Daya Shankar Pandey.

The film traces the journey of self discovery by an NRI Mohan Bhargava (played by Shahrukh Khan) who has come from abroad to an Indian village to search for his childhood maid who had raised him after the death of both his parents. He observes firsthand the abject poverty and deprivation of people in the villages, and decides to set up a power plant, during which he falls in love with a woman with whom his maid was staying. He eventually comes back permanently to the village, leaving his well-paid NASA job.

**Tamas** (Darkness) (1987)
Producer: Blaze Entertainment; Director: Govind Nihalani; Cast: Om Puri, Naseeruddin Shah, Saeed Jaffery, Amrish Puri, Deepa Sahi, Dina Pathak, A. K. Hangal, Bhisham Sahni.

A six-part TV drama based on the acclaimed novel of the same name by Bhisham Sahni, which highlights the violence and heartburn behind the holocaustic division of the nation. It tells the tale of a Sikh family, and the trauma of Partition and communal violence.

**Tango Charlie** (2005)
Producer: Gaurav Digital; Diretor: Mani Shankar; Cast: Sanjay Dutt, Suniel Shetty, Ajay Devgan, Bobby Deol, Tanisha, Sudesh Berry.

It is about a soldier Tarun Chauhan (code named Tango Charlie, played by Bobby Deol), who is posted in the North-East, then in Andhra and finally at Kargil to fight battles for the country. In the process, the film exposes both the insurgents and Indian armed forces.

**The Hero—Love Story of a Spy** (2003)
Producer: Nanjibhai Shah; Director: Anil Sharma; Cast: Sunny Deol, Preity Zinta, Priyanka Chopra, Amrish Puri.

Arun Khanna (Sunny Deol) is an undercover agent who goes to Kashmir to uncover Pakistani secret service's dangerous plans to seize Kashmir. He seeks help from a local village girl Reshma (Preity Zinta), who soon becomes a part of his network. They fall in love but an accident separates them. Arun continues his spying, befriending the daughter (Priyanka Chopra) of an ISI accomplice. He pretends to be a nuclear scientist to crack the ISI plan of launching a nuclear bomb.

**The Legend of Bhagat Singh** (2002)
Producer: Tips Films Pvt. Ltd; Director: Raj Kumar Santoshi; Cast: Ajay Devgan, Sushant Singh, Amrita Rao.

The film traces the story of well known freedom fighter Bhagat Singh, who believed in violent means to achieve freedom from the British and differed with Gandhi on the means to attain freedom.

*Upkar* (The Favour) (1965)

Producer and director: Manoj Kumar; Cast: Manoj Kumar, Asha Parekh, Pran, Prem Chopra.

Manoj Kumar was nicknamed 'Mr Bharat' (Mr India; implying a patriot) with this film. Two sons of a widowed mother live in a village. Bharat (played by Manoj Kumar) sacrifices his education and career, working in the fields so that Puran (played by Prem Chopra) can study abroad. But once back from abroad, Puran wants a share in the property so that he can live comfortably. Bharat's love interest is a village doctor played by Asha Parekh. Pran (who was until then usually used to playing negative characters), is, for the first time here, cast in a sympathetic role.

*Veer-Zaara* (2004)

Producer: Yashraj Films; Director: Yash Chopra; Cast: Shahrukh Khan, Preity Zinta, Rani Mukherjee, Amitabh Bachchan, Hema Malini, Kirron Kher, Manoj Bajpai, Boman Irani.

A love story between an Indian Air Force (Shahrukh Khan) officer and a Pakistani girl (Preity Zinta), who run into hurdles to their union because of her orthodox Muslim father and her unyielding fiancé. They have to wait for twenty-two years before they are united as a result of the untiring efforts of a feisty woman lawyer of Pakistan (Rani Mukherjee). The film has used music by the well-known Madan Mohan, decades after his death.

*Waqt* (Time) (1965)

Producer: B. R. Chopra; Director: Yash Chopra; Cast: Balraj Sahni, Sunil Dutt, Raj Kumar, Shashi Kapoor, Sadhna, Rehman, Shashikala.

The film traces the fortunes of the family of a rich businessman Lala Kedarnath (played by Balraj Sahni) who has three sons. He scoffs at the idea of destiny, and believes in free will. But then an earthquake transforms his life and separates his family from one another. The rest of the film moves through romantic and dramatic twists and turns towards the ultimate reunion of the family decades later.

***Zakhm*** (Wound) (1998)

Producer: Pooja Bhatt; Director: Mahesh Bhatt; Cast: Ajay Devgan, Pooja Bhatt, Sonali Bendre, Kunal Khemu, Nagarjuna, Ashutosh Rana, Saurabh Shukla, Sharat Saxena.

An autobiographical film by Mahesh Bhatt, it explores the tragic life of a Muslim woman played by Pooja Bhatt in love with a Hindu film director. The differences in faith come between them, making them move away from each other. She goes on to live as a Hindu with a Hindu man but yearns to be recognized as a devout Muslim. Her now grown-up son played by Ajay Devgan buries her like a Muslim on her death, finally getting her real peace.

# Bibliography

Advani, Pratibha. 2005. 'Patriotism in Indian Cinema', *Organiser* 56 (37).

Ahmad, Zarin. 2003. 'The Bihari Muslims of Bangladesh: In a State of Statelessness', in P. R. Chari, Mallika Joseph and Suba Chandran (eds), *Missing Boundaries: Refugees, Migrants, Stateless and Internally Displaced Persons in South Asia*, Delhi: Manohar, pp. 173–80.

Ahmed, Shoaib. 2006. 'Film conference will help film industry, says G. G. Jamal', *Daily Times*, 31 May 2006. Retrieved 3 June 2006, from http://www.dailytimes. com.pk.

Ahmed, Zubair. 2003. 'Bollywood War Film Taps Patriotism', *BBC Online*, 29 December 2003, <news.bbc.co.uk/2/hi/south_asia/3287369.stm>. Accessed 3 May 2005.

Altman, Rick. 1984. 'A Semantic/Syntactic Approach to Film Genre', *Cinema Journal* 23 (3).

Althusser, Louis. 2001. *Lenin, Philosophy and Other Essays.* Trans. Ben Brewster. New York: Monthly Review Press.

Anderson, Benedict. 1983. *Imagined Communities: Reflections on the Origin and Spread of Nationalism.* New York, NY: Verso.

Anon. 1999. 'Bollywood, please don't ride on Kargil', *The Times of India*, 9 July. Accessed 1 March 2006, from LexisNexis database.

———. 2004a. 'Bollywood's Oscar nominee director returns to tackle Indian brain drain', *Agence France Presse*, 16 December. Accessed 1 Mar 2006, from LexisNexis database.

———. 2004b. 'Bollywood justifies film on Indo–Pak war', *Press Trust of India*, 7 January. Accessed 1 Mar 2006, from LexisNexis database.

———. 2004c. 'War epic helped by finesse of star director', *Leicester Mercury*, 24 June. Accessed 6 February 2006, from LexisNexis database.

———. 2005. 'People like Bollywood family movies', *Daily Times*, 2 April, http://www. dailytimes.com.pk. Accessed 2 March 2006.

———. 2006a. 'India, Pakistan end culture talks', *Agence France Presse*, 2 June. Accessed 2 June 2006, from LexisNexis database.

———. 2006b. 'No more Indian films in cinemas', *Daily Times*, 27 May, http://www. dailytimes.com.pk. Accessed 1 March 2006.

Ansari, Shabana. 2004. 'Bollywood swaps war screenplay for peace', *Times of India*, 3 May. Accessed 1 March 2006, from LexisNexis database.

Anzaldua, Gloria. 1987. *Borderlands/La Frontera*. San Francisco: Aunt Lute Books.

Astruc, Alexandre. 1968. 'The birth of a new avant garde', in P. Graham (ed.), *The New Wave*, London: Secker and Warburg.

Athique, Adrian M. 2006. 'The Global Dispersal of Media: Identifying Non–Resident Audiences for Indian Films', in T. Holden and T. Scrase (eds) *Medi@sia: Communication in Society and Cultural Context (Asia's Transformations)*, London and New York: Routledge.

Auerbach, Erich. 1953. *Mimesis*. Trans. Willard R. Trask. Princeton: Princeton UP.

Bagchi, Jasodhara and Subhoranjan Dasgupta. 2002. 'The Problem', http://www.indiaseminar.com/2002/510/510%20the%20problem.htm.

—— (ed.). 2003. *The Trauma and the Triumph: Gender and Partition in Eastern India*. Calcutta: Stree.

Bahri, D. 2001. 'The Digital Diaspora: South Asians in the New *Pax Electronica*', in M. Paranjape (ed.), *Indiaspora: Theories, Histories, Texts*, New Delhi: Indialog Publications.

Bakhtin, M. (V. N. Voloshinov), et al. 1973. *Marxism and the Philosophy of Language*. New York: Seminar Press.

Bamzai, Kaveree. 2001. 'Filmmakers scale down war movies', *Times of India*, 22 October. Accessed 1 Mar 2006, from LexisNexis database.

Banaji, S. 2006. *Reading 'Bollywood': The Young Audience and Hindi Films*. Basingstoke: Palgrave–Macmillan.

Bannerjee, Paula, S. B. R. Chaudhury and S. K. Das (eds). 2005. *Internal Displacement in South Asia*. New Delhi: Sage.

Barker, C. and D. Galasiński. 2001. *Cultural Studies and Discourse Analysis*. London/ Thousand Oaks/ New Delhi: Sage.

Barthes, Roland. 1974. *S/Z*. Trans. Richard Miller. New York: Hill and Wang.

Benjamin, Walter. 1969. 'Theses on the Philosophy of History', *Illuminations: Essays and Reflections*. New York: Schocken.

Bhabha, Homi. 1990. *Nation and Narration*. London: Routledge.

Bhalla, Alok. 1999. 'Memory, History and Fictional Representations of the Partition' *Economic and Political Weekly* XXXIV, pp. 3199–3128.

—— (ed.). 2005. *Stories about the Partition of India*. 3 volumes. New Delhi: Indus.

Bharucha, R. 1995. 'Theatre, Cinema, Ghatak', in Prabodh Maitra Nandan, ed., *Hundred Years of Cinema*, Calcutta: Maitra Nandan Publications.

——. 1998. *In the Name of the Secular: Contemporary Cultural Activism in India*. New Delhi: Oxford University Press.

——. 2001. *The Politics of Cultural Practice: Thinking through Theatre in an Age of Globalization*. New Delhi: Oxford University Press.

Bhaskar, Ira. 1983. 'Myth and Ritual: Ghatak's *Meghe Dhaka Tara*', *Journal of Arts and Ideas* 3, pp. 43–50.

Bhatt, C. 2001. *Hindu Nationalism: Origins, Ideologies and Modern Myth*. Oxford and New York: Berg.

Bhattacharya, N. 2004. 'A Basement Cinephilia: Indian Diaspora Women Watch Bollywood', *South Asian Popular Culture* 2 (2), pp. 161–83.

BJP. 1998. 'Our Policy on Media, Cinema, Arts', http://www.bjp.org/manifes chap17htm.

Bordwell, David, Janet Staiger and Kristin Thompson. 1988. *The Classical Hollywood Cinema: Film Style & Mode of Production to 1960*, London: Routledge.

Braudy, L. and M. Cohen. 2004. *Film Theory and Criticism*. 6th edn. Oxford: Oxford University Press.

Browne, Malika. 2004. 'Together in electric dreams', *The Times*, 19 February. Accessed 1 March 2006, from the LexisNexis database.

Butalia, Urvashi. 1995. 'Muslims and Hindus, Men and Women: Communal Stereotypes and the Partition of India', in T. Sarkar and U. Butalia (eds), *Women and the Hindu Right: A Collection of Essays*, New Delhi: Kali for Women, pp. 58–81.

Butalia, Urvashi. 1998. *The Other Side of Silence: Voices from the Partition of India.* New Delhi: Penguin.

Butalia, Urvashi. 2000. *The Other Side of Silence: Voices from the Partition of India.* Durham, NC: Duke UP.

Carby, Hazel. 1986. 'White women listen! Black feminism and the boundaries of sisterhood', in Paul Gilroy (ed.), *The Empire Strikes Back: Race and Racism in 1970s Britain.* London: Hutchinson.

Caruth, Cathy. 1996. *Unclaimed Experience: Trauma, Narrative and History.* Baltimore: Johns Hopkins UP.

Chakravarty, Sumita. 2002. 'Fragmenting the Nation: Images of Terrorism in Indian Popular Cinema', in M. Hjort and S. Mackenzie (eds), *Cinema and Nation*, London and New York: Routledge, pp. 222–38.

Chakravarty, S.1993. *National Identity in Popular Indian Cinema, 1947–1987.* Austin: University of Texas Press.

Chambers, Iain. 1990. *Border Dialogues: Journeys in Postmodernity.* London: Routledge.

Chatterjee, Gayatri. 2002. *Mother India.* London: BFI Classic Series.

Chatterjee, Partha. 1994. *The Nation and its Fragments: Colonial and Postcolonial Histories.* New Delhi: Oxford University Press.

———. 2003. 'The Relentless Tragedy of Ritwik', *Himal Magazine*, http://www.himalmag.com/2003/november/essay.htm.

Chatterjee, Saibal. 2005. 'The new face of Bollywood', *Hindustan Times*, 29 March. Accessed 2 February 2006, from the LexisNexis database.

Chatterji, S. 2003. 'War films are right up the Parivar's street', *Hindustan Times*, 20 November.

Chatterji, Shoma A. 2004. *Ritwik Ghatak: The Celluloid Rebel.* New Delhi: Rupa.

Chaturvedi, Sanjay. 2001. 'Process Of Othering in the Case of India And Pakistan', *Tijdschrift Voor Economische En Sociale Geografie* 93 (2), pp. 149–59.

Chopra, Anupama. 2005. 'Young Indian producers make mark with B.O. hits', *Variety* 28 March. Accessed 6 February 2006, from the LexisNexis database.

Collier, J., and M. Collier. 1948. *Visual Anthropology: Photography as a Research Method.* Albuquerque: University of New Mexico Press.

Cowasjee, S. and K. S. Duggal (eds). 1995. *Orphans of the Storm: Stories on the Partition of India.* New Delhi: UBS.

Darpan, Mahesh (ed.). 2000. *Partition: Biswin Sadi ki Hindi Kahaniyan* (Partition: Twentieth Century Hindi Stories). New Delhi: Samayik Prakashan.

Das, Runa. 2006. 'Encountering Hindutva, Interrogating Religious Nationalism and (En)gendering a Hindu Patriarchy in India's Nuclear Policies', *International Feminist Journal of Politics* 8 (3), pp. 370–93.

Dasgupta, S. D. 1993. 'Feminist Consciousness in Woman–Centred Hindi Films', in Women of South Asian Descent Collective (eds), *Our Feet Walk the Sky*, San Francisco: Aunt Lute Books, pp. 56–64.

Davis, Darrell William. 1996. *Picturing Japaneseness: Monumental Style, National Identity, Japanese film.* New York; Chichester: Columbia University Press.

Deleuze, Gilles. 1986. *Cinema 1: The Movement–Image.* Trans. Hugh Tomlinson and Barbara Habberjam. New York: Continuum.

Derné, S. 2000. *Movies, Masculinity and Modernity: An Ethnography of Men's Film-going in India.* Westport, Conneticut; London: Greenwood Press.

Derrida, Jacques. 1992. *Acts of Literature.* New York: Routledge.

Deschaumes, Ghislaine Glasson and Rada Ivekovic (eds). 2003. *Divided Countries, Separated Cities: The Modern Legacy of Partition*. New Delhi: Oxford University Press.

Deshmukh, J. 2004. 'Bollywood builds Indo–Pak bridges', http://entertainment.iafrica.com/bollywood/news/399186.htm.

Deshmukh, Jay. 2002. 'Reel-life patriotism flops at the Indian box office', *Agence France Presse*, 6 February.

Dhareshwar, Vivek and Tejaswini Niranjana. 2000. 'Kaadalan and the Politics of Resignification: Fashion, Violence and the Body', in R. S. Vasudevan (ed.), *Making Meaning in Indian Cinema*, New Delhi: OUP.

Dick, B. 2002. *Anatomy of Film.* 4th edn. New York: Bedford/St. Martin's.

Didur, Jill. 2006. *Unsettling Partition: Literature, Gender, Memory.* Toronto: University of Toronto Press.

Dixon, W. W. 1997. *The Films of Jean Luc Godard.* USA: State University of New York Press.

Doval, Nikita. 2006. 'GenX patriotism: The new formula', *The Times of India*, 4 February. Accessed 6 February 2006, from LexisNexis database.

Dudrah, R. K. 2002. 'Vilayati Bollywood: Popular Hindi Cinema–going and Diasporic South–Asian Identity in Birmingham (UK)', *Javnost: The Public Journal of the European Institute for Communication and Culture* 9 (1), pp. 19–36.

———. 2006. *Bollywood: Sociology Goes to the Movies.* London and New Delhi: Sage.

Dwyer, Rachel. 2000. 'The Erotics of the Wet Sari in Hindi Films', *South Asia; Journal of South Asian Studies* 23 (2), pp. 143–59.

Fazila-Yacoobali, V. 2002. '*Yeh mulk hamara ghar*: The "National Order of Things" and Muslim Identity in John Mathew Mattan's *Sarfarosh*', *Contemporary South Asia* 11 (2), 183–98.

Feldman, Shelley. 1999. 'Feminist Interruptions: The Silence of East Bengal in the Stories of Partition', *Interventions* 1 (2), pp. 167–82.

Foucault, Michel. 1980. *The History of Sexuality.* Vol. 1. Trans. Robert Hurley. New York: Random House.

———. 1986. 'Of Other Spaces', *Diacritics*, Spring 1986, pp. 22–27.

Gahlot, D. 2001. '*Lagaan* is not about Cricket, *Gadar* is not about Love', 22 June. http://www.rediff.com/entertai/2001/jun/22deepa.htm. Accessed 28 January 2007.

Gangadhar, V. 2004. 'Who should decide?', *The Hindu*, 19 November. Accessed 10 Jun 2005.

Ganti, Tejaswini. 2004. *Bollywood: A Guidebook to Popular Hindi Cinema*. London: Routledge.

Gelder, Lawrence Van. 2004. 'Arts Briefing', *The New York Times*, 30 December Accessed 1 March 2006, from LexisNexis database.

Ghatak, Ritwik. 1975. Chitrabikshan Annual. Calcutta: Cine Central. Reprinted and translated in Ashish Rajadhyaksha and Amrit Gangar, eds, *Ghatak: Arguments and Stories* (Bombay: Screen Unit, 1987).

———. 1987. *Cinema and I.* Calcutta: Ritwik Memorial Trust.

———. 2000a. 'My Films', in *Rows and Rows of Fences: Ritwik Ghatak on Cinema*, Calcutta: Seagull Books.

———. 2000b. *Rows and Rows of Fences: Ritwik Ghatak on Cinema.* Foreword by Satyajit Ray. Calcutta: Seagull Books.

———. 2000c. 'Sound in Cinema', in *Rows and Rows of Fences: Ritwik Ghatak on Cinema*. Calcutta: Seagull Books.

Ghosh, S. 2002. 'Queer Pleasures for Queer People: Film, Television, and Queer Sexuality in India', in R. Vanita (ed.), *Queering India: Same-Sex Love and Eroticism in Indian Culture and Society*, London and New York: Routledge, pp. 207–21.

Giroux, Henry. 1992. *Border Crossings: Cultural Workers and the Politics of Education*. London: Routledge.

Goff, Le. 1992. *History and Memory*. New York: Columbia University Press.

Gokulsingh, K. Moti and Wimal Dissanayake. 1998. *Indian Popular Cinema: A Narrative of Cultural Change*. London: Trentham Books.

Gramsci, Antonio. 1996. *Selections from the Prison Notebooks of Antonio Gramsci*. Edited and translated by Quintin Hoare and Geoffrey Nowell Smith. Chennai: Orient Longman.

Guha, Jaganath. 2001. 'Conflict as Masala', <http://www.himalmag.com/march2001/analysis.html>. Accessed 7 July 2006.

Gupta, Hari Ram. 1967. *India–Pakistan War 1965*. Delhi: Hariyana Prakashan.

Hasan, Mushirul (ed.). 1997. *India Partitioned: The Other Face of Freedom*. Vol. 1–2. New Delhi: Roli Books.

———. 1998. 'Memories of a Fragmented Nation Rewriting the Histories of India's Partition', *Economic and Political Weekly* XXXIII, pp. 2662–668.

Hayward, S. 2001. *Cinema Studies: The Key Concepts*. 2nd edn. London: Routledge.

Higson, Andrew. 1989. 'The Concept of National Cinema', *Screen* 30 (4).

———. 1995. *Waving the Flag: Constructing a National Cinema in Britain*. Oxford Clarendon Press.

Hoffheimer, M. H. 2005. '*Veer–Zaara*: Love and Law in Bollywood', *Picturing Justice The On-Line Journal of Law and Popular Culture*, at http://www.usfca.edu/pj/veerzaara_hoffheimer.htm. Accessed 17 May 2006.

Hollway, W. 1989. *Subjectivity and Method in Psychology: Gender, Meaning and Science* London/Beverley Hills/New Delhi: Sage.

Hood, John. 2000. *The Essential Mystery, Major Filmmakers of Indian Art Cinema* New Delhi: Orient Longman.

Hooks, Bell. 1990. 'Sisterhood: Political Solidarity Between Women', in Sneja Gunew (ed.), *A Reader in Feminist Knowledge*, London: Routledge.

IMDb.com. 2001. 'IMDb User Comments for *Refugee*', http://dick.imdb.com/title/tt0250690/usercomments. Accessed 3 July 2006.

Jain, Madhu, Nandita Chowdhury and Namrata Joshi. 1999. 'War: There's no Biz like War Biz', *India Today*, 23 August. Accessed 1 Mar 2006 from LexisNexis database.

Jha, Subhash K. 2000a. 'Dutta's Penchant for Indo–Pak Themes', <http://movies.indiainfo.com/features/jpdutta.html>. Accessed 3 June 2006.

———. 2000b. '*Refugee* Director Lashes out at Media', <http://movies.indiainfo.com/features/jpdutta.html>. Accessed 3 June 2006.

———. 2003. 'War Veteran of Bollywood', *Deccan Herald*, 28 December 2003, <www.deccanherald.com/deccanherald/dec28/enter5.asp>. Accessed 3 June 2006.

Joshi, L. M. (ed.). 2004. 'Partition Films', *South Asian Cinema* 5–6. London: South Asian Cinema Foundation.

Joshi, Varsha. 1995. *Polygamy and Purdah: Women and Society among Rajputs*. Jaipur: Rawat.

Kabir, A. J. 2005. 'Gender, Memory, Trauma: Women's Novels on the Partition of India', *Comparative Studies of South Asia, Africa, and the Middle East* 25 (ii), 177–90.

Kabir, Nasreen Munni. 2001. *Bollywood: The Indian Cinema Story*. London: Channel 4 Books.

Kakar, S. 1996. *The Colours of Violence: Cultural Identities, Religion and Conflict*. Chicago and London: The University of Chicago Press.

Kakar, Sudhir. 1983. 'The Cinema as Collective Fantasy', in Aruna Vasudev and Philippe Lenglet (eds), *Indian Cinema Superbazaar*, New Delhi: Vikas Publishing House.

Kalra, Virinder and Navtej Purewal. 1999. 'The Strut of the Peacocks: Partition, Travel, and the Indo–Pak Border', in Raminder Kaur and John Hutnyk (eds), *Travel Worlds: Journeys in Contemporary Cultural Politics*, London: Zed Books, pp. 54–67.

Kamal, Muniba. 2004. 'The beginning of synergy', *The News on Sunday*, 12 December, http://www.jang.com.pk/thenews/dec2004–weekly/nos–12–12–2004/instep.htm. Accessed 1 March 2006.

Kaur, Raminder and Ajay J. Sinha (eds). 2005. *Bollywood: Popular Indian Cinema Through a Transnational Lens*. New Delhi: Sage.

Kazmi, Fareed. 1999. *The Politics of India's Commercial Cinema: Imaging a Universe, Subverting a Multiverse*. New Delhi: Sage.

Kazmi, N. 1998. *The Dream Merchants of Bollywood*. New Delhi: UBSPD.

Kazmi, Nikhat. 2005. 'Jhappis with the Jawans', *Times of India*, 23 March. Accessed 6 February 2006, from LexisNexis database.

Kennedy, Charles K. 1990. 'Islamization and Legal Reform in Pakistan:1979–1989', *Pacific Affairs* 63 (1), Spring, pp. 62–77.

Kenny, Michael G. 1991. 'A Place for Memory: The Interface between Individual and Collective History', *Comparative Studies in Society and History* 41, pp. 420–37.

Kermode, Mark. 2004. 'Bombay meets Boys Own', *Observer*, 27 June. Accessed 6 February 2006, from LexisNexis database.

Khan, Gerrard. 2001. 'Citizenship and Statelessness in South Asia', *New Issues in Refugee Research*, Working Paper No. 47, UNHCR.

Khanna, Anish. 2000. 'Refugee', *Planet Bollywood*, <http://www.planetbollywood. com/Film/refugee.html>. Accessed 3 July 2006.

Khubchandani, Lata. 2003. *Raj Kapoor, the Great Showman*. New Delhi: Rupa and Co.

Kinder, Marsha. 1993. *Blood Cinema: The Reconstruction of National Identity in Spain*. Berkeley; London: University of California Press.

Koves, Margit. 1997. 'Telling Stories of Partition and War', *Economic and Political Weekly*, August 16–23, pp. 2147–57.

Krishna, Sankaran. 1994. 'Cartographic Anxiety: Mapping the Body Politic in India', *Alternatives* 19, pp. 507–21.

———. 1996. 'Cartographic Anxiety: Mapping the Body Politic in India', in Alker Jr., Hayward and Shapiro, Michael (eds), *Challenging Boundaries: Global Flows, Territorial Identities*, Minneapolis, University of Minnesota Press, pp. 193–215.

Kumar, Priya. 1999. 'Testimonies of Loss and Memory: Partition and the Haunting of a Nation', *Interventions* 1 (2), pp. 201–15.

Kumar, Shanti and Michael Curtin. 2002. 'Made in India: In between Music, Television and Patriarchy', *Television & New Media* 3 (4).

Lanzoni, Remi Fournier. 2002. *French Cinema: From its Beginnings to the Present*. New York: Continuum.

Luhrmann, T. M. 1994. 'The Good Parsi: The Postcolonial 'Feminization' of a Colonial Elite', *Man* 29 (2), June, pp. 333–57.

Lukacs, Georg. 2002. 'Critical Realism and Socialist Realism', in Anand Prakash (ed.), *Approaches in Literary Theory: Marxism*, Delhi: Worldview.

Lutgendorf, Phillip. 2004. 'Is there an Indian Way of Film-making?' Unpublished manuscript.

Lutz, Lothar and Beatrix Pfleiderer (eds). 1985. *The Hindi Film: Agent and Re-agent of Cultural Change*. New Delhi: Manohar Publications.

Macdougall, David. 1998. *Transcultural Cinema*, Princeton, New Jersey: Princeton University Press.

Mahey, Arjun. 2001. 'Partition Narratives: Some Observations', in Ravikant and Tarun Kr Saint (eds), *Translating Partition*, New Delhi: Katha.

Mahmood, Saba. 2005. Politics of Piety: The Islamic Revival and the Feminist Subject. California: Princeton University Press.

Malhotra, Sheena and Tavishi Alagh. 2004. 'Dreaming the Nation: Domestic Dramas in Hindi Films Post–1990s', *South Asian Popular Culture* 2 (1), April, New York: Routledge, pp. 19–37.

Mankekar, P. 2000. *Screening Culture, Viewing Politics: Television, Womanhood and Nation in Modern India*. New Delhi/Bombay: Oxford University Press.

Markovits, Claude. 2003. 'The Partition of India', in Ghislaine Glasson Deschaumes and Rada Ivekovic (eds), *Divided Countries, Separated Cities: The Modern Legacy of Partition*, New Delhi: Oxford University Press.

Mathur, V. 2002. 'Women in Indian Cinema: Fictional Constructs', in J. Jain and S. Rai (eds.), *Films and Feminism: Essays in Indian Cinema*, Jaipur and New Delhi: Rawat Publications.

Mayne, J. 1993. *Cinema and Spectatorship*. London and New York: Routledge.

Mazumdar, Ranjini. 2005. 'Memory and History in the Politics of Adaptation: Revisiting the Partition in *Tamas*', in Robert Stam and Alessandra Raengo, *Literature and Film: A Guide to the Theory and Practice of Film Adaptation*, Oxford: Blackwell, pp.313–30.

Mehdi, Sikander Syed. 2003. 'Refugee Memory in India and Pakistan', in Ghislaine Glasson Deschaumes and Rada Ivekovic (eds), *Divided Countries, Separated Cities: The Modern Legacy of Partition*, New Delhi: Oxford University Press.

Menon, Ritu and K. Bhasin (eds). 1998. *Borders and Boundaries: Women in India's Partition*. New Delhi: Kali for Women.

Menon, Ritu. (ed.). 2004. *No Women's Land: Women from Pakistan, India and Bangladesh Write on the Partition of India*. New Delhi: Women Unlimited.

Michelson, A. 1984. *Kino-Eye: The Writings of Dziga Vertov*. London: University of California Press.

Michaelsen, Scott and David E. Johnson. 1997. *Border Theory: The Limits of Cultural Politics*. Minneapolis and London: University of Minnesota Press.

Minh-Ha, T. T. 1992. *Framer Framed*. London: Routledge.

Mirani, Leo. 2003. 'Bollywood to release big-ticket war films as India, Pakistan talk peace', *Agence France Presse*, 14 December. Accessed 6 February, 2006 from LexisNexis database.

Mishra, Vijay. 2002. *Bollywood Cinema: Temples of Desire*. London, New York: Routledge.

Mookerjea-Leonard, Debali. 2005. 'Divided Homelands, Hostile Homes: Partition, Women and Homelessness', *Journal Of Commonwealth Literature* 40 (2), pp. 141–54.

Monaco, J. 2000. *How to read a film.* 3rd edn. Oxford: Oxford University Press.

Mulvey, Laura. 1989. 'Visual Pleasures and Narrative Cinema', in *idem.*, *Visual and Other Pleasures: Theories of Representation and Difference.* Bloomington: Indiana University Press.

Mulyadi, Sukidi. 2006. 'Max Weber's Remarks on Islam: The Protestant Ethic among Muslim Puritans', in *Islam and Christian–Muslim Relations* 17 (ii), pp. 195–205.

Naficy, H. 2001. *Accented Cinema: Exilic and Diasporic Filmmaking.* USA: Princeton University Press.

Nair, Suresh. 2002. 'Playing a war hero is a dream role: JP Dutta', *The Economic Times*, 17 October. Accessed 1 March 2006, from LexisNexis database.

Nanda, Ritu. 2002. *Raj Kapoor Speaks.* With audio CD. New Delhi: Viking.

Nandy, A. 1996. The *Savage Freud and Other Essays on Possible and Retrievable Selves.* New Delhi: OUP.

Nandy, Ashis. 2003. 'Notes Towards an Agenda for the Next Generation of Film Theorists in India', *South Asian Popular Culture* 1 (i), April, pp. 79–84.

Narrain, Siddharth. 2004. 'Exit, Anupam Kher', *Frontline* 21 (23).

Neale, Steve. 1993. 'The Same Old Story: Stereotypes and Difference', in Manuel Alvarado, Edward Buscombe and Richard Collins (eds), *The Screen Education Reader*, London: Macmillan, pp. 41–7.

———. 1999. *Genre and Hollywood.* London: Routledge.

———. 2003. 'Questions of Genre', in B. K. Grant (ed.), *Film Genre Reader III*, Austin, Texas: University of Texas Press.

Nelmes, J. 2003. *An Introduction to Film Studies.* 3rd edn. London: Routledge.

O'Donnell, Erin. 2005. '"Woman" and "Homeland" in Ritwik Ghatak's Films: Constructing Post-Independence Bengali Cultural Identity', http://www.ejumpcut. org/archive/jc47.2005/ghatak/text.html.

Pacifici, Sergio J. 1956. 'Notes toward a Definition of Neorealism', *Yale French Studies* 17, pp. 50–51.

Pandey, Gyanendra. 1991. 'In Defence of the Fragment: Writing about Hindu–Muslim Riots in India Today', *Economic and Political Weekly*, Annual Number, March, pp. 559–72.

———. 2001. *Remembering Partition: Violence, Nationalism and History in India.* Cambridge: Cambridge University Press.

Pearson, Bryan. 2003–4. 'War pix storm theaters', *Variety*, 22 December 2003–2 January 2004. Accessed 1 March 2006, from LexisNexis database.

Pendakur, Manjunath. 2003. *Indian Popular Cinema: Industry, Ideology and Consciousness.* Cresskill, N.J.: Hampton Press.

Pisharoty, Sangeeta Barooah. 2005. 'Not just her father's daughter', *The Hindu*, 29 January. Accessed 1 March 2006, from LexisNexis database.

Potter, J. and M. Wetherell. 1987. *Discourse and Social Psychology: Beyond Attitudes and Behaviour.* London: Sage.

Prasad, M. Madhava. 1998. *Ideology of the Hindi Film: A Historical Construction.* Delhi: Oxford University Press.

Pritam, Amrita. 2003 [1950]. *Pinjar.* Delhi: Hind Pocket Books.

Purewal, Navtej. 2003. 'The Indo–Pak Border: Displacements, Aggressions and Transgressions', *Contemporary South Asia* 12 (4), pp. 539–56.

Pushkarna V. 2001. 'Courting Death', *The Week*, 9 September.

Rajadhyaksha, Ashish and Amrit Gangar (eds). 1987. *Ghatak: Arguments and Stories.* Bombay: Screen Unit.

Rajadhyaksha, Ashish and Paul Willemen (eds). 1999. *Encyclopedia of Indian Cinema* New Delhi: Oxford University Press.

Rajadhyaksha, Ashish. 1982. *Ritwik Ghatak: A Return to the Epic.* Bombay: Screen Unit.

Rajagopal, A. 2001. *Politics After Television: Hindu Nationalism and the Reshaping of the Public in India.* Cambridge, U. K.: Cambridge University Press.

Rajan, Julie. 2000. 'Cracking Sidhwa', interview of Bapsi Sidhwa, *Monsoon Magazine*, www.monsoonmag.com/interviews/i3intersidhwa.html. Accessed 1 July, 2006.

Ramasubramaniam, S. and M. B. Oliver. 2003. 'Portrayals of Sexual Violence in Popular Hindi Films, 1997–99', *Sex Roles* 48 (7/8), April: pp. 327–36.

Rao, Deepa. 2004. 'Im happy being who I am', *Times of India*, 20 April. Accessed 1 March 2006, from LexisNexis database.

Rao, K. Krishna (ed.). 1965. *The Kutch–Sind Border Question.* New Delhi: Indian Society Of International Law.

Ravikant and Tarun Kr Saint (eds). 2001. *Translating Partition.* New Delhi: Katha.

Raychaudhary, Ansua Basu. 2004. 'Nostalgia of "Desh": Memories of Partition', *Economic and Political Weekly*, Special Articles, 25 December.

Rehman Sheikh, Atta ur. 2005. 'Pakistan: Development and Disaster', in Paula Bannerjee, S. B. R. Chaudhury and S. K. Das (eds), *Internal Displacement in South Asia*, New Delhi: Sage.

Richter, William L. 1977. 'The Political Dynamics of Islamic Resurgence in Pakistan', *Asian Survey* 19 (6), June, pp. 547–57.

Rosaldo, Renato. 1989. *Culture and Truth: The Remaking of Social Analysis.* Boston Beacon Press.

Rosenstone, Robert A. 1988. 'History in Images/History in Words: Reflections on the Possibility of Really Putting History onto Film', *The American Historical Review* 93 (5), pp. 1173–85.

Russell, C. *Experimental Ethnography.* Durham and London: Duke University Press, 1999.

Sahni, Bhisham. 1988. *Tamas,* Delhi: Penguin.

Sarkar, T. 2001. *Hindu Wife, Hindu Nation: Community, Religion and Cultural Nationalism.* New Delhi: Permanent Black.

———. 2002. 'Semiotics of Terror', *Economic and Political Weekly* 37 (28), 13–19 July: pp. 2872–76.

Schatz, Thomas. 1981. *Hollywood Genres: Formulas, Filmmaking, and the Studio System* Boston, Mass.: McGraw Hill.

Scrase, Timothy J. 2002. 'Television, the Middle Classes and the Transformation of Cultural Identities in West Bengal, India', *Gazette* 64, August, pp. 323–42.

Seabrook, Jeremy. 2002. 'Confrontations of Fundamentalism', *Statesman*, 21 July.

'Sena Terms Muslim Protestors of *Gadar* Anti-national'. 2001. www.rediff.com, 25 June, http://www.rediff.com/entertai/2001/jun/25gad4.htm. Accessed 16 March 2006.

Semati, M. Mehdi and Patty J. Sotirin. 1999. 'Perspectives: Hollywood's Transnational Appeal: Hegemony and Democratic Potential?' *Journal of Popular Film & Television* 26 (4), pp. 176–88.

Sethi, M. 2002. 'Cine-Patriotism', *Samar* 15, Summer/Fall, http://www.samarmagazine org/archive/article.php?id=115. Accessed 18 May 2006.

Shedde, Meenakshi. 2004. 'Bollywood's Agenda Remains Apolitically Correct', *Economic Times*, 1 March.

Shohat, Ellen. 1997. 'Gender and Culture of Empire: Towards a Feminist Ethnography of Cinema', in Matthew Bernstein and Gaylyn Studlar (eds), *Visions of the East: Orientalism in Film*, New Brunswick, New Jersey: Rutgers University Press.

Shukla, A. 2005. 'Pakistan through the window: identity construction in Hindi cinema', http://culturewars.org.uk/2005–01/indopak.htm. Accessed 13 May 2006.

Sidhwa, Bapsi. 1990. *Ice-Candy-Man*. Penguin: New Delhi.

Singh, Harneet. 2004. 'A Bollygood Rewrite: From Pak-bashing to an Indo-Pak Bash', *The Indian Express*, 28 March. Accessed 1 Mar 2006, from LexisNexis database.

Singh, Shail Kumar. 2004. 'Bollywood repackages war film amid new goodwill towards Pakistan', *Agence France Presse*, 11 April. Accessed 1 March 2006, from LexisNexis database.

Singh, Sunny. 2005. 'From Kurukshetra to Ramarajya: A Comparative Analysis of the Star Personas of Amitabh Bachchan and Shahrukh Khan.' Unpublished manuscript.

Somayya, Bhawana. 1997. 'This penchant for patriotic themes', *The Hindu*, 18 July. Accessed 1 Mar 2006, from LexisNexis database.

Spate, O. H. K. 1947. 'The Partition of the Punjab and of Bengal', *The Geographical Journal* 110 (4–6), pp. 210–18.

Staiger, J. 2003. *Perverse Spectators: The Practices of Film Reception*. New York and London: New York University Press.

Stam, Robert and Alessandra Raengo. 2005. *Literature and Film: A Guide to the Theory and Practice of Film Adaptation*. Oxford: Blackwell.

Stam, Robert. 2000. *Film Theory: An Introduction*. Oxford: Blackwell.

'Storm over partition love story'. 2001. BBC News, 27 June, http://news.bbc.co.uk/1/hi/world/south_asia/1410142.stm. Accessed 20 March 2006.

Sumar, Sabiha. 2005. 'Talking to Sabiha Sumar about Khamosh Pani', 23 February, <http://www.chowk.com/show_article.cgi?aid=00004791 &channel=chaathouse. Accessed 1 May 2007.

Talukdar, Sudip. 2004. 'Bollywood Battlefield', *Times of India*, 31 March. Accessed 6 Feb. 2006, from LexisNexis database.

Terdiman, Richard. 1985. *Discourse/Counter-Discourse: The Theory and Practice of Symbolic Resistance in Nineteenth Century France*. London: Cornell UP.

Tyagi, Shivli. 2004. 'High on patriotism, low on success', *The Economic Times*, 8 January. Accessed 1 March 2006, from LexisNexis database.

Unnithan, Sandeep. 2003. 'Reliving Kargil', *India Today*, 24 November. Accessed 1 Mar 2006, from LexisNexis database.

Untewale, Mukund G. 1974. 'The Kutch–Sind Dispute: A Case Study in International Arbitration', *The International and Comparative Law Quarterly* 23 (4), pp. 818–39.

Valicha, K. 1988. *The Moving Image*. Bombay: Orient Longman.

Varma, Mitu. 1997. 'Indian film on war with Pakistan stirs passions', *Inter Press Service*, 5 July. Accessed 1 March 2006, from LexisNexis database.

Vasudevan, R. 2000. 'Another History Rises to the Surface: Melodrama Theory and Digital Simulation in *Hey! Ram*', *Media City/Film City*.

Vasudevan, Ravi S. 2000. 'The Politics of Cultural Address in a "Transitional" Cinema A Case Study of Indian Popular Cinema', in Christine Gledhill and Linda Williams (eds), *Reinventing Film Studies*, London: Arnold.

Verma, Meenakshi. 2004. *Aftermath: An Oral History of Partition*. New Delhi Penguin Books.

Verma, Sukanya. 2003., 'Indo, Pak governments will not gain from *Pinjar*', interview with Dr Chandraprakash Dwivedi, 22 October, rediff.com/movies/2003/oct/22chandra.html. Accessed 7 July 2006.

Virdi, Jyotika. 2003. *The Cinematic ImagiNation: Indian Popular Cinema as Social History*. New Brunswick: Rutgers University Press.

Vishwanath, G. 2002. 'Saffronizing the Silver Screen: The Right-Winged Nineties Film', in J. Jain and S. Rai (eds), *Films and Feminism: Essays in Indian Cinema*, Jaipur and New Delhi: Rawat Publications.

Vitali, V. 2000. 'The Families of Hindi Cinema: A Historical Approach to Film Studies', *Framework: The Journal of Cinema and Media* 42, Summer.

Waters, Malcolm. 2001. *Globalization: Malcolm Waters*. 2nd edn. London Routledge.

White, Hayden. 1973. *Metahistory: The Historical Imagination in Nineteenth-century Europe*. Baltimore: Johns Hopkins UP.

———. 1978. *Tropics of Discourse: Essays in Cultural Criticism*. Baltimore and London: Johns Hopkins UP.

———. 1988. 'Historiography and Historiophoty', *The American Historical Review* 93 (5), December, pp. 1193–199.

Yusufzai, Rahimullah. 2001. 'In which Lollywood gives Bollywood Those Ones', <http://www.himalmag.com/march2001/analysis.html>. Accessed 7 July 2006.

# About the Editors

**Meenakshi Bharat** is Reader at the Department of English, Sri Venkateswara College, University of Delhi. She is a translator, reviewer and critic. She is especially interested in children's literature, women's fiction and English studies — areas which she has extensively researched. She has published three books: *The Ultimate Colony* (2003), *Desert in Bloom: Indian Women Writers of Fiction in English* (2004), and recently, a new edition of George Eliot's *The Mill on the Floss*. Currently, she is engaged in translating a volume of Hindi short stories, and is also editing an anthology of Indo-Australian short stories. She has delivered a number of lectures on films in several universities in Australia and the UK. At present, she is exploring diasporic responses to Indian films in the UK (as Charles Wallace Fellow), and elsewhere.

**Nirmal Kumar** is Reader at the Department of History, Sri Venkateswara College, University of Delhi. He has worked on gender history of the eighteenth century and is in the process of editing a book on Muslim identities in Hindi films. Two of his edited volumes are forthcoming: *Essays in Medieval Indian History* and *Essays in Early Modern History of India*. He has been Associate Fellow at the Indian Institute of Advanced Studies, Shimla; Visiting Fellow at the Centre for Interdisciplinary Gender Studies, Leeds; and Fellow, Royal Asiatic Society, London.

# Notes on Contributors

**Adrian Athique** works on transnational media reception in Asia and Australasia, digital environments for teaching and research, and the sociology of the cinema in India. In his Ph. D. thesis, 'Non-resident Cinema: Transnational Audiences for Indian Films', he reconsiders the formulation of the movie audience as a social body and as a subject of social analysis, under the impact of media globalisation. Adrian has also been active as a practitioner of photography and digital design, and has previously worked as a learning and teaching technologies officer at the UK Open University. Adrian is currently researching the multiplex cinema in India.

**Aparna Sharma** is an independent, experimental filmmaker and cultural theorist studying at the Film Academy, University of Glamorgan, UK. She has recently been filming in the American southwest and interacting with native Indian tribes such as the Hopis.

**Arshad Amanullah** is a media practitioner and researcher based in New Delhi. He has studied the madrasa media as well as mainstream media with special reference to Muslim issues in India. His writings include 'Media Aur Musalman Azadi Ke Baad' (Media and Muslims since Independence, 2003). He blogs at http://madrasa.wordpress.com/. Before joining Jamia Millia Islamia, New Delhi, where he studied Mass Communications for his Masters degree, he spent nine years at Jamia Salafia, an Ahl-e-Hadis madrasa situated in Varanasi, to study Muslim theology and philosophy.

**Claudia Preckel** has studied Arabic and Islamic studies, and pedagogy at the University of Goettingen and Bochum. In 1997, she obtained her M. A. degree from Bochum University, on the Begums of Bhopal. Parts of this work has been translated into English, published as *The Begums of Bhopal* by Roli books in Delhi. She is currently working on her Ph. D. on Islamic scholarly networks in nineteenth-century Bhopal.

**Kamayani Kaushiva** is a research scholar in the department of Humanities and Social Sciences, Indian Institute of Technology, New Delhi. Her area of research is postcolonialism, with particular reference to Partition literature, with special focus on the works of Salman Rushdie, Amitav Ghosh and Bapsi Sidhwa. She has worked on the theme of trauma as represented through the cinematic mode, with reference to films on the holocaust (Claude Lanzmann's *Shoah*) and Partition.

**Kishore Budha** is actively engaged in research in film theory, film history and the film industry, and production, focusing on communication technologies, visual culture, and broadcasting and media production. He teaches at the University of Leeds and is currently engaged in a doctoral programme.

**Rajinder Dudrah** is Senior Lecturer in screen studies at the University of Manchester. His academic interests are Bollywood cinema, black British representation, popular music, diasporic and transnational media, television studies, cultural theory, and qualitative research methods as applied to popular culture. He is one of the founders and co-editors of the internationally peer-reviewed journal *South Asian Popular Culture* with Routledge publishers. He is also a script reader and adviser for Maverick Television, Birmingham.

**Savi Munjal** is currently pursuing her M. Phil. in English literature. She teaches undergraduate students at the University of Delhi. Her areas of interest include visual culture, the history and theory of the representational apparatus in world cinema, and the interdisciplinary aspects of eighteenth-century British print culture and literature.

**Shakuntala Banaji** is a researcher at the Centre for the Study of Children, Youth and Media, Institute of Education, University of London. She has taught English and media studies and lectured on Hindi film, taught on the media and society B.Sc. at South Bank University, and now teaches film theory in *Media Culture and Communication* at the Institute of Education and for the British Film Institute. She has worked as a researcher on the project 'After September 11th: TV News and Transnational Audiences', and has an abiding interest in diasporic relationships to national and international media. The main findings of her doctoral research into the meanings made by young viewers from representations of sex, gender and ethnicity in Hindi films may be found in *Reading Bollywood: The Young Audience and Hindi Films*, Palgrave Macmillan, 2006.

**Sunny Singh**, born in Varanasi, India, and educated in various parts of the world, teaches creative writing at the London Metropolitan University. She has worked as a journalist, teacher, and management executive for multinationals around the globe, finally giving up the corporate life for writing. Sunny is involved with several non-profit organisations like Club Masala, a Barcelona-based organisation for the promotion of South Asian culture. She is the founder of the Jhalak Foundation, an organisation that funds pediatric cardiac surgery for underprivileged children in India. Besides writing plays, she has just published a novel, *From Krishna's Eyes*.

**Tavishi Alagh** is an independent filmmaker. She has worked on the production and direction of ten films and programs in India, the US and other countries. She has delivered a series of lectures to the US State Department's Foreign Service Institute about Hindi film and Indian social and political issues; she has also organised a seminar series on Bollywood cinema with leading American universities. Her most recent article on Hindi cinema, 'Dreaming the Nation', appeared in *The Routledge Journal of South Asian Popular Culture*. She is working on a script for a feature with noted filmmaker Sudhir Mishra as well as developing a screenplay for her own features project.

# Index